MAC® OS X SECURITY

BRUCE POTTER
PRESTON NORVELL
BRIAN WOTRING

New Riders
www.newriders.com

201 West 103rd Street, Indianapolis, Indiana 46290
An Imprint of Pearson Education
Boston • Indianapolis • London • Munich • New York • San Francisco

Mac® OS X Security

International Standard Book Number: 0-7357-1348-0

Library of Congress Catalog Card Number: 2002115258

Printed in the United States of America

First edition: June 2003

06 05 04 03   7 6 5 4 3 2 1

Interpretation of the printing code: The rightmost double-digit number is the year of the book's printing; the rightmost single-digit number is the number of the book's printing. For example, the printing code 03-1 shows that the first printing of the book occurred in 2003.

Trademarks

Warning and Disclaimer

ASSOCIATE PUBLISHER
Stephanie Wall

MANAGING EDITOR
Gina Kanouse

SENIOR PRODUCT MARKETING MANAGER
Tammy Detrich

PUBLICITY MANAGER
Susan Nixon

SENIOR ACQUISITIONS EDITOR
Linda Anne Bump

DEVELOPMENT EDITOR
Chris Zahn

SENIOR PROJECT EDITOR
Lori Lyons

COPY EDITOR
Linda Seifert

SENIOR INDEXER
Cheryl Lenser

PROOFREADER
Teresa Stephens

INTERIOR DESIGN
Wil Cruz

COMPOSITION
Wil Cruz
Jake McFarland

MANUFACTURING COORDINATOR
Dan Uhrig

COVER DESIGNER
Aren Howell

Contents at a Glance

BRUCE POTTER

To my family.

PRESTON NORVELL

To my Grandfathers all.

BRIAN WOTRING

To my grandparents, Lyle and Mary Goodspeed.

Table of Contents

Part V   Auditing and Forensics

About the Authors

 **Bruce Potter** has a broad information security background. From application security assessments to low-level smartcard analysis to wireless network deployments, Bruce has worked in both the open- and closed-source communities. Trained in computer science at the University of Alaska Fairbanks, Bruce served as a senior technologist at several high-tech companies in Alaska and Virginia. He currently is employed as a Senior Software Security consultant with Cigital Inc. in Dulles, Virginia. Bruce is founder and President of Capital Area Wireless Network, a non-profit based in Washington, DC. CAWNet, an organization of community members and commercial wireless Internet Service Providers (WISPs), is attempting to create a large-scale public wireless network throughout the metro-DC area. In 1999 Bruce founded The Shmoo Group (TSG), an ad-hoc group of security professionals scattered throughout the world. Bruce's interests include wireless security, large-scale network architectures, open-source software assistance, and promotion of secure software engineering.

 **Preston Norvell** is a project and security engineer for Mercury Data Group, a large IT consulting firm serving the state of Alaska and locations abroad. Preston was educated in computer science at the University of Alaska Fairbanks and has since been a senior engineer at various IT firms in the state. A member of The Shmoo Group since 1999, Preston is the progenitor of TSG's MacSecurity.org web site. Preston's interests and experience includes open-source software, network design, heterogeneous systems integration, network and systems security, and practical bioinformatics.

 **Brian Wotring** is an experienced software engineer with an intense devotion to software security. Brian studied computer science and mathematics at both the University of Alaska and the University of Louisiana.

As a long-standing member of The Shmoo Group of security and privacy professionals, Brian has an interest in open-source software development, secure programming engineering, and file-integrity systems. He is responsible for the development of Osiris, a file-integrity management application. With the help of The Shmoo Group, Osiris is on the road to becoming a host-based intrusion detection system. Brian also founded and maintains knowngoods.org, an online database of file signatures for numerous operating systems.

About the Technical Reviewers

These reviewers contributed their considerable hands-on expertise to the entire development process for *Mac OS X Security*. As the book was being written, these dedicated professionals reviewed all the material for technical content, organization, and flow. Their feedback was critical to ensuring that *Mac OS X Security* fits our reader's need for the highest-quality technical information.

 **John Viega** is an internationally recognized expert on software security. He has co-authored three books in the field, including *Building Secure Software* (Addison-Wesley, 2001), *Network Security with OpenSSL* (O'Reilly, 2002), and *Secure C Programming Cookbook* (O'Reilly, 2003). John is the founder and Chief Scientist of Secure Software (www.securesoftware.com), an Adjunct Professor at Virginia Tech, and a Senior Research Scientist at the Cyberspace Security Policy and Research Institute. He also serves on the board of directors for the Secure Trusted OS Consortium (STOS).

 **Roland Miller** is an information security manager at a large research university. His background includes business management as well as MS and BS degrees in Mechanical Engineering. He has significant experience with Windows NT/2000 and Mac OS/Mac OS X in terms of security, integration, and support. He currently holds CISSP, GCFA, GSEC, MCSE, and MCP+I certifications.

Acknowledgments

I would first like to thank my wife, Heidi, and two children, Terran and Robert. They gave me the time and support needed to research and write this book. Without them, I never would have made it. I would like to thank the members of The Shmoo Group. You guys and gals have been the foundation for much of my technical work for the last few years. Also, the team at New Riders has been great. Thanks to Linda Bump and Chris Zahn for their outstanding effort in getting this book published, as well as our technical reviewers John Viega and Roland Miller.

My first introduction to OS X was at a place called FortNOCS where I worked with Preston and Brian. We spent many a long day porting standard UNIX applications to OS X Server. OS X Server had just been released and Client was still a year away. We learned a lot about the innards of OS X and how great an operating system it was shaping up to be. Preston and Brian taught me an incredible amount about the history of Macs, the hardware, and the future of OS X. The knowledge they instilled in me has been invaluable in my continuing experience with OS X. I am lucky to have them as teachers, co-authors, and friends. Thanks, guys.

—Bruce Potter

I would like to thank my friends, family, and co-workers for their patience and understanding during this process—it was more appreciated than I ever conveyed. I would like to thank a junior high school friend named Steve Ball, wherever he is, for introducing me to Macintoshes. Thanks also go out to my grandmother, Peggy Linder, for giving me my first Mac, a Macintosh XL (which actually ran Xenix, but that is another story for another day). And then there are thanks to my parents who gave me my first modern Mac (with a ginchy new PowerPC in it) as well as doing all that other stuff great parents do.

I would especially like to thank my co-writers for their work and their patience. I met Bruce many moons ago at the university in Fairbanks, Alaska. He was responsible for me getting my first real IT job, as well as getting me interested in security when we were reunited a couple years later at a company named FortNOCS. It was there that I was also introduced to Brian, a momentous occasion of small proportions that I am sure he rues to this day. They are both good friends and comrades-at-arms, and I can think of no two people with whom I would rather write a book.

Last, I would like to thank the New Riders crew (Linda Bump and Chris Zahn), and our technical editors (John Viega and Roland Miller) for their patience, guidance, and expertise—without their help this book would not be what it is.

—**Preston Norvell**

First, I would like to thank my wonderful wife, Kaleigh. My part in this book would not have been possible without her patience and support over the last months.

I would like to thank The Shmoo Group for all that I have learned from them over the years. I want to thank Paul Holman for being such a faithful friend and mentor, and for turning me on to OpenStep when I was in school.

Thanks to Bruce and Preston for being excellent technical partners and co-authors. Working on this book reminded me how much I have learned as a result of us having been co-workers, and co-conspirators to various projects. Thank you both for your friendship, and for the technical adventures we've had over the years.

Many thanks to New Riders, specifically Chris Zahn and Linda Bump for all their efforts in making this book come together. Thanks to Roland Miller for his role as technical reviewer and for helping out with various Mac OS X issues.

Finally, I would like to personally thank John Viega for his expertise and insight, as a technical editor for this book, and as a contributor to the field of computer security. This book has truly benefited from his time and input.

—**Brian Wotring**

Tell Us What You Think

As the reader of this book, you are the most important critic and commentator. We value your opinion and want to know what we're doing right, what we could do better, what areas you'd like to see us publish in, and any other words of wisdom you're willing to pass our way.

As the senior Acquisitions Editor for this book, I welcome your comments. You can fax, email, or write me directly to let me know what you did or didn't like about this book—as well as what we can do to make our books stronger. When you write, please be sure to include this book's title, ISBN, and author, as well as your name and phone or fax number. I will carefully review your comments and share them with the author and editors who worked on the book.

Please note that I cannot help you with technical problems related to the topic of this book, and that due to the high volume of email I receive, I might not be able to reply to every message.

Fax: 317-581-4663

Email: linda.bump@newriders.com

Mail: Linda Anne Bump
          Acquisitions Editor
          New Riders Publishing
          201 West 103rd Street
          Indianapolis, IN 46290 USA

INTRODUCTION

This book is about security. Specifically, it is about understanding security issues with Mac OS X. From the basic framework of the operating system, to host-based security, to integration into an enterprise network, this book covers it all.

Mac OS X is a powerful operating system. It contains new security features that go above and beyond previous versions of Mac OS. There are keychains to store passwords. Disk volumes can be encrypted so other users cannot read your data. Permissions on files and directories can be controlled on a user and group basis. It is interoperable with more industry standards and operating systems than previous versions of Mac OS ever aspired to. With NetInfo, large-scale users and resource management is reality. Mac OS X systems can be integrated into enterprise directory services, such as Active Directory and Apple's own Open Directory for management of users and resources.

Mac OS X is also more dangerous to use than previous Apple operating systems if not installed and configured correctly. Without understanding how various configuration files and commands alter the state of the machine, a user can quickly break down any security barriers that existed in the default install and leave themselves open to attack.

We will not only cover the tools and security issues, but also provide practical application and configurations where needed. By the end of this book, you will understand how to defend and audit a Mac OS X installation and how to avoid common mistakes that can expose you to security risks.

Organization and Content

We have divided this book into five major parts. In the following sections, we provide a brief overview of each part that makes up this book.

Part I: The Basics

Part I begins with an overview of security and the fundamentals of Mac OS X security. Chapter 1, "Security Foundations," covers some basic risks and the user/group model. Chapter 2, "Installation," highlights the issues surrounding various installations of the operating system, including guides for both the client and server versions of Mac OS X.

Part II: System Security

Part II focuses on Mac OS X on the workstation. When used as a workstation, Mac OS X has specific security considerations that need to be addressed on a per-user and per-application basis. Chapter 3, "Mac OS X Client General Security Practices," covers general practices, such as dual booting and patching the operating system. Chapter 4, "What Is This UNIX Thing?," introduces the UNIX-layer by detailing file permissions and the security risks associated with a UNIX operating system. Many applications that ship with Mac OS X have their own particular security domains. Chapter 5, "User Applications," covers application-level security, including risks and solutions for securing commonly used applications.

Part III: Network Security

Along with the powerful UNIX underpinnings comes a host of new networking capabilities. These are addressed in Part III. Chapter 6, "Internet Services," explores the major facets of Mac OS X's network services, their peculiarities, and how they can be deployed in a secure fashion. Chapter 7, "File Sharing," deals with issues related to file sharing, including NFS, AFS, SMB, and WebDAV services. Chapter 8, "Network Services," focuses on the tools and configuration options that can be used to defend a Mac OS X system from network attacks and reduce network vulnerabilities. This includes topics such as VPNs, firewalls, and wireless security.

Part IV: Enterprise Security

Part IV of this book addresses Mac OS X security on a larger scale. Apple is positioning Mac OS X Server as the keystone in their enterprise architecture. Maintaining an enterprise full of workstations and servers can be a daunting task. This section covers the security issues that administrators encounter when using Mac OS X Server as the core of their infrastructure. Chapter 9, "Enterprise Host Configuration," includes Kerberos Integration, Rendezvous, and WebDAV management. Chapter 10, "Directory Services," explores Mac OS X's capability to integrate into enterprise directory services. The three directory services covered in this chapter are Active Directory, Open Directory, and NetInfo.

Part V: Auditing and Forensics

Part V deals primarily with verifying the integrity of a Mac OS X-based infrastructure, and what to do when a system is compromised. No matter how secure a Mac OS X installation is, it may be broken into over time. Without understanding how to audit hosts and respond to attacks, all the previous sections in this book are near useless. Auditing tends to be forgotten in the realm of computer security. Chapter 11, "Auditing," explains the built in logging facilities of Mac OS X, how to set up logging correctly, and how to monitor logs. Chapter 12, "Forensics," explores forensic solutions for Mac OS X. This includes host integrity management and post-mortem analysis tools. Finally, Chapter 13, "Incident Response," covers incident recognition, response, and prevention issues from both a user and an administrative perspective.

Part VI: Appendixes

For information that did not fit well in any of the chapters, we have provided appendixes: Appendix A, "SUID and SGID Files," Appendix B, "Common Data Security Architecture," and Appendix C, "Further Reading."

Target Audience

This book is aimed at intermediate to advanced Mac OS X users. It was our goal to make this book something that anyone from a home user to an administrator would find valuable.

We assume the reader has a working knowledge of Mac OS X. Due to the technical variety of this audience, some of the material assumes a knowledge of basic UNIX commands. For readers new to UNIX, we recommend the book *Learning UNIX for Mac OS X*, 2nd Edition, by Dave Taylor and Brian Jepson (O'Reilly & Associates).

Mac OS X Security may also be of interest to advanced users of other operating systems such as Windows or Linux, system administrators, and security administrators. Due to the UNIX core, Mac OS X is now a viable option to deploy in large-scale desktop and server environments. Administrators need to understand the innermost details of the operating system to be able to secure hundreds of hosts at a time.

Additionally, we have set up a web site containing resources and information that was not practical to include in this book. This site also contains updated information, an errata listing, links to applications, and references related to the material mentioned throughout the text. Check it out at

```
http://www.macsecurity.org/osx-book
```

Send email to

```
osx-book@macsecurity.org
```

Code Convention Used in This Book

We've designed Mac OS X Security to be easy to use. One thing we'd like to point out is the use of code continuation characters in code lines. When code lines wrap to a second or third line, you will see a \ at the end of the first line, and -> at the beginning of the runover lines:

```
bash-2.05a$ sudo osiris -f /var/db/osiris/configs/daily.conf \
->-o /var/db/osiris/base.osi

bash-2.05a$ mactime -z MST7MDT -b seizure-copy1.mac > \
->seizure-copy1.timeline
```

PART I
THE BASICS

## CHAPTER 1

SECURITY FOUNDATIONS

"The loftier the building, the deeper must the foundation be laid."
—*Thomas Kempis*

The most recent version of Mac OS is a multitasking, multithreaded, multiuser, and multiprocessing operating system. Yesterday, Macintosh users were using a relatively simplistic system, while today they are using a powerful UNIX-based operating system that may become a prime target for attackers. The security knowledge of an average Mac user is currently very limited; the historical security of the Mac OS operating system and the focus on ease of use conspire to make it so.

Mac OS X contains many security features, but without an understanding of what those features are, and how to put them in place, users can quickly leave themselves open to attack. This book is about understanding the risks, as well as the procedures and tools to reduce those risks.

We begin with an overview of the risks, why these risks are real, and what technologies exist to address those risks. Finally, we explore the basics of the UNIX security model as it applies to Mac OS X. The material covered in this chapter provides a basis to aid in the understanding of the remainder of the material covered in this book. Those with strong UNIX backgrounds might be tempted to skip over this chapter; however, many peculiarities of Mac OS X are covered, so you are encouraged to stick around.

The Basics

Security is not something that you achieve by following a sequence of steps, or by keeping up to date with patches. It does not make sense to say only that an operating system is secure, just like you would not simply say, "Bob is protected." Bob is protected from what? A goat falling on his head? The meaning of security varies from person to person and it varies depending on the situation. To describe an operating system or a piece of software as "secure" requires an understanding of the context.

Security means applying a policy or plan specifying what elements in your environment are important, and how those elements will be protected. Your policy may be a formal written document or an implicit set of guidelines that you follow.

Also, certain aspects of security will be important to some more than others. Mac OS X is being deployed into many different environments, with different usage models. Your environment might be a single computer for home use. It might be a lab environment, or a cluster of Xserve boxes.

Therefore, before jumping into the details of commands and configuration files, it is necessary to understand the nature of certain risks, the ideas behind reducing those risks, and what tools are available for doing so.

Threats and Risk

Mac OS X is in a unique position. The operating system has many cosmetic and behavioral similarities to previous versions of Mac OS; however, underneath the hood it is a full bore UNIX system. As a result, the user base is a collection of disparate technical backgrounds and computing cultures. The risks involved vary significantly from system to system.

Common Misconceptions

A common mistake made with respect to computer security is an underestimation of the potential for disaster. Some question whether people would go through (seemingly) so much trouble to attack a system. Still, others are ignorant of the nature of many of those attacks. The fact is, attacks do occur. Malicious users are willing to spend the time and energy, as unreal as it might seem.

Another concept that is not always apparent is that the mind behind an attack is not always one of brilliant technical prowess. Once the details of vulnerabilities are made known, the recipe for execution can often be packaged and inflicted with little effort. An attacker might not even understand the details of the attack. On more than one occasion we have been witness to attacks of this nature whereby the intrusion was obviously executed by a party who did not really know what they were doing—yet the intrusion was some-what successful.

Complete security of an operating system is not obtainable. It makes no sense to say that an installation of Mac OS X is completely "secure." Given enough time and resources, the security of that installation can be compromised. Never assume a system is completely immune to a compromise in security.

Computers do not get tired or bored. They can be made to spend all day scanning network traffic, looking for vulnerable aspects of systems, or to just wait for you to make a mistake. It only takes one mistake, and the consequences of that mistake can be realized in seconds.

The Nature of Attacks

The motivations behind attacks on computers really don't stray much from those of the real world. People steal money. People spray graffiti on walls. People impersonate others for personal gain. When thought of in this manner, it is not hard to realize the motivations behind some of these computer attacks.

Destructive attacks primarily seek to destroy digital property, and disrupt services. The denial of service attacks that took place against the Yahoo! and Amazon servers in early 2000 are good examples of this.

Many security applications serve to protect the privacy of information. Email, file transfers, remote logins, instant messaging, and web browsing, are all common applications susceptible to eavesdropping.

With the popularity of online banking, monetary theft is a definite risk. Account management software can leave sensitive financial information on hard disks; the usage of online account management and bill payment systems needs to be secured and verified.

Still, other attacks make use of compromised hosts as a means to gain access to another, bigger target. University networks and Internet service providers can be targeted simply to gain access to other connected networks or resources. Therefore, just using these types of systems makes you a target.

What is done after a host is compromised can vary as well. Well-thought-out attacks often attempt to stay under the radar and gather information, such as passwords. Attacks perpetrated by those who really don't know what they are doing often lead to random acts of mischief.

Most attacks occur as a result of placing your computer(s) on a network. The security of a system does involve more than network security, but in most cases, this is where the majority of the threats begin. One key distinction with Mac OS X is that the networking infrastructure is based on that of the 4.4BSD UNIX operating system. This is good because the BSD system is mature and is considered robust by many. However, this now brings with it a variety of security concerns. Because of its importance, this issue is addressed throughout the book.

Understanding the Technology

There is more to reducing security risks than just throwing cryptography at them. The encryption technologies and tools currently at the disposal of the Mac OS X user are awesome, but the importance of knowing how to apply those technologies should not be minimized. *The key to effectively reducing a security risk involves having an understanding of how the tools involved attempt to solve the problem.* For example, certain encryption algorithms are considered more resilient to brute force attacks based on current trends in computing power. More than likely, it is not sufficient to simply say you are encrypting data. This is not to say that you must understand the details of the encryption algorithm, but that the limitations and peculiarities of the tools used are very important.

Understanding the technology is really more a matter of adopting a mindset, not just a mapping of tools to situations or problems. For example, using the Telnet program to log in to a remote machine is often considered unwise, primarily, because your password (and more) is sent unencrypted over the network. This issue can be addressed by using a replacement for Telnet. The Secure Shell program (SSH) encrypts the communication between the two computers. Simply knowing to use SSH instead of Telnet is fine, but isn't the most important aspect of this example. When learning of new vulnerabilities and risks, make a note of what the crux of the issue is first; the tools used to solve the problem will follow. As a result, taking this approach helps you understand and solve other security issues, whether you are an average user or an administrator.

Each chapter in this book highlights the underlying nature of the various topics, as opposed to just exposing the problems and solutions.

The Tools

With the rise in awareness toward computer security, the tools that serve to address the problems are finding their way onto the desktops of many systems. This includes secure replacements for common applications, to toolkits that contain strong cryptography. Mac OS X is no exception. The tools and the security architecture that reside on Mac OS X show that security is important to Apple. Understanding and effectively taking advantage of those tools, however, is left to users and administrators.

Due to the importance of network security, many of the built-in security features of Mac OS X serve to address this topic. Stopping malicious activity at this level is very important to maintaining a safe environment. After an attacker has gained access to a host, it is simply a matter of time before he elevates his privileges or gains root access.

Firewalls serve to filter data coming in and out of the attached networks on a computer. Mac OS X comes installed with a firewall called ipfw. This firewall can even be configured through the graphical interface. However, out of the box, it is not as effective as it could be. Details about firewalls are covered in Chapter 8, "Network Services."

Another network security tool installed with Mac OS X is OpenSSL. OpenSSL is a popular toolkit used to secure TCP-based network communications. It includes a multipurpose cryptographic library and a secure transport library that enables developers to secure network applications. It also includes a set of command line utilities for the rest of us. Use of the OpenSSL command line is covered in Chapter 4, "What Is This UNIX Thing?"

Wireless networks are becoming popular, and are not uncommon on laptops with Mac OS X installed. There are certain protocols that exist to address wireless security; however, they are not without their limitations and problems. This and other issues related to wireless security are covered in Chapter 8.

Virtual Private Networking (VPN) allows for the secure communication between networks over an untrusted medium, such as the Internet. It also allows for secure remote access to a network. Mac OS X has the capability to do secure host-to-host communications, as well as participate as a remote access client. The VPN capabilities of Mac OS X are explored in Chapter 8.

File encryption enables users to maintain the confidentiality of the contents of their files. Having the capability to encrypt files can be useful in the case of theft, network penetration, or just as a precautionary measure when using a multiuser machine. Mac OS X allows for file encryption through the use of the Disk Copy.app, which can create a secure encrypted file system. This application is covered in Chapter 3, "OS X Client General Security Practices." The Keychain Access.app allows for the encrypted storage of passwords for applications and web sites. Details of the Keychain Access.app are covered in Chapter 5, "User Applications."

In the unfortunate case of a compromised host, there are tools that can be used to determine how the compromise was achieved, and what damage was done. Mac OS X has system logs that can be used to pinpoint malicious activity. File integrity applications can be used to determine what files have been modified, if any. Still, more specific tools such as TASK can be used to play the forensics expert to a digital crime scene. Although Mac OS X does not come with any real forensics tools, an explanation of where to obtain some and how to use them effectively are covered in Chapter 12, "Forensics."

Darwin

Darwin is an open-source UNIX operating system built from the 4.4BSD distribution and FreeBSD 3.2. This makes up the foundation of the operating system, including the drivers, the kernel, and the command line applications. Darwin does not include any of the graphical components to Mac OS X such as the Quartz or Aqua interfaces.

Apple created the open-source Darwin project in the spring of 1999. The goal was to release the source code of the core of the operating system to the development community. This way, the implementation could be reviewed and improved by more than just Apple engineers. The debate over whether open-source software is beneficial is ongoing; however, Mac OS X is certainly benefiting from the architecture it shares with other open-source operating systems. Detection and resolution of security vulnerabilities is one benefit.

Mac OS X is built on top of Darwin. Throughout this book many of the concepts that are covered apply to standalone Darwin systems as well. When Darwin is specifically mentioned, this includes only the components released by Apple under the Darwin Project.

More information about Darwin and how it relates to Mac OS X can be found on Apple's open-source development site:

```
http://developer.apple.com/darwin/history.html
http://developer.apple.com/darwin/projects/darwin
```

The Command Line

Throughout this book (including this chapter) many references and examples use command line applications. To be effective in understanding some of the concepts discussed, you will have to get your hands dirty with the command line interface. The application Terminal.app (see Figure 1.1) obtains a command line interface. This application is located in /Applications/Utilities/Terminal.app.

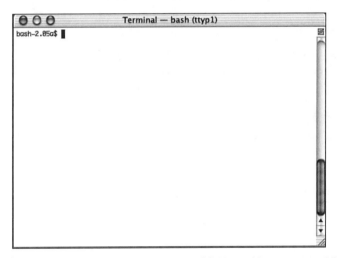

FIGURE 1.1   The Terminal application in Mac OS X provides command line access.

When you launch this application, you are presented with a prompt that allows you to enter commands to be executed by the operating system. Multiple instances of the terminal application can be opened simultaneously. Detailed information about the Terminal.app is given in Chapter 4. There are many commands, and discussing them all is outside the focus of this book. Refer to the book *UNIX for Mac OS X* by Dave Taylor and Jerry Peek (O'Reilly & Associates) for a good introduction to many UNIX commands. Also, the web site www.osxfaq.com contains many introductory articles and tutorials on the UNIX command line found on Mac OS X.

The command line interface also has a help system, man pages. To get help about a particular command, the syntax is man *command*. Replace *command* with the name of the command you need help with. In addition, you can search for keywords in the man pages by using man -k keyword. This provides a list of commands that match that keyword.

UNIX Security

Under the hood, Mac OS X is a full-fledged UNIX operating system. UNIX was originally designed as a programming environment, with no real focus on security. Over time, efforts have been made to address security concerns, but the reality is that the UNIX security model is a trusting one enforced mainly by applying security to files. Every file is owned by a specific user. Every application runs as a specific user. This section covers the basics of users and groups. Detailed information about file permissions will be covered in Chapter 4.

Users and Groups

Similar to other flavors of UNIX, Mac OS X implements a simple user/group model where users and groups are each represented by an integer, known as a user identifier (UID) and group identifier (GID). The UID and GID are what the operating system uses for identification purposes, and in turn, to enforce access control. UID and GID values are stored as 32-bit integers on Mac OS X with a maximum UID value of 2,147,483,647. Users and groups are also assigned names, but they are more for convenience purposes.

UID assignments do not have to be unique, but in most cases they are. If multiple user accounts share the same UID, there is no distinction between their owned files. Likewise, if two groups share the same GID, there is no real distinction between those groups (other than possibly their name). If a duplicate identifier is found, it should certainly be investigated.

IDENTICAL UIDs

Using the same UID for multiple user accounts is sometimes done to provide a backup root account in the case of disaster, or to provide root accounts for multiple administrators. However, doing this should not be necessary and it is not recommended. Regular users should always have unique UID values. Ascribing privileges to a set of users can usually be accomplished by using groups.

Users are members of one or more groups. Each user has a primary group to which they belong. You can view the groups that you are currently a member of with the `groups` command:

```
bash-2.05a$ groups
staff admin
bash-2.05a$
```

This user is a member of the staff and admin groups. The primary group for this user is the staff group, but this cannot be determined from the preceding output. For more detailed information, use the BSD `id` command:

```
bash-2.05a$ id
uid=501(brian) gid=20(staff) groups=20(staff), 80(admin)
```

This command is more forthcoming with information and can be quite handy. The names as well as the ID values associated with the user are displayed. Additionally, the primary group for the user is revealed. This command optionally accepts a username as an argument so you can see this same information for a specific user—for example:

```
bash-2.05a$ id root
uid=0(root) gid=0(wheel) groups=0(wheel) 1(daemon) 2(kmem) 3(sys)
4(tty) 5(operator) 20(staff) 31(guest) 80(admin)
```

Types of Users

In the UNIX world, there are typically two types of users: normal users and root. Out of the box, Mac OS X sets up a root user and a single admin user who is capable of root privileges.

Root, the Super-User

Without a doubt, the most important account on the system is the root user (UID 0), because the root user can do almost anything. This is the account that is used to handle logins, load and unload kernel extensions, control devices, and manage the file system and network, among other system level functions. This account is also referred to as "System" in the Finder. Due to the potential for disaster, this account is *not* to be used as a regular account, even by administrators.

Understanding User Roles

To reduce the risk of compromise, you should adhere to a policy of least privilege. Ideally, this leaves only a single account with administrative privileges. Administrative tasks are accomplished by temporarily elevating this account to root privileges (with the `sudo` command). Apple endorses this policy by making the root account on Mac OS X disabled by default. That is, it is not possible to log in as root from the login window. Note that there are still ways root access can be obtained; more on this in Chapter 4. The user created during the installation is considered an admin user. This user is in the admin group, and therefore given `sudo` capabilities. The details and risks surrounding `sudo` will also be covered in Chapter 4.

By default, the root account is disabled and does not have a password. Immediately upon installation, the root account should be initialized. This involves enabling the account (see Figure 1.2), setting root's password (see Figure 1.3), and then disabling the account again (see Figure 1.4). This can all be done with the NetInfo Manager application (`/Applications/Utilities/NetInfo Manager.app`).

After launching NetInfo Manager, you must authenticate with an admin username and password.

Now the root account is disabled and nobody can log in to the system as root. Also, the root password is now set and (hopefully) known only to an administrator.

With Mac OS X Server, the root account is enabled by default so, obviously, the preceding process does not apply. The main point is that all steps should be taken to prevent logins into the root account by disabling it.

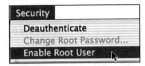

FIGURE 1.2   Authenticate and enable the root account.

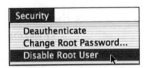

FIGURE 1.3   Change the root password.

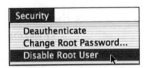

FIGURE 1.4   Authenticate and disable the root account.

Administrative Users

The user that was created during the installation is considered an administrator. What this means, specifically, is that this user is granted sudo abilities and membership to the admin group. The only other members of this group are the root user and possibly other admin users. Membership to this group enables the administrator to view log files and install programs under the /Applications directory. All other users have only read and execute permissions to the applications directory. That is, they are unable to save, modify, or delete any of the files.

On Mac OS X Server, the user created during the installation is also an admin user. However, the password given during the creation of that administrative account is also the initial password of the root account. That is, the root account has a password and is enabled. Likewise, it is recommended that the root password be changed so that it is not the same as the admin account, and then disabled.

By default, all members of the admin group are given sudo access. In keeping with the spirit of only allowing access as needed, it is recommended that the sudo privileges be allowed only to a single admin user. However, because all administrative users on Mac OS X are granted sudo access by default, changing this takes some modification of system files. The details surrounding the enforcement of this policy are also covered in Chapter 4.

Special Users

When users are created through the Accounts pane of the System Preferences application, UIDs are automatically generated starting at 501. On most UNIX systems, lower UID values are reserved for system use. On Mac OS X, this is the case for all UID values below 100. These system accounts are used for various purposes and vary with each type of UNIX distribution. The basic idea is that system level applications need to be given privileges to perform their service, and nothing more. A user is created for each service and is usually designated the owner of files related to that service.

Table 1.1 lists the system accounts that are installed with Mac OS X. Some of these accounts are not created; for example, the mmuser account is created only after the Macintosh Managemnet Server is initialized.

TABLE 1.1   Special System Users

UID	SHORT NAME	DESCRIPTION
–17	mmuser	Manages the Macintosh Management Server (Mac OS X Server only).
–2	nobody	An unprivileged account with no home directory or file ownership.
0	root	The user with highest privileges, the super-user.
1	daemon	Manages certain system services with limited privileges.
25	smmsp	The user that runs the sendmail processes.
70	www	The user that runs the Apache web server processes.
74	mysql	The user that runs the MySQL database server processes.
75	sshd	The user that runs the secure shell server processes.
98	ftp	The user assigned to anonymous incoming ftp users.
99	unknown	Used for unknown volumes.

Special Groups

Just as there are special user accounts for system use, there are system groups used to limit certain resources to a particular set of users. This also makes it possible to allow other users on the system to have access to files related to a specific system service.

Table 1.2 lists the system groups that are installed with Mac OS X. Some of the groups in the table are legacy UNIX groups that are not really used.

TABLE 1.2 Special System Groups

GID	NAME	DESCRIPTION
–2	nobody	Used for various system services.
–1	nogroup	Used for various system services.
0	wheel	The primary group for root.
1	daemon	Used for certain system services with limited privileges.
2	kmem	Used for kernel memory, for example, /dev/mem and /dev/kmem.
3	sys	Not used.
4	tty	Used for managing files associated with remote logins and certain applications.
5	operator	Not used.
6	mail	The group for managing mail files.
7	bin	A legacy group for owning binary files.
20	staff	The primary group for all normal users.
25	smmsp	The group that runs the sendmail processes.
31	guest	An Unprivileged user that owns no files.
45	utmp	Not used.
66	uucp	A group for handling uucp transactions.
68	dialer	The group used for managing modems.
69	network	Not used.
70	www	The group that runs the Apache web server processes.
74	mysql	The group that runs the MySQL database server processes.

continues

TABLE 1.2 Continued

GID	NAME	DESCRIPTION
75	sshd	The user that runs the secure shell server processes.
80	admin	Used for managing admin users. By default, this group is given sudo capabilities.
99	unknown	A group used for mounted volumes.

Introducing NetInfo

So far, this chapter has covered the basic concepts of the user/group model particular to Mac OS X. Now, we will take a look at how these users and groups are managed. Most UNIX systems make use of flat files to store information about users, groups, networks, and other resources. Files such as /etc/passwd, /etc/group, and /etc/hosts contain line entries of users, groups, and network names. Mac OS X does the same by using an organized directory structure called NetInfo. NetInfo is a remnant of the NeXTStep operating system, where Mac OS X has its roots. In addition to managing users and groups, NetInfo also manages resources such as devices, networks, services, and filesystem shares.

With a few adjustments, the traditional flat files can be used for user and group management. However, Mac OS X is set up to use NetInfo by default. NetInfo has a GUI-based management application—NetInfo Manager.app (see Figure 1.5). The interface organizes the information similar to a file system, with "/" as the top level of the domain.

Securing the management of users and groups when using flat files is fairly straightforward. The files in question are set up in such a way that normal users do not have direct write privileges. In most cases, these files serve to manage users local to the system. NetInfo is quite different.

NetInfo was designed to interact and share information with other NetInfo databases in a hierarchical fashion across a network. Thus, instead of a local file being queried for login credentials, the query is now sent to a distributed database, possibly over a network. In turn, the infrastructure for channeling these types of requests prevails in many of the applications and system services. The capability to deal with users and groups across a network of machines is handy, but it is also overkill for the casual user. For example, NetInfo is useful in the context of a university lab of Mac OS X machines, but the average home user will probably never know of or care about the capabilities of NetInfo.

FIGURE 1.5   NetInfo Manager.app showing the root of the directory hierarchy.

Although Mac OS X installations are not always part of a greater NetInfo network, a local NetInfo domain still serves requests in similar fashion. Let's examine some risks involved in using NetInfo, and steps you can take to reduce those risks.

NetInfo Security

One of the issues with NetInfo that has raised a great deal of concern is the capability for normal users to read the encrypted password values of other users, including the root password. Normally password shadowing prevents such attacks by preventing normal users from having read access to the encrypted passwords. However, the `nidump` command line application gives any local user the capability to read this information from a local NetInfo database. For example, this example prints the list of users and their attributes, including the encrypted passwords:

```
bash-2.05a$ nidump passwd /
nobody:*:-2:-2::0:0:Unprivileged User:/dev/null:/dev/null
root:*uN59qX0Z5X5Pc:0:0::0:0:System Administrator:/var/root:/bin/tcsh
```

continues

```
daemon:*:1:1::0:0:System Services:/var/root:/dev/null
unknown:*:99:99::0:0:Unknown User:/dev/null:/dev/null
smmsp:*:25:25::0:0:Sendmail User:/private/etc/mail:/dev/null
www:*:70:70::0:0:World Wide Web Server:/Library/WebServer:/dev/null
mysql:*:74:74::0:0:MySQL Server:/dev/null:/dev/null
sshd:*:75:75::0:0:sshd Privilege separation:/var/empty:/dev/null
bob:FMw7rHeeS3Sjo:501:20::0:0:Bob Smith:/Users/brian:/bin/tcsh
bash-2.05a$
```

A malicious user can then take the portion that represents the encrypted password, and try to decrypt it. The attack is a brute force attack, but nonetheless effective. For example, the following demonstrates dumping the user information from NetInfo using `nidump`, then running John the Ripper to crack some obviously weak passwords:

```
bash-2.05a$ nidump passwd . > /tmp/pw.dump
bash-2.05a$ ./john /tmp/pw.dump
Loaded 2 passwords with 2 different salts (Standard DES [24/32 4K])
password      (bob)
cheese        (root)
guesses: 2 time: 0:00:00:00 100% (2) c/s: 3142 trying: ginger -
gizmo
```

JOHN THE RIPPER

John the Ripper is a brute force password cracking command line tool. Given a password file, the tool attempts to decrypt and uncover the passwords. Initially, a dictionary attack is made. This involves checking to see if the password is a real English word. Many people unwisely choose words for their passwords. If that fails, a brute force attack is conducted which involves trying all possible character combinations.

John the Ripper is not included with Mac OS X, but it can easily be obtained and compiled. For information and downloads, visit: `http://www.openwall.com/john`.

The risk here is different depending on the nature of the system. For example, a multiuser system in an office environment probably warrants more concern than a student lugging around an iBook for school papers. In any case, the fact that users have the capability to compile and run UNIX software, such as password crackers, is representative of the risks of which users coming from a Macintosh background now need to be aware.

There is no sure solution to the NetInfo password problem that exists with the current implementation of NetInfo. This is unfortunate. However, steps can be taken to reduce the risks involved.

Begin with passwords. Do not use weak passwords! This is the most effective way to combat this problem. Given the nature of the attack, words found in the dictionary can be cracked faster than you can utter your password. The preceding example took less than a second. Use passwords with numbers and multiple symbols within the first eight characters.

Change the permissions of the command line NetInfo applications such that normal users do not have any access rights for the files. The details for changing permissions on files in this manner are discussed in Chapter 4. The list of NetInfo related applications includes

- `/usr/bin/niutil`
- `/usr/bin/nicl`
- `/usr/bin/nidump`
- `/usr/bin/niload`
- `/usr/bin/nifind`
- `/usr/bin/nireport`
- `/usr/bin/nigrep`
- `/usr/sbin/nidomain`

In addition, the NetInfo management application (NetInfo Manager.app) is run as root regardless of who actually launches the application. This is known as a Set User ID root application (SUID). It is recommended that the permissions be changed for this application as well. A detailed discussion of what SUID means, the dangers of SUID applications, and what files on Mac OS X are SUID are covered in Chapter 4.

Do not use important passwords that you use elsewhere. In the event that a password is compromised, you can bet your accounts on other systems will become immediate targets (for example, your mail server).

Do not reuse passwords. If you change your password, never go back to a password you used two passwords ago. This defeats the purpose of periodically changing your password and increases the risk of a compromise.

The problem is not with the "ni" applications or with the NetInfoManager.app in particular. The problem is that the local netinfo domain places limited access restrictions on the information it stores. It is important to understand that users can still copy over and run the "ni" applications, or even write their own applications to talk to the netinfo domain. See man `netinfo(3)` for more details. However, changing the permissions as suggested previously will not be in vain. If somebody wants to get into my house with a lock-picking kit, they can, yet I still lock my doors. Locking the doors is not a deterrent for all, but it is for some. The logic here applies.

Generally, read-access to NetInfo data is given to all local users, while write-access requires administrative privileges. Network access to the data is turned off by default. Also, the local NetInfo domain will not seek out other master NetInfo domains. This has also been turned off by default. Allowing access to the NetInfo domain from other hosts requires an administrator to explicitly add that host to an access control list. However, it is interesting to note that this was not always the case. Early versions of NeXTStep allowed even remote access to the NetInfo domain by default.

Another risk with NetInfo involves the use of a master NetInfo domain to manage a network of hosts and users. It is very apparent that the forefathers of this system were most concerned with providing a scalable directory service that was easy to set up and integrate into existing networks. Security, as it often does, took a back seat. All communications between NetInfo domains happens in clear text. This includes user authentications. For this reason, even Apple specifically recommends an alternative for managing authorization and authentication, such as a SSL/LDAP solution. Detailed information about NetInfo administration is covered in Chapter 10, "Directory Services."

Summary

The first step toward securing Mac OS X starts with an understanding of the risks. Only then can you begin to effectively reduce those risks. The disparate user base of Mac OS X users makes this job even harder. Users and administrators must understand the root of the security issues and develop a security mindset as opposed to just knowing to use certain tools.

The power of its UNIX core makes Mac OS X very appealing to users as well as to attackers. Understanding the UNIX roots found in this operating system is key to being effective in the securing process. That being the case, an entire chapter is dedicated to this subject.

Out of the box, Mac OS X is not horribly insecure, but obviously there are holes to be plugged and issues to be addressed. In the remainder of this book, we will explore and resolve the critical issues needed to establish a secure computing environment, for users and administrators alike.

## CHAPTER 2

INSTALLATION

"A bad beginning makes a bad ending."
—Euripides, Aegeus

There are many steps on the path to creating a secure host. Some steps, like those discussed in the previous chapter, happen prior to our having to touch the software. Years of development and maturation have brought the securability of UNIX to Mac OS X. Thousands of man-hours of design and implementation have created Apple's Security Framework and the applications that use it. But all this work simply provides a way for we users and administrators to create a measure of security for our Macs. The remaining steps in creating a secure host are left to us, who use these systems on a daily basis, using the tools given to us by those who walked the first, few paces down the path. And for us, this path begins at installation.

It may seem that the installation process would be an area where one wouldn't really have to think about security. So much of an administrator's time and emphasis in securing a host is done after an operating system is installed, that many forget the choices to be made during installation. This chapter discusses the decision points encountered during the install procedure, and provides some additional background on some of the particulars. The first two sections cover the BSD Subsystem and choosing a filesystem format. The final section provides a step-by-step walk-through of the installation process for both Mac OS X and Mac OS X Server.

"...BUT MY SYSTEM IS ALREADY INSTALLED."

Some readers might be saying to themselves, "But I've already installed my system...." or "My system came pre-installed, why do I need to read this chapter?" If you have a system that is already in production, it may be a good idea to read on, if nothing else than to reassure yourself that you made the right decisions during the install. If you have a system that came pre-installed, it is probably best to see if there are any unacceptable risks in the default install. It is very possible that your system complies with your security policy, but it would be wiser to check the assumption than suffer the consequences when that assumption fails.

To BSD or Not to BSD

Like most modern operating systems, Mac OS X consists of more than one API that developers may use for programming their applications. In fact, Apple supports five different APIs for development on Mac OS X: Classic, Carbon, Cocoa, Java, and UNIX. The Classic API is the standard Mac API for Mac operating systems prior to Mac OS X and is used solely by the Classic compatibility environment, which we will discuss in more detail in Chapter 3, "Mac OS X Client General Security Practices." The Carbon API is a modernized version of the Classic API that provides developers experienced in programming for Mac OS X's predecessors a relatively quick way to bring their applications to the new OS. The Cocoa and Java APIs are object-oriented APIs that allow for the creation of new legacy-free applications. The final API is UNIX, which among other things, is the API the BSD Subsystem relies on.

What exactly is the BSD Subsystem? Simplistically, it is approximately 130MB of applications and services optionally installed during the Mac OS X install process. Some readers may be asking how the BSD Subsystem could be an optional install on a UNIX-based operating system. After all, Apple touts the UNIX core of their newest OS, and removing the BSD Subsystem would seem to be removing the core of the operating system.

As it turns out, the BSD Subsystem is a confusing and poorly chosen name for a collection of applications that might be better termed "BSD Tools and Services." The 130MB, optional install package translates into approximately 4,300 applications, daemons, and support files. For most administrators and users familiar with UNIX, this probably sounds like a lot. And indeed it is.

Without the BSD Subsystem, many of the basic tools users come to expect become unavailable. No grep. No man pages. The nonessential aspects of the /etc configuration directory are gone. All the daemons typically started by the inetd superserver are not installed.

Although many of the common applications are unavailable without the BSD Subsystem installed, not all are missing. All the "must have" applications are there; ls, chmod, chown, vi and friends are all still there. For those users familiar with UNIX system, it is possible to liken the reduced command line environment to the subset of commands available when booted into single user mode on most UNIX-like operating systems.

Although the elimination of the BSD Subsystem would seem to be largely a functional issue, it has definite security implications as well. Every application a user can use on a system is an application that can be abused by that user. This is not to say that users necessarily, actively abuse the system. Sometimes the evilness is perpetrated by a process on behalf of the user (such as a virus or trojan), but other times it is a user doing something they should not. The BSD Subsystem is in a sense 4,300 potential weak points in a system's security. The law of averages says that a few of the applications have undiscovered vulnerabilities. Some of this risk could be mitigated if the computer code has undergone a rigorous security audit, which can eliminate some of the bugs that are abused, but not every application has such an audit. In most situations this added risk is small given that most of the tools do not provide elevated privileges and are not accessible from a network. In fact, were the average application exploited, it would at worst be able to affect the items the user has access to. Yet another reason not to log in as the root user.

With much of the UNIX core of Mac OS X being provided by open-source developers (a much-touted feature), Apple is relying on the various programmers not directly under their control to produce code without vulnerabilities. We as users then trust Apple to deliver an operating system as free from security issues as they can make it. As administrators, our users trust us to provide them with stable and secure systems to do their work.

Despite everyone's best intentions, bugs do appear. In fact, to date, there have been more than 30 discovered vulnerabilities in applications that are included with Mac OS X. Fortunately, Apple has been relatively quick to release patches and updates to fix the discovered vulnerabilities. Certainly it would seem that not installing the large number of applications in the BSD Subsystem eliminates the risks from any potential vulnerability in its 130MB of compiled code, even if Apple is lax on releasing a patch for a discovered vulnerability.

On the face of it, this might seem to be a great step forward for the security of a system. However, depending on your situation, this may not necessarily be true. Security often ends up being in a classic trade-off with usability, and the decision on whether to install the BSD Subsystem is no different.

For users, eliminating the wealth of tools in the package eliminates some of the power of the operating system. These missing applications could make users' jobs easier, the users themselves more efficient, and their systems more adaptable. History has shown that users will download whatever it is they think they are missing; this may be more dangerous than allowing them access to known, sanctioned versions of the same applications.

For many administrators, the ability to run "standard" UNIX applications is a huge drawing point. Among the many applications missing if the BSD Subsystem is not installed are those that many administrators often rely on to integrate and manage hosts into a network. Also missing are applications typically used for assessing, monitoring, and managing security of servers and workstations. If the BSD bits are not installed, a user or administrator will also find it impossibly difficult to compile patches for any applications that may require it.

The bottom line is that even though removing the BSD Subsystem eliminates 4,300+ potential problem applications, most users and administrators are going to want to have it installed. The applications are too useful for users in their everyday work, and too useful for administrators in maintaining and securing the systems. On top of this, of the applications included with Mac OS X found to have vulnerabilities, most are not even part of the BSD Subsystem, but a part of the base install.

There are those users who pride themselves on never using the command line; perhaps these users do not need the BSD Subsystem, but for the most part anyone serious about security on Mac OS X will find some use for some of the applications found in the BSD Subsystem. If an administrator happens to have a situation where his users are unlikely to ever want to use the missing applications or the environment requires an extra level paranoia, then not installing the tools is a reasonable idea. Otherwise, it is best left as the default, which is to install the tools.

Filesystems—HFS+ Versus UFS

Apple supports two different filesystems on which to install Mac OS X: HFS+ and UFS. Much like the decision on whether to install the BSD Subsystem, this would seem like a question of functionality and not security, but as we shall see, there is indeed a component of security in the choice.

A Tale of Two Filesystems

HFS+, also known as Mac OS Extended format, made its debut with Mac OS 8.1 in 1998. It was developed to replace the venerable HFS (Hierarchical File System, also known as Mac OS Standard format), which had been in use by the Mac OS since 1986. The original HFS supports separate data and resource "forks," and file type and creator metadata. The volume format is also case-insensitive, and case-preserving (more on this in a bit). Among the features HFS+ brought were improved file allocation (2^{32} file allocation blocks, up from 2^{16}), long filenames (255 characters, up from 32), Unicode filename support, extensible metadata, and larger maximum file size. By default, Apple ships their systems with HFS+ formatted volumes, and Mac OS X chooses this as its default filesystem format during the install.

UFS (also known as UNIX File System) shipped for the first time in a modern Mac operating system in 1999, when Mac OS X Server v1.0 shipped. It is a POSIX-compliant volume format based on the 4.4BSD Fast File System (FFS), and is similar to the native filesystems for most UNIX-like operating systems. It is a case-sensitive filesystem that cannot natively store multiple file forks. UFS is ignored and invisible to Mac OS 9.x and its predecessors, though UFS formatted volumes are visible and functional in the Classic compatibility environment.

Security Considerations

The two major issues in deciding which filesystem to use for an installation involve the Mac OS Extended format's resource forks and its case-insensitivity.

As we stated previously, HFS+ and its predecessor support multiple forks for file data and resource data. The data fork generally contains what users think of when they think of a file; for documents it is the content (words, pictures, and so on) a user manipulates, and for applications it usually contains executable computer code. The resource fork contains additional data, such as localization data, a document preview image, application code, or custom icons. Not all files have resource forks attached but many do, the most common being applications.

Security becomes an issue when applications that are ignorant of resource forks try to modify files that have a resource fork. If a file is copied, moved, or deleted by the Finder, the Finder knows how to properly deal the resource forks. But when a less-sophisticated application (such as cp, mv, or rm) is used, it does not know how to deal with the extra fork, and typically copies, moves, or deletes just the data fork. This orphans any data in the resource fork, leaving it inaccessible by normal means. This means any "secure" erase program has to be aware of the proper method of clearing the data. It also means any host intrusion detection software also needs to be cognizant of the issue to be fully functional. This also pertains to disaster recovery in that backup programs must know how to both back up and restore the forked files. On top of all this, it may also be possible that the resource fork could be used to hide malicious code from some security or virus scanners.

UFS, because it does not support resource forks, avoids this issue by default. Apple's Finder does allow UFS to store the data that would be in the resource fork not as a fork, but in another file on the filesystem. This allows data from an HFS formatted volume to be safely copied to a UFS volume, without losing any of the resource data. These files take the form ._sporkeaters.tiff, where sporkeaters.tiff is the original filename. Because the Finder and the command line do not by default show files that begin with a period, this conversion is relatively transparent to the user. It also has the side effect of allowing normal command line utilities (such as cp, mv, or rm) to manipulate the resource forks. There is no explicit relationship between the original file and the resource file though, so care must still be taken during such operations.

The other aspect of security affecting filesystem choice is the case-insensitivity of HFS+. This means that when a file is saved to the filesystem, the case (as in uppercase and lowercase letters) of the saved filename is preserved. However, if a file named fortunesfools.doc is saved to the filesystem, and another file named FortunesFools.doc is written, fortunesfools.doc will be overwritten. This is the right and expected functionality for existing Mac OS users and their applications. The issue comes up again with applications that were not designed to handle case-insensitive filesystems.

One of the earliest Mac OS X security patches (Mac OS X Web Sharing Update 1.0) was for a potential vulnerability that involved the way the built-in Apache web server handled file security. Because Apache assumed it was running on a case-sensitive volume format, such as UFS, its file and directory security mechanisms did not take into account that a file named .htaccess could be the same file as one named .Htaccess. In this case the file, .htaccess, is considered a sensitive file that may have authentication tokens for accessing the web site and a description of the permissions Apache places on various file system objects that make up the web site. Because of the security implications of allowing potential attackers access to this file, Apache disallows access to it by default. But, since Apache was not disallowing access to all the case-variant permutations of .htaccess (.Htaccess, .HTaccess, .hTaccess, and others), an attacker could just change the case of one letter of the filename and get access to information she should not have. Any files or directories protected using Apache's mechanisms were vulnerable to the same attack, unless extreme care was taken to write the access control. Apple eventually solved this problem by shipping an Apache module (mod_hfs_apple.so) that fixed part of the issue, but still required additional configuration changes to provide a more complete solution.

But this is a just one application's problem. There are undoubtedly others that administrators may run into when trying to run legacy UNIX applications on HFS+.

So, is the solution to both resource forks and case-insensitivity to install all our systems on UFS formatted volumes? Not necessarily. With the solution comes some complication to using Mac OS X. One of the biggest issues client systems will have is that Mac OS 9 cannot be installed on a UFS partition, and thus would preclude any dual booting or use of the Classic Environment, unless at least one HFS+ partition were available. Some Carbon applications also are not compatible with the filesystem, and others are not "supported" on such volumes.

Apple recommends that a user not install UFS unless he or she absolutely must work with the filesystem. This is likely due to compatibility issues with Carbon applications as stated previously. We cannot fault Apple for this suggestion, at least for client systems. Client machines run a wider array of software that may not be compatible with UFS, may dual boot into Mac OS 9, or may run the Classic Environment. For these reasons it may well make sense to leave the system with the default Mac OS Extended format, but for those users who will be developing or compiling applications, we recommend that users consider utilizing at least one UFS partition for this work. For Mac OS X Server installations, where the need to dual boot (one hopes) is eliminated, the likelihood that the Classic Environment needs to be run is diminished, and the variety of applications being run is limited, we think UFS is indicated. That is unless specific applications require an HFS+ filesystem, in which case it might be wiser to add a second partition with the format.

Mac OS X Install Step-by-Step

Mac OS X is one of the easiest installs for any UNIX-like operating system. With just a few clicks on throbbing, translucent buttons, a user can have a complete, buzzword-compliant operating system installed and running. Often lost in this point-and-click wonderland are a number of options that directly affect the function and security of the host being installed. This section takes users through a complete installation of their operating system, while pointing out the options often missed during the installation. Where necessary, we will point out any issues specific to the Mac OS X Server installation.

Physical Setup

Setting up Macs (and most PCs) is pretty easy these days, so we will not bore users with such specifics. We will mention however, that installers will need a supported computer with an Apple OEM video card—and unless they own a laptop, they need a USB keyboard and mouse, an SVGA (minimally) monitor, and adequate power for all of the above. Also required is about an hour to perform the installation. One thing readers might think is missing here is a network connection. This is not an error of omission, but an attempt to eliminate the effect of any potential vulnerability that may be attackable during the installation process. It also has the side effect of keeping Apple's automatic registration process from contacting Apple's servers, should this be a concern.

Beginning the Installation

After the computer is put together and all the cables and devices are plugged into their appropriate interfaces, it is time to get started with the actual installation.

1. Boot the machine from the Mac OS X installation CD.

   Placing the CD into the CD-ROM drive, and then holding down the 'c' key as the machine boots, easily does this. Assuming all is right with the world, the computer should soon start to boot from the media.

2. The first several installation screens are either informational or pertain to the presentation of the installer interface itself. The first dialog to appear is one that sets the language that will be used for the rest of the install (see Figure 2.1).

3. After selecting the language, and a "Welcome to the Mac OS X Installer" screen, there is a short wait, and then the Mac OS X "Read Me" is displayed. Once past this screen, you are presented with the EULA and asked whether you agree to all of its components.

FIGURE 2.1   The first dialog of the Mac OS X installer.

Choosing and Partitioning the Disk

Assume that those responsible for the installation indeed agree with all the provisions of the EULA and have pressed the Continue button.

1. The next screen is where you choose the destination disk for the installation (see Figure 2.2).

   As discussed in the previous section entitled "Filesystems—HFS+ Versus UFS," there are two different filesystems on which you can choose to install Mac OS X. If the disk has been partitioned appropriately already, you can simply select the icon representing the partition on which you want to install.

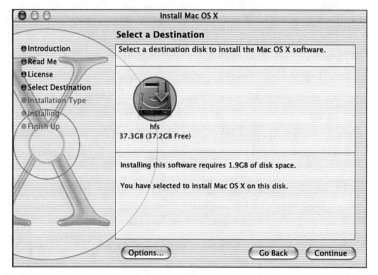

FIGURE 2.2   The Mac OS X installer querying for the target partition.

2. If the disk has not been partitioned yet, this can be done by selecting the target disk, and then clicking the Options button in the lower-left corner of the dialog. This presents the sheet seen in Figure 2.3.

   This sheet also presents three different methods of installation you can choose. The first option either upgrades Mac OS X or installs it for the first time, depending on whether or not the program can locate a previous Mac OS X install on the selected volume. The middle option allows you to benefit from a clean installation while still preserving most of your existing configuration information. This option is grayed out as it is in Figure 2.3 if there is not an existing installation, and the option does not exist in the Mac OS X Server installer. The final option, Erase and Install, allows users to format their drives with the filesystem type of their choice and install a completely new copy of Mac OS X.

   Unfortunately, this final option is useful only if a user wants to dedicate an entire disk to a single volume format.

FIGURE 2.3   The Mac OS X installer displaying options for partitioning the target disk.

3. For more complicated installations where multiple partitions (with or without differing volume formats) are needed, the Disk Utility application must be used. This can be accessed by selecting Installer, Open Disk Utility from the menu bar, which will then start an instance of Disk Utility (see Figure 2.4). With this utility it is possible to create multiple partitions on a disk and format them with various different volume formats.

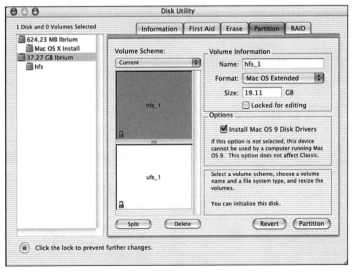

FIGURE 2.4   You can create multiple partitions with the Disk Utility.

4. To partition and format a disk in Disk Utility, first select the target disk from the left pane, and then the Partition tab on the right. This automatically shows the existing partitioning scheme on the disk.

5. To change this, select the number of partitions from the pop-up menu in the Volume Scheme section. This splits the pane beneath into the requested number of partitions. The separators between the partitions have thumbs that can be dragged to change their sizes as needed (the default is to make all partitions the same size).

   Volume name and format are set in the Volume Information section on the top right of the page. It should be noted that although Disk Utility allows you to format a partition as Mac OS Standard (HFS), this should not be selected unless a version of Mac OS earlier than 8.1 (or some other operating system that is not compatible with HFS+) must be supported. There is also a Install Mac OS 9 Drivers check box, which if unchecked will prevent the drive from being available to Apple Macintosh operating systems prior to Mac OS X. Any system dedicated to booting only into Mac OS X can safely clear this check box (it does not affect the Classic environment).

6. After the partition sizes, formats, and names are set, a click of the Partition button at the lower right of the page initializes the disk accordingly (after an obligatory "Are you sure?" dialog).

7. After the formatting is complete, quitting Disk Utility returns you to the installer. The newly prepared volumes should now be selectable in the installer interface.

Customizing the Install

After the target partition is selected, a click of the Continue button moves the user to the next phase of the install process, selecting the packages to be installed.

1. To manually select the packages to be installed, as opposed to accepting the defaults, you must click the Customize button on the dialog. This changes the dialog to list each of the optional packages (see Figure 2.5).

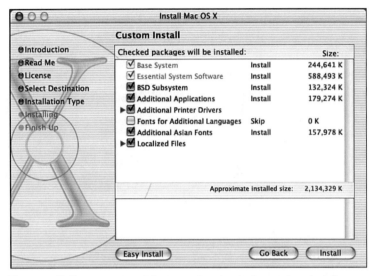

FIGURE 2.5   The Mac OS X installer displaying optional packages.

Mac OS X includes about a dozen optional packages in its installer. We discussed the BSD Subsystem in the previous section "To BSD or Not To BSD," so we will not go into it here other than to say this is where it can be removed from the installation. The Additional Applications package is a collection of applications such as iPhoto, iMovie, iTunes, and Adobe Acrobat Reader, which most users will likely want installed. The Additional Printer Drivers group of packages is a bunch of printer drivers (logically) that most users will want installed unless the installation partition is short on space. The rest of the optional packages, made up of the Fonts for Additional Languages and Additional Asian Fonts packages, and the Localized Files package group, are there primarily for installations for non-English speaking users, or those who work with foreign languages.

The Mac OS X Server installer has only four optional packages: BSD Subsystem, Japanese Localized Files, German Localized Files, and French Localized Files (see Figure 2.6). As we discussed in the previous section on the BSD Subsystem, most server installations are going to want this package installed. The remaining three packages are for localization of various applications within Mac OS X. Whether or not these packages are installed is primarily a functional concern, but not doing so does save about 60MB of disk space.

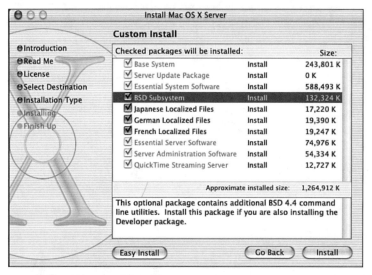

FIGURE 2.6   The Mac OS X Server installer displaying optional packages.

2. After the desired packages have been selected (and any undesired packages deselected), and the Install button clicked, installation proceeds with copying the requested files onto the target partition. Depending on which packages were chosen and the speed of the hardware involved, this phase of the installation can take anywhere from 15 minutes to the better part of an hour. After installation of files from the first disk is complete, the system will automatically reboot.

3. What happens next depends on which packages were chosen for install and which version of the operating system is being installed. Most of the optional packages are installed from a second disk included in the Mac OS X distribution. If any packages are needed from this second disk, a secondary installer will query for Disk 2. After the packages are installed, the computer reboots once more.

The Setup Assistant (Mac OS X Client)

Having installed all the selected software, the installation progresses to setting up the system for initial use.

1. After you are treated to some nifty screen magic and music, the system asks what region of the world you are from, and which keyboard type to use.

2. You are then requested to fill out a registration form (which will also be entered into the user's address book).

   Because you did not plug in the system to the network, the registration process will timeout after a short while, but allow the setup assistant to continue.

3. After you have answered those burning questions on the registration form, it is time to set up the first account on the system (see Figure 2.7).

   This first account is an administrative account that has the capability to perform privileged actions, such as creating accounts, configuring networking, and installing applications and drivers. This account is also made a member of the groups admin and staff (as well as the wheel group prior to Mac OS X v 10.2) and has all the privileges provided thereby as discussed in Chapter 1. If possible, we would suggest that the account not be used to log on to the system for daily operation. Some users will find the inability to install applications into /Applications or new drivers to be intolerable. Depending on the situation, this may be a valid concern, but it should be avoided if at all possible.

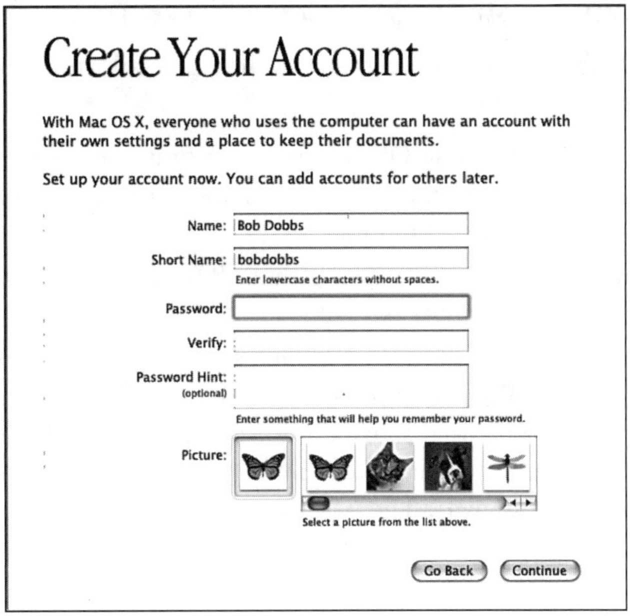

FIGURE 2.7   The Mac OS X Client setup assistant.

The account setup dialog is mostly self-explanatory. There is a field for the user's full name, a short name (what most users will think of as their username), the password, a hint (which we suggest not utilizing), and a picture icon (which secure installations will not be using).

4. The screen that follows the account setup dialog asks how the machine connects to the Internet (ethernet, DSL, and so on). This connection method is used by the installer to register the software, as well.

5. The next couple of dialogs complete the configuration of the Internet connection. This is followed by the optional setup of a .Mac account, configuration of Mail.app, and setting of the local time zone, date, and time.

6. If an Internet connection was unavailable to complete registration, the final screen is a reminder to be a good user and register your software at a later date.

    The secondary installer then promptly finishes and leaves the user in the Finder, ready to start working.

The Setup Assistant (Mac OS X Server)

Mac OS X Server's setup assistant is a little less colorful and more utilitarian, but no less functional.

1. Similar to the Mac OS X Client assistant, we are greeted by a "Welcome" screen and questions about the keyboard setup and the software serial number.

2. This is followed by a dialog that allows you to create the administrator account for the server.

    We would suggest not assigning this account to a particular user (say, "Bob Smith") to be used on a daily basis, but create it as a separate account to be used sparingly for administrative duties. Users should not be logging onto the server directly for anything other than administrative work anyway. The password chosen for this first account is also used for the root account, which unlike in the client edition, is enabled by default.

3. The next set of screens configure the network functionality of the server.

    First is configuration of the system's hostname, its DNS servers, search domain, and computer name. The last is used for AppleTalk connectivity, as opposed to the hostname, which is used by other IP-based protocols.

This is followed by configuration of the various ethernet ports on the system, starting with the network protocols that will be used on each (TCP/IP and AppleTalk). Administrators should choose only the protocols they will be using on their network. Most modern networks require TCP/IP, which is enabled on all interfaces by default. AppleTalk is a protocol used to support some legacy systems (including older Macs and printers). AppleTalk is not enabled by default. Next comes configuration of the individual interfaces for IP for those ethernet ports selected to run TCP/IP.

4. The second to last screen allows administrators to select the network services their server will be providing.

   All the services are disabled by default and will be activated only by selecting the appropriate check box. Any service can also be enabled or disabled later as an administrator sees fit. The Apple file service uses the Apple File Protocol (AFP) to share resources (directories and files) with Mac OS (8, 9, and X) clients. Print service can share printers to clients via a variety of protocols (AppleTalk, SMB, and LPR). The Web service is a common http server (Apache, actually) for sharing web-based content. It can also be configured to provide WebDAV capabilities, which among other things provides for file sharing via the web server. We will discuss WebDAV in more depth in Chapter 7, "File Sharing." Macintosh Manager provides a method for centrally managing Mac OS 8 and Mac OS 9 client computers. Email services are provided by Mail service. Streaming media content (video, music, and so on) is served by the QuickTime Streaming Server (QTSS).

5. Whether or not QTSS is enabled during installation, the last of the networking configuration screens requires you to set up an administrator account for it. This account is separate from the administrator account you created earlier during the installation and only provides for administration of the QTSS service.

6. The final dialogs of the setup assistant set the server's time zone, and its date and time.

7. The next screen displays the configuration the assistant is about to apply (allowing an administrator to save a copy of this configuration as well), and a button to allow you to Go Ahead and apply it.

8. After the configuration is applied, the assistant provides some helpful information on where to find the applications to manage the various services provided by Mac OS X Server. Clicking the Continue button

dismisses the setup assistant and starts another application, the Open Directory Assistant.

The Open Directory Assistant starts with the ubiquitous "Welcome" dialog (see Figure 2.8). Open Directory is Apple's extensible architecture for storing network and system configuration and management information. It is similar to Microsoft's Active Directory or Novell's Novell Directory Service (NDS). A full description of proper configuration and use of Open Directory is beyond the scope of this book, although we will go into enterprise configuration and integration in Chapter 10, "Directory Services."

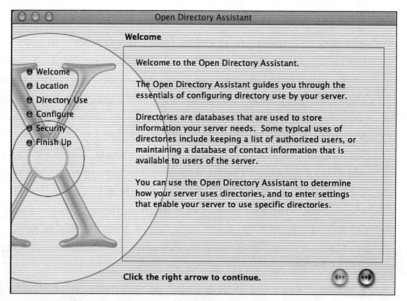

FIGURE 2.8   The Open Directory Assistant "Welcome" dialog.

9. The second screen of the Open Directory Assistant describes that the functionality it provides depends on a number of factors, including whether the server is using a statically assigned IP address (see Figure 2.9).

10. Assuming the server has a static address (servers should generally have static addresses on their local network), the next dialog allows you to choose how the directory is configured (see Figure 2.10).

For this installation, you can assume that no other directories exist and that you want to provide directory information to other computers on the network (the third option).

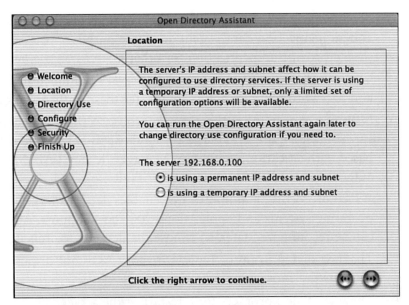

FIGURE 2.9   Setting how the server's IP is determined.

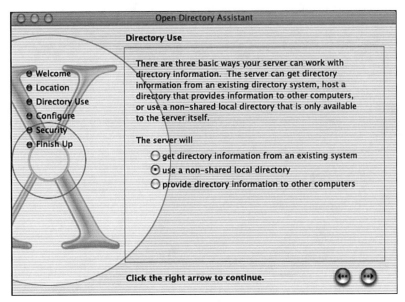

FIGURE 2.10   Setting how the directory is configured.

11. The next screen allows you to turn on LDAP support, which is recommended, and which you should do.

12. Next is configuration of how the directory gets or provides password and authentication data. Again, for these purposes you can assume you should provide authentication for other systems on the network.

13. The next dialog notifies you that the server's administrator username and password will be used to administer these authentication services.

14. Next you choose the authentication protocols the server will support (see Figure 2.11). These include SMB-NT (modern NT-based authentication), SMB-Lan Manager (legacy LAN Manager-based authentication), CRAM-MD5, and APOP.

    Which protocols an administrator enables depends largely on the client operating systems and applications they must support. All these options can be reconfigured later, so choose the defaults for this installation.

15. The next dialog from the Open Directory Assistant displays and commits the chosen configuration.

16. The final dialog prompts for a restart of the server.

    A quick reboot and the server boots to the login window, ready to start serving.

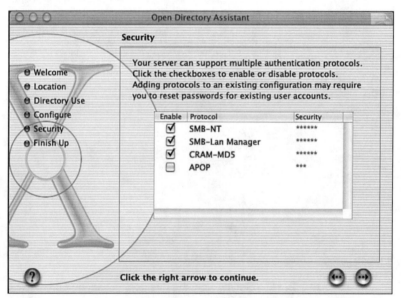

FIGURE 2.11   Setting authentication protocols in the Open Directory Assistant.

Developer Tools

There is one more optional package in the installation of Mac OS X—the Developer Tools. The Developer Tools is the third CD in the Mac OS X distribution. It contains a number of applications used to develop, test, and debug applications for the Mac OS X platform. Systems that will be regularly downloading source packages for compilation and installation will require Developer Tools to be installed. For those shared systems where the capability of untrusted users to compile applications is too risky and mitigation by strengthened permissions is difficult, it may be proper to leave the package uninstalled. Most single-user computers will need the software installed to allow power users to get the most out of their systems.

Summary

Apple has done a nice job of making Mac OS X as easy to install as it is to use. This ease of installation belies the importance of some of the decisions made during the install. Installation of optional applications and tools, choice of filesystem, and use of accounts and other choices all affect the security of the host before it is even put into production. Knowing how these decisions affect overall security and making the best choices for a given installation will help the installed system to be a secure base and hopefully keep it from coming to a bad ending.

But installation is only the first step on the path. Now that the system is installed, it is time to move on to the next step and Chapter 3, "Mac OS X Client General Security Practices."

PART II
SYSTEM SECURITY

## CHAPTER 3

MAC OS X CLIENT GENERAL SECURITY PRACTICES

"I think I'll call him Stampy."
—Bart Simpson

To have a secured workstation, all aspects of the machines' security need to be considered. From physical security to account management to boot options, the quality of the base configuration of your operating system makes a huge difference in the overall security of the host. There are many analogies that can be used to describe the need for secure OS configuration; A house needs a solid foundation to survive a storm, a chain is only as good as its weakest link, a tree with shallow roots is easily toppled. Regardless of which analogy you prefer, realize that the more effort and attention to detail you provide to your base configuration, the more secure and reliable your host will be.

This advice holds particularly true for Mac OS X. OS X is a powerful, modern operating system with a UNIX core. When using the operating system for day-to-day activities, it is easy to use and provides a stable platform for your applications. However, in the hands of a malicious user attempting to gain access to your data or resources, it is powerful and dangerous. Through proper configuration and maintenance, your Mac OS X workstation can provide a stable and *secure* platform for your applications.

Mac OS X as it ships out of the box is designed to be user friendly. However, to be user friendly, some sacrifices have been made that make it less secure. Also, there are some common configuration practices that can further reduce the overall security of the core operating system. This chapter presents techniques that you can employ that make Mac OS X more secure and have a minimal impact on the usability of the system.

Concerns About Physical Access

Physical security is a trait often overlooked when attempting to secure a host. However, it is an important aspect of information security. Lack of physical security in a workplace can allow illicit and almost untraceable access. According to various reports, between 38% and 70% of all computer attacks are *insider attacks*. Insider attacks are violations of the security of a resource by someone within your organization. These attacks are common because not only will an insider potentially have the motivation to attack, they will have easier access to trusted resources than an outside entity. Controlling physical access to a host is the first step in preventing an insider attack.

PHYSICAL SECURITY IN THE WORKPLACE

At a previous job, one of us (Bruce) shared an office with seven other system administrators. They worked around the clock on a shift basis, so it was not unusual for only one or two people to be in the office at a time. This gave some workers unsupervised physical access to their coworkers machines for hours on end. They took great joy in breaking into each others' computers and performing various acts of mischief. Over time, the administrators became skilled at locking down their workstations to make it difficult for those trying to play tricks on them. It was increasingly a real cat-and-mouse game as their defensive and offensive skills became refined.

In the end, the activity caused the workers to become much more security conscious and better administrators. Luckily, they were all friends and knew their boundaries with each other and the company. However, if the situation had been slightly different and there was a malicious user in the group, there could have been great harm done. It is easy to imagine situations where someone could impersonate a coworker in an effort to get them fired or harm the company. Many insider attacks are actually due to a disgruntled employee. Physical security is not simply a matter for data centers and security systems. It is something every employee needs to be concerned with.

Doors, Locks, and Guards

The first step in keeping a machine secure from prying fingers is keeping the host in a restricted location. How restricted you keep the host depends on the risk and potential loss of someone gaining illicit physical access. Depending on your level of risk, you may use locked doors, electronic security systems, or even armed guards. Even in an office environment, a coworker may be your worst enemy. Simply closing and locking your office door while you are away from your host may be enough to keep your machine secure from prying hands and eyes.

Remember, you are not securing only your host. Any resource your host can access is vulnerable if your host is compromised. Your host is only a link in a chain.

Open Firmware Password

Assuming someone gains access to your host, all is not lost. There are ways to prevent a person from gaining various types of access. Unfortunately, there are things that you can't stop. A malicious user can steal a whole machine or open it up and steal sensitive parts such as the hard drive or other storage media. Some computer cases have locks or places where antitheft devices can be attached. These mechanisms can make theft much more difficult for the casual attacker. The antitheft techniques differ from machine to machine, so consult the documentation that came with your computer.

Your Mac's bootstrapping process is controlled by something called Open Firmware. Open Firmware is a small program contained on a chip within your computer that controls its boot process. Open Firmware was developed many years ago and is used for many different computing platforms, including Sun and Apple's Macintosh series. It is similar to a BIOS on a PC but provides much more functionality and extensibility than a typical BIOS implementation.

Newer versions of Open Firmware password-protect your boot process. To make use of this functionality, you must be running Open Firmware version 4.1.7 or newer. You can find what version your machine is running by launching System Profiler and looking for the Boot ROM Version section (see Figure 3.1). If you need to upgrade your Open Firmware, go to `http://www.info.apple.com/` and search for the correct upgrade based on your platform. Alternatively, firmware updates are also available on your Mac OS X 10.2 installation CD.

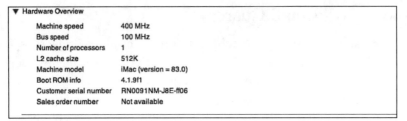

▼ Hardware Overview

Machine speed	400 MHz
Bus speed	100 MHz
Number of processors	1
L2 cache size	512K
Machine model	iMac (version = 83.0)
Boot ROM info	4.1.9f1
Customer serial number	RN0091NM-J8E-ff06
Sales order number	Not available

FIGURE 3.1   Open Firmware information from System Profiler.

After you have updated your machine, download the Open Firmware Password application from `http://docs.info.apple.com/article.html?artnum=120095` or install it from the Mac OS X 10.2 installation CD. This application allows you to password-protect certain functions of Open Firmware when the system is being booted, including

- Booting to CD-ROM, NetBoot, or a specific disk
- Booting in verbose mode
- Booting into single user mode
- Booting to the Open Firmware prompt (Command-Option-O-F at startup) and issuing commands

Figure 3.2 shows the Open Firmware Password utility in action. Be sure you use a difficult-to-guess password.

These features are great in a lab environment when a normal unattended boot is desired, but booting to a CD would generally only be done by a malicious user. Unfortunately, many people would like to have a higher degree of security by requiring a password at boot time to simply bring the operating system up. This functionality is analogous to a POST password on a PC. Although Apple does not supply a tool for directly configuring a boot password, Open Firmware does support this concept.

FIGURE 3.2   Setting an Open Firmware password.

nvram is a program accessible via the Terminal program that displays the contents of many variables stored within Open Firmware. Running it as a normal user allows you to view the public values and not modify any of the values. Running it via sudo nvram prints any private fields, such as the password, and allows modification of the Open Firmware contents. The –p flag prints the contents of Open Firmware:

```
bash-2.05a$ sudo nvram -p
Password:
... a great deal of output...
security-mode     command
... more output...
security-password     %e8%cc%d2%cf%c1%c1
```

Rather than use the nvram command, a machine can be booted directly to the Open Firmware prompt. Pressing Command-Option-O-F as a machine is being booted, bypasses the normal boot process and provides you with a prompt that directly controls Open Firmware. The security mode can be reset to none by issuing the setenv security-mode none command at the Open Firmware prompt. printenv displays all Open Firmware variables. Typing **reset-all** reboots the host after resetting the password. For a complete discussion of Open Firmware commands, see Apple Tech Note 1061 at http://developer.apple.com/technotes/tn/tn1061.html.

The security mode set by the Apple Open Firmware Password application is set to command. This provides the level of functionality listed earlier. To set the security mode to the original value that shipped with your machine, execute sudo nvram security-mode="none". To enable password protection for *all* Open Firmware activities, including booting to the default disk, set the security-mode to full. This forces a user who wants to boot a machine to know the Open Firmware password to access the normal operating system. To make brute forcing the password unlikely, be sure to set a password that is difficult to guess and contains a variety of characters.

> **NOTE**
>
> The security password displayed by the nvram command is not a cryptographically secured password. The password is simply displayed in its hexadecimal representation. This is merely an obfuscation of the password, not actual protection. Be aware that a user with administrative privileges can easily decrypt this password and use it later without your knowledge.

Password-protecting Open Firmware does not ensure the host cannot be booted in a manner counter to what you intend. An attacker who can open the case of the computer can force a password reset. By adding or removing memory, the host is put into a mode where it is possible to reset the PRAM by pressing Command-Option-P-R at boot time. Once the PRAM is reset three times, the password protection is removed. This quirk in the Open Firmware architecture underscores the reason for physical locks on your hosts.

Also, a utility called FWSucker allows an attacker, once logged in to a host, to harvest the Open Firmware password. Even guest users can decrypt the password. FWSucker is available from http://www.msec.net/software/. Again, Open Firmware password protection must be treated as a tool in protecting your host, not absolute protection.

Login Window

If a malicious user manages to successfully boot your machine, there are still more configuration options that will make their life difficult. By default, Mac OS X logs in automatically to the primary account on the machine. This gives anyone with the capability to boot the machine full access to the operating system. This can be disabled in the Accounts System Preferences panel. Under the Users tab, uncheck the line labeled Log in Automatically as [username]. This causes a login window to be displayed after the next boot.

In the Login Options tab (see Figure 3.3), there are several other default options that should be changed. The Login Window can display a list of user accounts on the machine and allow you to select one or it can simply display a blank username input field. By selecting Name and password you force a local attacker to know both the account name *and* the password. This might not be a huge barrier, but it is one more thing the attacker must know. Please note that starting in Mac OS X 10.2, the previous login name is not shown.

You also might want to check the Hide the Restart and Shutdown Buttons check box. This prevents users from shutting down or restarting the machine by one mouse click from the login screen. However, be aware that the power button still works so it is still possible to power off the machine.

Finally, uncheck the check box for Show Password Hint After 3 Attempts to Enter a Password. Selecting this causes the hint that was entered when the user was created to be displayed on the login screen. This can be handy if you have forgotten your password, but it can also be handy for an attacker. Make a point of remembering your password and you will need this option. Besides, after you get used to logging into your machine, entering your password will become second nature to you.

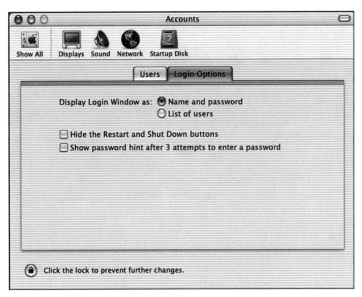

FIGURE 3.3 Login options.

Screen Locking

All these configuration steps are useful if an attacker gains access to a host that is powered off. Things are a bit different when you are logged into a host and have stepped away for a moment. If you leave your machine unattended while you are logged in, you have bypassed all boot security mechanisms for an attacker with physical access.

Luckily, the screen saver for Mac OS X can be password-protected. Under the Activation tab in the Screen Effects Preferences panel there is a radio button to force the screen saver to ask for your password when normal operation resumes (see Figure 3.4). This effectively locks the screen while Screen Effects are active. There is also a slider on the same tab that controls how long the machine needs to be idle before the screen is locked.

This timer is great in instances when you forget to lock your workstation. However, it is not practical to stand watch over your machine for a series of minutes while you wait for Screen Effects to turn on. On the Hot Corners tab of the Screen Effects Preferences panel you can specify a corner (or corners) where you can drag your mouse to lock your screen. This allows you to lock your workstation at will without having to wait.

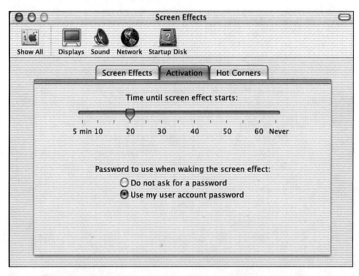

FIGURE 3.4   The Screen Effects Preferences panel.

MAC OS X SCREEN LOCKING

Mac OS X screen locking is not as robust and secure as other operating systems' locking mechanisms. Under Windows XP you must press Control-Alt-Delete, a special key sequence that sends an interrupt to the core processor to make sure some other application is not pretending to be the Windows Lock screen. OS X has no such mechanisms. In fact, you can send some commands to the operating system while the screen is locked. For instance, you can force the system to take a screen capture of the lock screen by pressing Command-Shift-3. It is obvious that the OS X password protected Screen Effects does not provide the highest level of security in locked screen. However, it is important to note that the attacker at this point would have physical access anyway so even a bulletproof screen lock can be bypassed with a screwdriver and a few minutes to pry out the hard drive.

System Preferences Locking

You may have noticed a lock in the bottom-left corner of some System Preferences panes. The capability to lock a preference pane is present in the Network and System panes primarily and may also be available in panes provided by third-party software. This lock enables you to password-protect sensitive system settings, preventing unauthorized or unintentional changes. By clicking the lock within a pane, users of the workstation cannot change the configuration of that pane. When a change needs to be made, click the lock again and you will be prompted for a username and password. Type the credentials of your administrative user account and the pane will once again allow modification. Figure 3.5 shows a pane as it looks before and after locking has been utilized. The locking mechanism provided by the preferences lock only applies to the current user. It is not a global lock for all users, therefore its utility is limited. Use specific attributes for user rights to control their ability to modify Preferences panes. See User Accounts and Access Control later in this chapter for more information on per user access control.

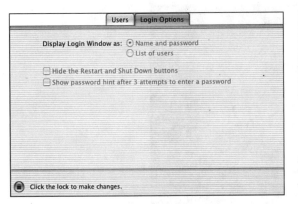 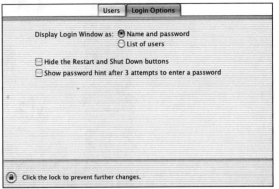

FIGURE 3.5   Comparison of locked and unlocked Accounts panel.

Dual Booting and the Classic Environment

The idea of running more than one operating system on a single host is a relatively new idea to mainstream Mac users. The idea of *dual booting* a host where you can select from several operating systems at boot time has been common on the PC platform for years. PC users may commonly have several operating systems they use depending on their needs, especially if the user periodically uses Linux.

Classic and Mac OS 9

With the advent of Mac OS X, running two operating systems became a fact of life for most Mac OS X users. Mac OS X is a completely different operating system from previous versions of Mac OS. Rather than attempt to provide backward compatibility with previous Mac OS applications directly within Mac OS X, Apple opted for what it calls the *Classic Environment*. Classic provides support for previous apps by actually running a previous version of Mac OS on top of Mac OS X. Mac OS X effectively provides an emulation environment for Mac OS 9 to run in as a complete operating system. Mac OS 9 runs as a process within Mac OS X.

When a Classic application launches, Mac OS X automatically launches Classic to provide an environment for the application to run in. If you click the collapsible triangle, you can actually see Mac OS 9 booting within Mac OS X (see Figure 3.6).

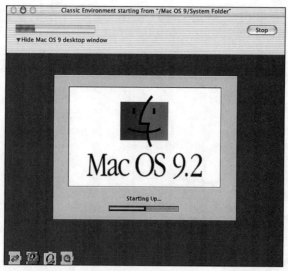

FIGURE 3.6   The hidden Mac OS 9 startup window.

Classic requires a great deal of system resources to run. Because you are running two complete operating systems at one time, your machine's resources are split between them. Most notably, Mac OS 9 uses a large amount of RAM. Mac OS X gives Classic hooks to other resources, such as disks and network interfaces.

Like any other application, it is best to remove or not install Classic if you do not require it. Even though Classic is run through emulation on the host, it has access to many of the system's sensitive devices. Mac OS X attempts to intercept access to restricted data or devices through the Security Services interface. However, this method may not be bulletproof to all types of attacks.

OS 9 AND OS X 10.2

Starting with OS X 10.2, Apple no longer ships an OS 9 disk with the main operating system. This is a step by Apple toward phasing out OS 9 support. If you need Classic support under 10.2, you will need to install media purchased separately. Going forward this move by Apple means there will be fewer and fewer OS X machines with the Classic environment.

Dual Booting Dangers

The Mac platform provides a means to boot multiple operating systems on the same host. This capability is controlled by the Startup Disk control panel. If you have Classic installed on a host, you have the opportunity to boot directly to Mac OS 9. This option is provided for applications that require direct hardware access under Mac OS 9. Mac OS X runs Classic through an emulator. This emulator abstracts the hardware from Mac OS 9 applications. If an application uses special hardware or needs low-level access, booting directly to Mac OS 9 provides a means for these specific applications to work. For example, a video game may have been written to directly access a joystick connected to a host. This game will not work properly under Mac OS X.

Mac OS 9 has very few security features compared to Mac OS X. When Mac OS 9 is booted on a host that also contains Mac OS X, many of the security features of Mac OS X are completely bypassed. Mac OS 9 has complete access to all the hardware on a host, and subsequently has access to all the data on that hardware. Filesystem level access control, such as files limited to only the superuser account, can be bypassed within Mac OS 9.

If you require Classic applications without direct hardware access, you can install Mac OS 9 into a disk image created with DiskCopy. This disk image will automatically be mounted by Mac OS X when it needs to launch the Classic environment. However, because the disk image is a file within Mac OS X, it prevents direct booting to Mac OS 9. If you require direct hardware access in Mac OS 9, be sure you install an OpenFirmware password to prevent unauthorized booting.

> **NOTE**
>
> Starting sometime in 2003, hardware shipped from Apple will no longer have the capability to boot to OS 9 directly. It will allow OS 9 access only through Classic regardless of how OS 9 is installed.

To help mitigate the risk of an Mac OS 9 application accessing Mac OS X data, you should ensure Mac OS X is installed on a UFS partition. Mac OS 9 cannot natively read UFS filesystems. Therefore, data stored on the UFS partition will be safe from modification due to Mac OS 9 applications.

Other operating systems, such as Linux, can be booted on a Mac. These other operating systems may also have the capability to bypass the security model of Mac OS X because they have direct access to the hardware. Even worse, the Mac OS X installation can be used to boot a host and reset the root password. Again, the best option if you have to boot to two bootable operating systems on a host is to require an Open Firmware password.

Staying Current with Mac OS X

Any operating system, regardless of who wrote it and on what platform it runs, will eventually be found to be vulnerable to some type of attack. After these vulnerabilities are found, it is important for vendors to release a patch in a timely manner. It is also important for administrators to have an intuitive and effective way to stay current with the latest patch levels.

Apple has gone through a bit of a revolution in how it handles patches. In the early days of Mac OS X, patches were slow to arrive and the patching mechanism provided within Mac OS X was not secure. However, based on user feedback, Apple is now much more responsive about releasing security patches. They have also updated their patching mechanism to provide assurances of the integrity of the patch and where it came from.

Due to the UNIX core of Mac OS X, many of the vulnerabilities that affect other UNIX variants, such as FreeBSD and Linux, will also affect Mac OS X. Mac OS X has also had its fair share of vulnerabilities specific to itself. It is important to stay current with the patches released by Apple to protect yourself from attackers attempting to utilize known vulnerabilities.

The Software Update Preferences pane controls Mac OS X's automatic update features. The Update Software tab controls the frequency of when Software Update runs. Set this to daily to be as current as reasonably possible. If you feel you need to check for updates by hand, there is a Check Now button that will run Software Update manually. When Software Update runs, it queries a server at Apple for any patches and fixes available for software installed on your computer (see Figure 3.7). If it finds anything that requires updates, it will display them to you and verify that you want the updates installed. After Software Update has run, run it manually another time. Due to dependencies on other updates, some updates may not be installed the first time. By running Software Update a second time, any packages with previous dependencies should be installed.

FIGURE 3.7   The Software Update panel.

After you have selected the updates you want to install, Software Update downloads the patches and installs them. Generally the core security updates will require a reboot of your machine, so be sure you have saved all your work before you start the update process. Depending on how far behind on patches you are, you may have to run Software Update several times.

There is also a command line software update program, softwareupdate, that can be run from the Terminal application. When run without any parameters passed to it, it will contact the servers at Apple and determine what patches need to be installed:

```
bash-2.05a$ sudo softwareupdate
Software Update Tool
Copyright 2002 Apple Computer, Inc.
Software Update found the following new or updated software:
   - 3359
         QuickTime (6.0.2), 19620K - restart required
   - 3339
         StuffIt Expander Security Update (7.0), 4420K
```

To install a particular patch, reference it by name as a parameter. For example sudo softwareupdate 3339 will install the StuffIt Expander Security Update. softwareupdate is convenient if you are maintaining workstations remotely and need to update them without terminal access.

User Accounts and Access Control

One of the driving principles of information security is the idea of *Least Privilege*. Least Privilege is the concept that an entity should be given only the fewest possible rights to perform its required activity and no more. For instance, if a user only needs to surf the Internet, he does not need the capability to change the system's IP address or add new users. By giving a user more access than he requires, you are opening the door to, at the very least, system instability and possibly security compromises. Unfortunately, most modern operating systems were not designed from the ground up to adhere to Least Privilege. Usability and extensibility won the day. Locking down users to a small subset of commands is a difficult job. Thinking about what your users need to accomplish and being diligent with systems configuration will drive up the security of your systems.

When Mac OS X is first installed on a host, a user is created with administrator privileges. This user has a great deal of control of the workstation, either directly through the various System Preferences panes or through other mechanisms such as sudo. Mac OS X attempts to limit the direct access this administrative user has by requiring an administrative password be supplied when an especially sensitive activity is performed. For example, when installing a third-party application that needs to modify your network stack, Mac OS X will launch an authentication screen to verify the activity. When launching commands through the Terminal program sudo, you are prompted for a password as well.

However, there are still a great number of activities that an admin user can perform that you may not want to allow everyone to do. Mac OS X comes with a robust user creation utility that allows you to have a reasonable amount of control over what users can and cannot do. If someone other than yourself will use your host, for example, a coworker or relative, it is advisable to create a user account specifically for that person which grants only the access they require.

ROLE ACCOUNTS

A *role account* is an account that multiple people use to gain access to a host. Role accounts are common in an office environment where a group of individuals require the same type of access. For example, everyone in finance may use the *finance* account to connect to an ftp server. Although this simplifies account management, it makes tracking illicit use very difficult. Every person accessing a system should have his or her own unique account. This provides a more complete audit trail for you to examine when something bad happens to the machine.

The Users tab in the Accounts System Preferences pane controls all user accounts on the system. Adding a new user is as simple as clicking New User and filling in all the required fields (see Figure 3.8). The Name field is what is commonly known in the UNIX world as the GECOS field. This should contain the user's full name and any relevant contact information. The Short Name field corresponds to the UNIX username. When filling in the password field, be sure to use a strong password. A strong password is not guessable and should contain a combination of letters, numbers, and special characters. Be sure the user changes her password when she first logs on to the host.

Leave the Password Hint field blank. As mentioned before this will be of great help to an attacker and should be disabled for the login screen. If need be, give the user administration privileges, but only do so if absolutely required. Also, you can allow the user to log in from a Windows host via SMB. This enables SMB access for the entire host and grants that user access to his or her files on the system. Again, only grant this access if it is required for your network. For more information on SMB and other network services, see Chapter 6, "Internet Services."

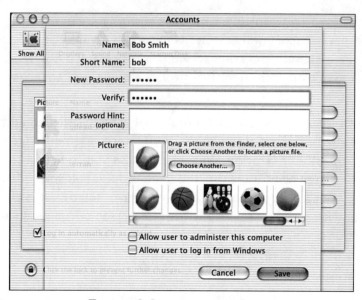

FIGURE 3.8   Adding a new user.

After the user has been added to the system you can further limit his access by clicking Capabilities in the Accounts pane. This allows for fine-grained control over what the user can and cannot do on the host. You can control whether the user can modify system settings, burn CDs, or even launch certain programs. Note that the Capabilities button is not available if the new user has administrator privileges. There is an option to enable the Simple Finder for the user. Simple Finder allows you to limit what applications a user can see. By selecting applications in the Applications list view, Simple Finder will only display the allowed applications. Also, Simple Finder can only open documents containing the users Documents folder in their Home. The Simple Finder cannot open ordinary folders.

The underlying mechanism that controls user accounts is not the standard UNIX /etc/password architecture. NetInfo is a distributed user management system that is employed by Mac OS X for authentication and authorization issues. When making changes to a user, you are really making the changes to the NetInfo database. For more information on NetInfo see NetInfo in Chapter 10, "Directory Services." The UNIX /etc/password construct is used by Mac OS X only in the event of booting to single user mode.

LIMITING ACCESS IS HARD TO DO

Restricting access to a subset of programs is not always bulletproof. Remember Bruce's mischievous coworkers who were constantly breaking into each other's workstations? Well, they were also finding ways to break through various restrictions on their user accounts imposed on them based on Least Privilege. Through the `sudo` tool they were granted rights to the UNIX editor `vi` so they could edit various sensitive system files when needed. However, `vi` could be used to view files they were not supposed to view. It was also able to launch other programs from within itself. So using the higher privilege level of the `vi` process, they could run other programs which were not explicitly allowed to them under `sudo`.

The problem was due to transitivity of trust from `sudo` to `vi` to other external programs. By giving them explicit rights to use `vi`, `sudo` was actually giving them rights to all the programs on the host. Luckily, rather than be malicious about the excess trust, they used it as a tool to learn more about locking down user accounts. One of them would modify `sudo` to further limit access while still allowing everyone to do their jobs and the rest of them would try to break out of the little "jail" that was created. It taught them the good and bad about Least Privilege and trying to enforce it.

Remember, just because a user does not have explicit access to a program through his account does not mean he will not find a way to access it.

Filesystem Encryption

Even when an attacker has complete access to your host, you can still use encryption to protect your most sensitive data. Properly implemented, encrypting files is a great way to keep private data from being read by the wrong people. Historically, however, encrypting data you use on a regular basis has been a difficult and awkward process. The tools available for most operating systems were very complex and required the user to have deep knowledge of cryptography and system administration.

Thankfully, modern operating systems have made huge advances in useable encryption. Microsoft Windows XP and Mac OS X both have the capability to encrypt user data in a manner that is secure and relatively transparent. This is a great leap forward as it allows for your data to be secure even in the event of theft. Previously this was only possible with very specialized software or with a great deal of effort.

At the heart of filesystem encryption in Mac OS X are two applications: DiskCopy and KeychainAccess. DiskCopy is used to create and copy disk images to drives. KeychainAccess is used to automatically handle passwords and passphrases for programs and web sites. KeychainAccess is discussed in detail in Chapter 5, "User Applications."

Primarily DiskCopy is used to burn CD-R and DVD-RAM discs. However, it can also create disk images that will exist on top of a normal hard disk filesystem. These disk images are convenient for storing personal data and moving it between machines. Images created by DiskCopy are also used for software distribution. Many popular freeware and shareware software packages ship as disk images that can be mounted on a machine, used to install the software, then discarded. The disk image, typically with a .dmg extension, is downloaded and saved to a local disk. When the image is activated, DiskCopy will verify the checksum of the image, and then mount the volume contained in the image on the desktop. You can then access the data in the volume like any disk. When you are done with the volume, it can be unmounted by ejecting it as if it were removable media.

DiskCopy also allows for these disk images to be encrypted using AES to protect the data inside. AES, the *Advanced Encryption Standard*, is a symmetric cryptographic mechanism endorsed by the United States government. AES has gone through detailed analysis and is generally considered secure. For most uses it is secure enough to be unbreakable.

Before you make your new volume, determine how large you need it to be. If you are going to be storing email or other small files only, a few megabytes should work fine. If you are going to be storing multimedia files and other types of large data, you may need to allocate several hundred megabytes. Be aware that when you make the disk image it uses all the space when it is created. It does not grow based on your needs up to a maximum nor can it be grown later if you fill it up. It should be big enough to hold the data you need but not so much to run yourself out of space.

To create an encrypted volume, launch DiskCopy from the Utilities folder. Create a new disk image by selecting File, New, Blank Image. A window pops up enabling you to configure properties for the new image (see Figure 3.9). The Save As field is the name of the file in which the image will be saved. The Volume Name is the name the volume will have once it is mounted. Choose the format required for your workstation. For a discussion of the differences between HFS+ and UFS and why you would choose one or the other, see Chapter 2, "Installation." Finally, set the required size, select AES encryption, and click Create.

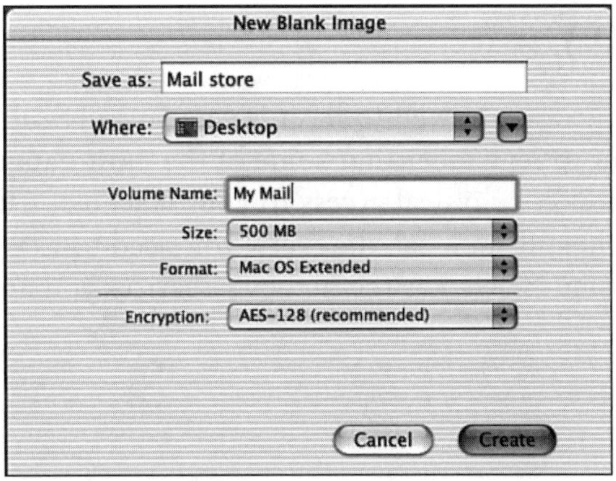

FIGURE 3.9   Creating a blank image with DiskCopy.

DiskCopy will then create and format the image. It will then prompt you for a passphrase for the image. This password is what will protect your sensitive data, so be sure it is a strong password with a combination of letters, numbers, and special characters. If the Remember Password check box is checked, this passphrase will then be stored in your keychain so you do not have to type it in every time you need to mount the volume. After the passphrase is entered and verified, the volume will be mounted and you can begin using it.

After your next reboot, the volume will not be mounted automatically. To use the volume, double-click on the disk image. DiskCopy launches, accesses your keychain with your log-in credentials, and decrypts and mounts the volume. If you need to unmount the volume, simply drag it to the trash or type Command-E to (virtually) eject it.

ENCRYPTED FILES AND FILESYSTEMS IN WINDOWS XP VERSUS OS X

Windows XP handles encrypted files and filesystems much differently than OS X. In OS X, files cannot be encrypted individually. Rather, you must go through the preceding process with DiskCopy and create a standalone volume. In Windows XP, you can encrypt a file, a directory, or an entire filesystem. This allows for much greater flexibility in only encrypting exactly what you need.

In Windows XP, if a file is moved from an encrypted directory to an unencrypted directory, the file retains its encrypted attribute. That ensures that you do not inadvertently remove protection from a sensitive file. Like OS X, the files are effectively "unlocked" using your log-in credentials when you authenticate to the operating system. However, there is no standalone keychain application that manages this access. Access is controlled by the core authentication mechanisms within Windows XP.

Summary

In the networked world we live in, it is easy to forget about console security. It is important to remember that some of the most dangerous attackers are the ones with direct physical access to your machine. After you have properly secured your host from local attackers, you need to examine the applications you will be using, as well as the network services you are running.

## CHAPTER 4

WHAT IS THIS UNIX THING?

"UNIX is simple. It just takes a genius to understand its simplicity."
—Dennis Ritchie

Behind the advanced Aqua interface, and the glitter of the Quartz windowing system, Mac OS X is a modern UNIX operating system. By now you have probably heard this a million times. This chapter focuses on the most critical aspects of UNIX security and, specifically, those aspects particular to Mac OS X. Those with a UNIX background will benefit most from the exposed peculiarities of this system. Those who come from more of a Mac OS background will benefit most from learning about the awesome difference in power and, in turn, the incredible responsibilities that go along with this new version of Mac OS.

First, we will cover the basics of the command line interface, and the security concerns surrounding the use of the terminal application that ships with Mac OS X. Next, we will cover some key command line applications that can be helpful in managing the security of Mac OS X system(s). Topics in this chapter also include the details of modifying file permissions and file ownership, as well as an exploration of the nature of certain files that are installed with the OS.

Finally, we will cover some common UNIX security topics, including administrative issues surrounding the sudo application.

Now that we have a full-bore UNIX operating system to toy with, it is important to know how to do so without burning ourselves in the process.

The Command Line Interface

The first versions of UNIX did not have complex graphical interfaces. In fact, they had no real graphical interfaces at all. The human computer interaction that took place was always through a command line interface. Most modern UNIX systems still use the command line as the primary interface, treating graphical interfaces as an optional set of applications. Mac OS X is a little different in this respect; the user is automatically presented with a graphical interface as the primary interface on boot.

Apple has probably done the best job yet of placing a usable graphical interface on top of a UNIX system. However, under the hood Mac OS X is still a UNIX-based system. Throughout this book, we will be concerned with issues of security and often these issues cannot be fully addressed without making use of the command line interface.

Apple has also done a decent job of securing Mac OS X right out of the box. Keeping it secure requires knowledge and understanding of the UNIX foundation that supports this operating system. This understanding begins with the command line interface.

Command Line Access

There are different ways to obtain command line access on a Mac OS X system. You can gain access via remote login, you can use the Terminal.app from within the Aqua interface, you can boot into single user mode as described in Chapter 3, "Mac OS X Client General Security Practices," or you can log in to the console directly.

CONSOLE LOGIN

To log in to the console directly and bypass the Aqua interface, use >console as a username (see Figure 4.1). Do not enter a password. This exits the graphical login application, shuts down the window server and leaves you with a command line interface. Initially, this will be just a login prompt. This and login options similar to this one will be covered in detail in Chapter 9, "Enterprise Host Configuration."

FIGURE 4.1   Logging in to the Mac OS X console for command line access.

By default, the legacy UNIX remote access methods, including `telnet`, remote shell (`rsh`), and remote login (`rlogin`) are disabled. This is a good thing. All these access methods present security risks to your system and are ideal targets for attackers. With `telnet`, the login process is conducted without encryption, as is all subsequent communication. By default, `rlogin` and `rsh` suffer the same problem.

Secure Shell (SSH) solves these issues, and more. SSH protects the authentication process, as well as all communication between the client and the remote host. SSH is essentially a secure replacement for these legacy UNIX access methods. SSH is also disabled by default but can easily be enabled through the GUI, using `System Preferences.app`. In the Sharing pane, select the Services tab. Select the Remote Login service and click the Start button (see Figure 4.2). This will perform the steps needed to start the SSH server. Apple calls the SSH server the "Secure Login Server." From that point on, the server will be started automatically at boot time until specifically disabled.

Mac OS X is inherently a multiuser operating system. Thus, multiple users can be logged in simultaneously with access to a command line interface. This, combined with the operating system's networking capabilities, makes Mac OS X more of a target for attackers than previous versions of Mac OS. It is important to be aware of other users on the system, and their actions. This is covered more later in this chapter when we discuss the `who` and `ps` commands.

FIGURE 4.2   Enabling the SSH server for secure remote shell access.

As an administrator, it is essential that you understand the details of remote and direct access and how to control them. As a user it is important to understand the risks involved with command line access. Information pertaining to securing system services will be discussed throughout the remainder of this book.

Command Line Security

`Terminal.app` reveals a familiar UNIX command line interface (see Figure 4.3). This interface provides access to applications that modify important files and change the state of the system. In fact, many of these operations can be done only on the command line. The potential for disaster is probably more potent than any other application installed with the operating system. While it is possible to unintentionally wreak havoc on a system through the GUI, it is generally a lot harder. This is especially true with Mac OS X. The graphical interface is very user friendly. This is often not the case with the command line interface.

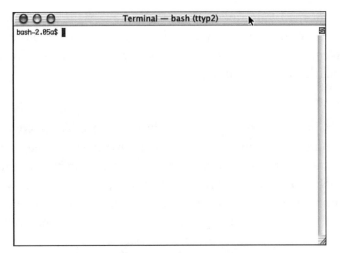

FIGURE 4.3 The Mac OS X Terminal.app.

A good rule to follow is: Never run terminal commands unless you know the effects they will have on the system and other users. This is especially important while executing commands as root. An administrator armed with root privileges can be very dangerous. With a single command the root user can destroy a system, or render it unable to boot. A root shell is like a gun. It must be handled very carefully or you can wind up shooting yourself in the foot. If you have doubts about a certain command, consult the man page for details about its behavior.

In the same vein, never hastily paste commands into a terminal window unless you know what you are doing. With the growing popularity of Mac OS X, many online resources exist that provide tips and tricks for tweaking the system or manipulating the file system. The command line interface is a lot less forgiving of mistakes. The Finder, for example, will often prompt in the case of deleting a file. By default, most shells will simply delete the file(s).

It is also important to understand how your shell interprets special characters. Filenames can contain characters that the shell might interpret in a different way than you might think. Here is a simple example. Suppose you want to delete a file named "*a"; you could use the rm command:

```
bash-2.05a$ rm *a
```

This deletes the file in question, as well as every file ending in "a"! The correct way to remove only the intended file would be to escape the asterisk, which would force the shell not to treat it as a special character. To escape a character, use a backslash, for example:

```
bash-2.05a$ rm \*a
```

Also, refrain from entering sensitive information, like passwords, as arguments to commands. For convenience purposes, many shells keep a history file of recent commands. Sensitive information entered on the command line would then be left in such a file. More importantly, the operating system maintains a list of running commands in the system process list. Tools exist that allow users to view the currently running applications, including the arguments. These tools are available to all users on the system.

COMMAND LINE ARGUMENTS

At a former job, one of us (Brian) worked on a certain application that accepted command line arguments to allow users to specify both a username and a password on the command line. This was done as a convenience so that users could script the use of the application.

Features like this encourage the exercise of poor judgment. Just because an application allows for something like this does not mean it is wise.

Often there are ways around the password issue. For example, some applications that require passwords accept command line arguments that cause the application to prompt for a password instead of forcing the user to enter it as part of the command.

There also are various convoluted ways to attempt to remove such information from the process list, but none of them are completely safe. It is best to assume that any arguments given to commands can be seen by other users.

Directories, Permissions, and File Ownership

The crux of the UNIX security model has to do with enforcing file permissions. Everything, including devices and memory has a file representation of some kind. In turn, access to files is restricted based upon user and group credentials. Understanding how this model works is essential for anyone concerned with protecting his or her data.

This section covers the details of Mac OS X file permissions, including how to modify ownership, access control, and certain special attributes of files.

File Security and Permissions

Every file belongs to a single user and a group. In addition, every file has an associated set of permissions. These permissions define who can access the file and what types of operations are permitted. The "who" aspect of these permissions include:

- The owner of the file
- The group that owns the file
- All other users

For each of these three elements, the permissions further define allowable modes of access for that user type. These modes are

- Read
- Write
- Execute

Each file has permissions data attached to it. These permissions consist of a sequence of bits that reflect the preceding elements. Thus, we have nine bits designating read, write, and execute privileges. Actually, every file has twelve permissions bits associated with it. The other three are the Set User ID bit, the Set Group ID bit, and the sticky bit, covered later in this chapter.

Permissions are usually represented as a string reading from left to right. This string is organized into three main sections (see Figure 4.4). The first section denotes permissions for the owner, the second section for the file's group, and the last section for all other users.

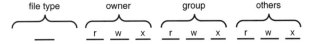

FIGURE 4.4   Breakdown of a string that represents file permissions.

Each section contains three elements, one for each access type. The "–" symbol denotes the denial of access. Table 4.1 illustrates the possible values for a section.

TABLE 4.1   File Permission String Sections and Their Meanings

VALUE	ALLOWED ACCESS
---	no access
--x	execute
-w-	write
-wx	write, execute
r--	read
r-x	read, execute
rw-	read, write
rwx	read, write, execute

The permissions for a file can be displayed with the ls command line application, using the -l option (meaning long listing). For example:

```
bash-2.05a$ ls -l /usr/bin/grep
-rwxr-xr-x  1 root   wheel   93348 Nov 22 16:44  /usr/bin/grep
```

The first item is the permissions string, in this case (rwxr-xr-x). With this file, the owner is root and has read, write, and execute privileges (rwx). The wheel group has read and execute privileges (r-x). All other users have read and execute privileges (r-x).

Read access to a file means the contents of that file can be revealed. Read access to a directory means that the contents of the directory can be listed.

Write access to a file means that the contents of the file can be altered. Write access to a directory allows the addition and removal of files contained in that directory.

Execute privileges for a file means that the file can be loaded and run as a program. The capability to execute a directory means it can be entered with the cd command, or searched.

From Figure 4.4, you can see that the leftmost element of the permissions string denotes the file type.

Everything in UNIX is represented as a file. As a result, there are certain files that must comply with specific format or purpose. Some files serve to represent devices; other files represent memory. These files are known as special files.

Most files on Mac OS X are so-called regular files, meaning they contain an arbitrary format of binary or textual data. Regular files are represented by a dash (-) in the permissions string.

Block and *Character files* are usually tied to a device or a piece of hardware. Sometimes this is to a pseudo device, such as a terminal application. These files are used as a means of communication between the device and the operating system. Block files communicate in blocks, or multiple characters of data at a time. Character devices communicate one character at a time. Block and Character files are represented in a permissions string by the letters "b" and "c," respectively.

Directories contain files. A *directory* is more or less a regular file, but it has a specific format, or structure. Directories are represented in a permissions string by the letter "d."

A *symbolic link* is a reference to some other file that may or may not exist. The symbolic link file basically contains a path. A symbolic link has permissions, but they are meaningless. Symbolic links can point to other files, other directories, or even other symbolic links. Symbolic links are represented in a permissions string by the letter "l."

A *socket file* is used to facilitate the communication of data between two applications running on the same machine. Socket files are represented in a permissions string by the letter "s."

This system of file access control is relatively simple, and for many UNIX folks, not unfamiliar. However, there are some caveats to watch for:

- If a user owns a file, and is also a group owner, the group permissions are ignored and the user permissions apply.
- Read access to a directory does not affect the permissions of the files contained in that directory. Read permissions provide access to the directory attributes. This includes the capability to list the files that the directory contains. Disabling read access does not necessarily prevent the contained files from being opened, modified, or even deleted.
- Write access to a directory enables a user to delete any file in that directory regardless of the permissions for the files (except when the "sticky bit"—see the later section, "Sticky Bits").
- Disabling write access to a directory does not affect the capability to write to existing files in the directory, but does deny the capability to create or remove files.

- Execute permissions on a directory allows access to the contents of that directory. Regardless of the permissions of the files contained, denying executable permissions on a directory prevents access to those files (and prevents shells from entering the directory).

LINKS AND ALIASES

Most operating systems include some form of links, aliases, or shortcuts. Mac OS X supports hard links, symbolic links, and aliases.

A *hard link* is a direct reference to a file somewhere on the same filesystem. A file can have any number of hard links to it, but there is only a single copy of the file. Therefore, any changes to a hard link affect the referenced file. Another way to think of a hard link is that it is another name for the same file. When you create a hard link, the directory where you created the link now contains the header information for the file. It is not possible to create a hard link to a directory, or to a file on a different filesystem.

Symbolic links are different than hard links in that when a symbolic link is created, a special file is created for that link. This new file contains the path to another file. Because a symbolic link is nothing more than a path, it is possible to create symbolic links to directories, and to files on different filesystems. Because symbolic links are files themselves, it can be confusing trying to distinguish between the link file and the target file. With most applications, when access is made to a symbolic link, the access is made of the target file, not the symbolic link file. This is called *traversing* the link. Most command line applications traverse the link. A few do not. The `rm`, `mv`, `ls`, and `file` commands do not traverse symbolic links. That is, they operate on the link file itself. As mentioned previously, the permissions of a symbolic link are meaningless.

An *alias* is another indirect reference to a file, like a symbolic link. Symbolic and hard links are products of the UNIX environment, but aliases are unique to Mac OS X and its predecessors. Like a symbolic link, an alias can be modified, including deleting it, without modifying the actual file. However, unlike a symbolic link, the file an alias references can be moved without breaking the alias. An alias stores information about the file, including the path, in the resource fork of the alias file. As a result, aliases can only be used on HFS filesystems. Also, command line tools such as `find` will not be able to traverse an alias file.

Special File Permissions

So far, we have covered only nine of the twelve permissions bits. The permissions that deal with read, write, and execute privileges are fairly straightforward. However, there are three additional elements to a file's permissions that are not as simple.

Set User ID

Normally, a process runs with the same privileges as the user who executed the application. The Set User ID bit allows a file to execute as if the owner of the file had executed it. That is, the resultant process always runs with the same privileges as the file's owner.

Every process has a real UID and an effective UID associated with it. The real UID is the ID of the user that started the process. The effective UID determines user privileges for the process. The effective UID can change during the life of a process, but usually, the real and effective UID values are the same. The Set User ID bit causes the effective UID of the process to be that of the owner of the file. A file with the Set User ID bit set is commonly referred to as SUID.

Directories can be SUID; but on Mac OS X, this has no effect. On some UNIX systems, creating a directory SUID makes any new files in the directory automatically owned by the owner of the directory.

A file that is SUID is represented as such in the *owner* executable portion of the permissions string. Although it does affect the execution of a file, the SUID bit is distinct from the owner execute bit; however, they both occupy the same position in the permissions string. Because of this, there are certain symbols to denote which bits are set. Table 4.2 shows the possible values for the owner executable portion of a permissions string.

TABLE 4.2 File Owner Execute Bit Possible Values

VALUE	MEANING
–	Not executable by owner, not SUID
x	Executable by owner, not SUID
s	Executable by owner, and SUID
S	SUID, not executable by owner

An example of a SUID file is the `passwd` application:

```
bash-2.05a$ ls -la /usr/bin/passwd
-r-sr-xr-x  1 root  wheel  30492 Nov 22 16:45 /usr/bin/passwd
```

Sometimes it is necessary to give unprivileged users access to system files. For example, many UNIX systems have a password file that is owned by root, and can only be read or written to by the root. Users need read access to this file when logging in, for verification of their password. They need write access to the file when changing their password. For obvious security reasons, it makes no sense to allow normal users the capability to arbitrarily read and write to such a file. However, by making the `login` and `passwd` programs SUID, users have the capability to read and write to the file in a (hopefully) controlled fashion. The difference is that these programs place constraints on the nature of the access. They dictate exactly what can be read or written, and how.

This is a benefit of the SUID bit, but there are also dangers associated with this permissions attribute that will be covered later in this chapter.

Set Group ID

The Set Group ID bit serves the same function as the Set User ID bit, only it applies to group privileges. Likewise, it is often referred to as the SGID bit. When a SGID file is executed, the effective group ID of the process is the same as the GID of the file. As with the SUID bit, setting the SGID bit on a directory in Mac OS X has no effect.

The SGID bit is represented in the permissions string the same way as the SUID bit. The only difference is that it is represented in the *group* executable position. An example of a SGID file is the uptime application that shows how long the operating system has been running:

```
bash-2.05a$ ls -la /usr/bin/uptime
-r-xr-sr-x  1 root   kmem   19536 Nov 22 16:44 /usr/bin/uptime
```

Sticky Bits

The sticky bit applies to directories on Mac OS X, and is used to further restrict write access to files. In a sticky directory, only root and the owner are allowed write access to each file. This is true even if the owner allows write access to all other users. This is commonly used for temp directories, and Mac OS X is no exception with the /tmp directory being a sticky directory.

On older UNIX systems, it is possible to set the sticky bit on regular files with a completely different effect. Some systems still allow this. On Mac OS X, setting the sticky bit only affects directories.

A directory that is sticky is represented as such in the *others* executable portion of the permissions string. The sticky bit is distinct from the *others* execute bit. Because of this, there are certain symbols to denote which bits are set. Table 4.3 shows the possible values for the *others* executable portion of a permissions string.

TABLE 4.3 File *other* Execute Bit Possible Values

VALUE	ALLOWED ACCESS
–	Not executable by owner, not sticky
x	Executable by others, not sticky
t	Executable by others, and sticky
T	Sticky, not executable by others

Another example of a sticky directory is the /cores directory:

```
drwxrwxrwt   2 root    wheel          68 Jul 14 00:20 cores/
```

Hidden File Flags

The permissions we have covered so far are apparent to users. That is, they are seen with most of the applications used to display file permissions. However, there are other flags associated with files that are not so apparent. These flags are inherited from BSD, and most derivatives of BSD implement some permutation of these hidden flags. Linux users familiar with the `chattr` command might recognize some of these flags. Mac OS X supports the flags shown in Table 4.4.

TABLE 4.4 Hidden File Flags

FLAG	DESCRIPTION	PRIVILEGES REQUIRED
uchg	user immutable	owner or root
schg	system immutable	root only
uappnd	user append-only	owner or root
sappnd	system append-only	root only
nodump	nodump flag	owner or root
arch	allow to archive	root only
opaque	opaque directory	owner or root

These flags can actually be seen with the `-lo` options to the `ls` command. For example,

```
bash-2.05a$ ls -lo /tmp/myuchgfile
-rw-r--r--  1 brian  wheel  uchg 0 Nov 29 22:32 myuchgfile
```

The user immutable flag (`uchg`) prevents the user from modifying the file in any way, regardless of the permissions.

The system immutable flag (`schg`) prevents any user (including root) from modifying the file. After the system immutable bit has been set, even root cannot change it back. The only way to reset the bit, or remove the file, is to boot into single user mode.

The `appnd` flags only allow data to be appended to the file; the existing content in the file cannot be altered. Like the `schg` flag, the `sappnd` flag can only be set by root and removed by root in single user mode.

The dump flag signals to the dump(8) utility to skip this file when conducting backups.

The arch and opaque flags set attributes that do not deal with access control.

The flags to be most concerned with are the immutable (uchg/schg) and append (uappnd/sappnd) flags. In fact, some BSD distributions make use of the chg flags for critical system files. The basic idea is that intruders are unable to modify schg files unless they have physical access to the box and know the root password. If this is ever the case you have bigger problems to worry about. The best thing to do in such a situation is panic.

The capability to remove some of these flags is directly related to the security level of the kernel. Booting into single user mode reduces the kernel security level thereby allowing these bits to be altered. Kernel security levels will be covered later in this chapter.

How to Modify Permissions and Ownership

So far we have seen how file permissions are organized, and the types of access control available to files on Mac OS X. Here we reveal the tools used to modify permissions and ownerships of files.

Using chmod

The chmod command line application can be used to modify file permissions. This includes all twelve of the permission bits. The hidden flags, such as uchg and uappnd, cannot be modified by chmod. Only the owner and root can change the permissions of a file.

There are basically two methodologies that can be used with chmod: the octal method or the symbolic method. In either case, the basic syntax is

```
chmod mode file
```

The symbolic method uses the characters u, g, and o to represent the user (owner), group, and others section of the permissions. The characters r, w, x, s, and t represent the same bits they do in the permissions string. This is best explained with some examples:

```
chmod u=rwx,g=rx,o=r foo.txt
```

These permissions give read, write, and execute privileges to the owner, read and execute privileges to the group, and read access to all other users.

```
chmod g+x foo.exe
```

This sets the group execute bit; all other permissions remain the same.

```
chmod o-w foo.exe
```

This makes the file foo.exe not writeable by other users. All other permissions stay the same.

```
chmod u+s foo.exe
```

This sets the foo.exe application to be SUID. All other permissions stay the same.

When using the octal method, the mode is a sequence of four integers that define the value for each of the twelve permission bits. The first number applies to the SUID, SGID, and sticky bits. Table 4.5 shows the possible values for this first number.

TABLE 4.5   File Permissions Octal Mode Values for SUID/SGID and Sticky Bits

MODE VALUE	PERMISSIONS
0	No bits set
1	Sticky bit
2	SGID
3	Sticky and SGID
4	SUID
5	SUID and sticky bit
6	SUID and SGID
7	SUID, SGID, and sticky bit set

The second number applies to the *owner* permissions, the third number to *group* permissions, and the final number for the *other* section of the permissions. Table 4.6 shows the possible mode values, and associated permissions.

TABLE 4.6   File Permissions Octal Mode Values for *read, write, execute* Bits

MODE VALUE	PERMISSIONS STRING
0	---
1	--x
2	-w-
3	-wx
4	r--
5	r-x

continues

TABLE 4.6 Continued

MODE VALUE	PERMISSIONS STRING
6	rw-
7	rwx

Here are some examples using the octal method, and the corresponding permissions strings:

```
chmod 0744 foo.exe        becomes: rwxr--r--
chmod 4755 foo.exe        becomes: rwsr-xr-x
chmod 0777 foo.exe        becomes: rwxrwxrwx
chmod 2655 foo.exe        becomes: rw-r-sr-x
```

The chmod command also can be applied recursively to all files in a directory using the -R option.

Using the octal method is nice because all twelve permissions bits can be changed with a relatively short command. This can also be viewed as a more safe way to change file permissions; because you specify a value for each element of the permissions, there is less of a chance that you will accidentally allow unintentional access to a file. The downside is that it can be cumbersome to remember what the numbers actually mean. For some, the symbolic method for changing permissions is a lot easier to remember. Reference the chmod man page for detailed usage information.

Using chown and chgrp

The chown command changes the owner (UID) and/or the group owner (GID) of a file. For security reasons, only the root user can change the ownership of a file. The basic syntax is as follows:

```
chown user:group file
```

With this command, it is possible to change a file's owner, group, or both. For example:

```
bash-2.05a$ cd /tmp
bash-2.05a$ touch myfile
bash-2.05a$ ls -l myfile
-rw-r--r--  1 brian  wheel  0 Dec  1 00:32 myfile
bash-2.05a$ sudo chown root:staff myfile
Password:
bash-2.05a$ ls -l myfile
-rw-r--r--  1 root   staff  0 Dec  1 00:32 myfile
```

DEFAULT PERMISSIONS (UMASK)

The `chmod` command allows you to use symbolic representations for elements of permissions, such as "g" for group and "u" for user. However, octal representations are more inline with how the operating system deals with file permissions. As a result, there are situations where knowing what an octal value actually means with respect to permissions can be useful. One prime example is the concept of default permissions, or the umask. By default, the permissions of a new file on Mac OS X are set to 0666, and 0777 for directories. The way umask works is that the umask value is subtracted from the default which results in a new default permissions value. For example, if your current umask value is 0022, your default file permissions will be (0666 – 0022), which is 0644 (rw-r--r--).

To view your current umask value, type umask in a shell:

```
bash-2.05a$ umask

0022
```

To set your umask value, specify a single octal argument:

```
bash-2.05a$ umask 0022
```

To permanently change your shell's umask value, edit your shell's startup script and add the desired umask value the same way you would at your shell prompt.

The umask value is important for security as well as for convenience. It also can prevent having to worry about race conditions between the time a file is created and the use of `chmod` to set the desired permissions. The default umask value on Mac OS X (0022) is appropriate in most cases; only the owner has write privileges to newly created files and directories.

The `chgrp` command changes the group owner (GID) of a file. Only the owner or the root user can change the GID of a file. In addition, the user changing the group must also be a member of the new group. The basic syntax is

`chgrp group file`

For example:

```
bash-2.05a$ cd /tmp
bash-2.05a$ touch myfile
bash-2.05a$ ls -l myfile
-rw-r--r--  1 brian  wheel  0 Dec  1 00:20 myfile
bash-2.05a$ chgrp staff myfile
bash-2.05a$ ls -l myfile
-rw-r--r--  1 brian  staff  0 Dec  1 00:20 myfile
```

Just like `chmod`, the `chown` and `chgrp` commands also can be applied recursively.

Using chflags

The hidden file flags cannot be changed with the chmod command. Instead, use the chflags command. To set a flag, use the flag name listed in Table 4.4. To remove a flag, prefix the keyword with no (Except for nodump; to remove this flag use dump). For example, to set the user immutable flag:

```
chflags uchg <file>
```

To remove that same flag:

```
chflags nouchg <file>
```

This might be a bit confusing at first because you use uchg to not allow changes, and nouchg to allow them. To verify the flags set on a file, use the -lo options to the ls command:

```
bash-2.05a$ ls -lo
total 0
drwx-wx-wx   3 brian   staff   -                102 Oct 16 13:27 ./
drwxr-xr-x  22 brian   staff   -                748 Oct 16 13:22 ../
-rw-r--r--   1 brian   staff   uappnd,uchg        0 Oct 16 13:27 random_file
bash-2.05a$
```

The flags to be most concerned with are the uchg/schg and uappnd/sappnd flags. In fact, some BSD distributions use the chg flags for critical system files. The basic idea is that intruders are unable to modify schg files unless they have physical access to the box and know the root password. If this ever is the case, your best recourse is to panic.

See chflags(1) for more information about these flags. For developers, see chflags(2).

> **NOTE**
>
> For developers, note that there is no mention of the arguments for changing the arch and opaque flags in chflags(2). Other BSD derivatives, FreeBSD for example, have since updated their man pages accordingly. The flags to use are UF_OPAQUE and UF_OPAQUE. This can be verified by referencing <sys/stat.h>.

Using Get Info to Modify Permissions

Permissions also can be modified through the Finder using the Get Info dialog. After selecting a file, the Get Info dialog can be invoked in three ways. Select the Get Info option from the File menu, Control-click the file and choose Get Info, or use the Command-I keyboard sequence.

Use the Ownership & Permissions section (see Figure 4.5) of this dialog to modify the owner, group, and basic file permissions.

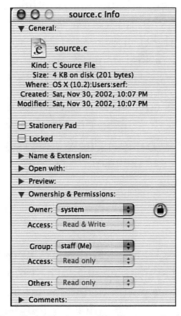

FIGURE 4.5   Using Get Info to modify file permissions from the Finder.

This dialog provides the capability to set read and write privileges. It also allows the owner and the group for the file to be changed. The root user is referred to as "system" in this dialog. Likewise, the wheel group is referred to as "system."

The "Locked" check box, when checked, sets the uchg flag of the file in question. None of the other special flags can be set with this dialog.

Obviously, Get Info does not come close to providing the same degree of control over file permissions as with the chmod application. Some basic permutations of the read and write bits can be set, but with this dialog it is not possible to alter the SUID or SGID bits. Likewise, the Get Info dialog does not reveal a lot of important permissions bits.

Common UNIX Commands

Mac OS X is littered with useful command line applications. Some of these applications can be very useful from a security perspective. They shed light on the happenings of the UNIX layer of Mac OS X. They allow a user or an administrator to monitor and manage system behavior. In this section we will cover a few such commands.

Most of the commands covered here accept many options and can be used in various ways. The following sections are not complete descriptions of each command; they serve to point out how these commands can be used, including some examples. Reference the man pages for a complete and detailed explanation of these commands.

top

The `top` command (see Figure 4.6) displays information and statistics about running processes and system memory. The information is divided into two main sections. The upper portion contains information about the overall system memory and CPU usage. The bottom portion displays information about specific processes. This application takes over your console (or terminal window) and keeps running until you press the Q key.

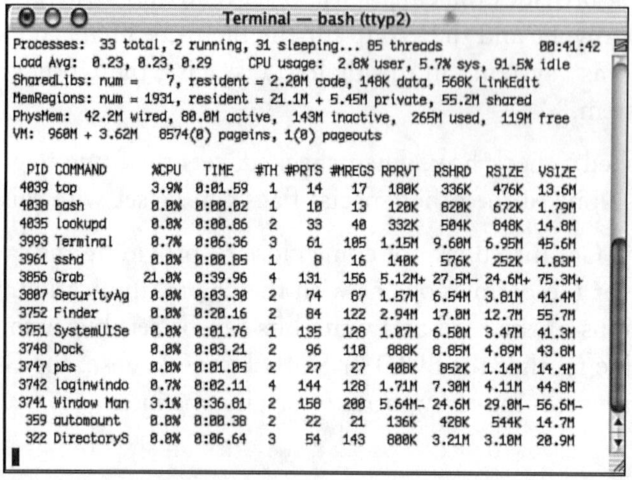

```
Terminal — bash (ttyp2)
Processes:  33 total, 2 running, 31 sleeping... 85 threads            00:41:42
Load Avg:  0.23, 0.23, 0.29     CPU usage:  2.8% user, 5.7% sys, 91.5% idle
SharedLibs: num =    7, resident = 2.20M code, 148K data, 568K LinkEdit
MemRegions: num = 1931, resident = 21.1M + 5.45M private, 55.2M shared
PhysMem:  42.2M wired, 80.0M active,  143M inactive,  265M used,  119M free
VM:  960M + 3.62M   8574(0) pageins, 1(0) pageouts

  PID COMMAND      %CPU   TIME   #TH #PRTS #MREGS RPRVT  RSHRD  RSIZE  VSIZE
 4039 top          3.9%  0:01.59   1    14    17   180K   336K   476K  13.6M
 4038 bash         0.0%  0:00.02   1    10    13   120K   820K   672K  1.79M
 4035 lookupd      0.0%  0:00.86   2    33    40   332K   504K   848K  14.8M
 3993 Terminal     0.7%  0:06.36   3    61   105  1.15M  9.60M  6.95M  45.6M
 3961 sshd         0.0%  0:00.85   1     8    16   140K   576K   252K  1.83M
 3856 Grab        21.0%  0:39.96   4   131   156  5.12M+ 27.5M- 24.6M+ 75.3M+
 3807 SecurityAg   0.0%  0:03.30   2    74    87  1.57M  6.54M  3.81M  41.4M
 3752 Finder       0.0%  0:20.16   2    84   122  2.94M  17.0M  12.7M  55.7M
 3751 SystemUISe   0.0%  0:01.76   1   135   128  1.07M  6.50M  3.47M  41.3M
 3748 Dock         0.0%  0:03.21   2    96   110   888K  8.85M  4.89M  43.8M
 3747 pbs          0.0%  0:01.05   2    27    27   408K   852K  1.14M  14.4M
 3742 loginwindo   0.7%  0:02.11   4   144   128  1.71M  7.30M  4.11M  44.8M
 3741 Window Man   3.1%  0:36.81   2   158   200  5.64M- 24.6M  29.0M- 56.6M-
  359 automount    0.0%  0:00.38   2    22    21   136K   428K   544K  14.7M
  322 DirectoryS   0.0%  0:06.64   3    54   143   800K  3.21M  3.10M  20.9M
```

FIGURE 4.6 The `top` application shows usage statistics and process information.

The good thing about `top` is that it can provide quick access to updated information about multiple processes. Thus, you can do a quick sanity check of overall system behavior. By default, `top` sorts the processes by PID with the highest PID value at the top. You also can sort the list by the most CPU-intensive applications with the `-u` command line option. As a result, the `top` application is a good place to pinpoint, for example, a process that is consuming too many system resources.

By default, `top` updates the information displayed in the table every second. You can set the update interval in seconds by using the `-s` command line argument. The defaults to `top` are usually sufficient.

ps

The `ps` command also is used to get information about running processes. Although `top` is usually used as a means to get a rough overview of the system, `ps` is used to get much more detailed information about specific process or set of processes. The `ps` command enables the user or administrator to gain important information about who is running what applications, and how those applications are effecting the state of the system. See the man page for the list of process attributes available with this command.

The following are some simple examples:

`ps -uU root`

This displays all the commands currently being run by the root user, including the command line arguments. A command like this can be used to quickly view the applications being run by any specific user.

`ps -auxe`

This displays every command running on the system, and the environment for each command.

`ps -aux | grep telnet`

This displays information about any currently running `telnet` command, started by any user.

These examples show how easy it is to obtain information about running processes. The output from `ps` also includes all the command line arguments to applications and the environment in which the application is running. On Mac OS X, *the root user is not excluded from this*. Also, some UNIX systems only allow root to see the environments of other user processes. On Mac OS X, all users can see the environment of any process.

Mac OS X also has a graphical application called the Process Viewer.app that functions similar to the ps command (see Figure 4.7). This application is located in /Applications/Utilities/Process Viewer.app. However, compared to ps it does not provide the same level of detail.

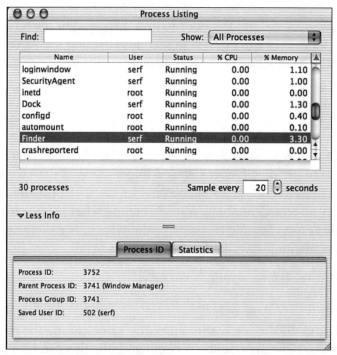

FIGURE 4.7 The Process Viewer is a graphical version of the ps command.

kill and killall

The kill and killall commands are used to send various types of signals to running processes. Signals are a way to notify a process about important events. The signal interrupts the execution of the application and the application must then react to the signal. The operating system can issue signals, and processes can send signals to each other. There are many different signals, only some of which can actually kill the process. These commands can be used to stop out of control applications, or any application that poses a threat to the security of the system.

To see the list of available signal types, use the `-l` command line option:

```
bash-2.05a$ kill -l
 1) SIGHUP        2) SIGINT       3) SIGQUIT      4) SIGILL
 5) SIGTRAP       6) SIGABRT      7) SIGEMT       8) SIGFPE
 9) SIGKILL      10) SIGBUS      11) SIGSEGV     12) SIGSYS
13) SIGPIPE      14) SIGALRM     15) SIGTERM     16) SIGURG
17) SIGSTOP      18) SIGTSTP     19) SIGCONT     20) SIGCHLD
21) SIGTTIN      22) SIGTTOU     23) SIGIO       24) SIGXCPU
25) SIGXFSZ      26) SIGVTALRM   27) SIGPROF     28) SIGWINCH
29) SIGINFO      30) SIGUSR1     31) SIGUSR2
```

To send a signal, specify the signal type, then the process ID that should receive the signal. The process ID is often referred to as a PID, and can be acquired with an application like ps or top. The signal numbers can be used instead of the name. For example, to try to kill a process with PID 6677 by sending the TERM signal do the following:

```
kill -TERM 6677
```

> or

```
kill -15 6677
```

The default behavior for the TERM signal is for the application to quit. Applications can ignore signals, but the SIGSTOP and SIGKILL signals cannot be ignored. The Force Quit option from the Apple menu is equivalent to issuing a kill -KILL, the non-ignorable terminate signal. This also is known as a kill -9 and can be very useful to halt an application that has stopped responding.

The kill application is not SUID root. Therefore, users can only kill processes that they own, but the root user can kill any process.

The killall command is different from the kill command. This command can kill all applications owned by a specific user, attached to a specific tty, or matching a name. For example, this command would kill all instances of ping:

```
killall ping
```

The default signal is the TERM signal, but you also can specify a signal type to send.

last and *who*

The last application displays a list of logins, some of which may still be active. The list includes the username, terminal port, hostname, start and stop dates, and the duration of the login session. The file /var/log/wtmp is where login session information is stored. The list displays the more recent logins first. Usually, the output of this command is quite verbose. To see the 10 most recent logins, pipe the output through the head command. For example:

```
bash-2.05a$ last | head
brian        ttyp1                          Tue Dec  3 19:49    still logged in
brian        ttyp1                          Tue Dec  3 19:49 - 19:49  (00:00)
brian        ttyp1                          Tue Dec  3 19:21 - 19:49  (00:27)
brian        ttyp1                          Tue Dec  3 19:21 - 19:21  (00:00)
brian        ttyp1                          Tue Dec  3 16:24 - 19:21  (02:57)
brian        ttyp1                          Tue Dec  3 16:24 - 16:24  (00:00)
brian        ttyp1                          Tue Dec  3 16:21 - 16:24  (00:02)
brian        ttyp1                          Tue Dec  3 16:21 - 16:21  (00:00)
brian        ttyp1                          Tue Dec  3 15:59 - 16:21  (00:21)
brian        ttyp1                          Tue Dec  3 15:59 - 15:59  (00:00)
```

The who command displays a list of users who are currently logged in, including remote login sessions. The list includes the username, terminal port, the login time, and a hostname if the user is logged in remotely.

The who command, as with the file where the information is stored, is only visible to root and admin users.

find

The find command locates files. It recursively searches a list of directories and produces a listing of files that match specific search criteria. Aside from the obvious day-to-day activities that a command like this would be useful for, the find command can be very helpful in maintaining host security. Also, the file search capabilities in the Finder do not come close to the capabilities of find.

The find command can be used to easily locate files that might be considered risky, such as SUID root files. It can be used to identify files of a specific type, or that have specific permissions, size, group membership, or owner. The use of this command is better explained with some examples. The following examples search for files starting from the root level directory.

```
find / -user root \( -perm -001 -or -perm -010 -or -perm -100 \)
```

Find all the executable files on the system that are owned by root, and executable. The -perm option allows you to restrict the find operation to the specified permissions mode. In this case, any file that has any executable bits set is included.

```
find / -type f \( -perm -02000 -or -perm -04000 \)
```

Find any files with the SUID or SGID bit set. The -type f option allows the search to be limited to regular files. Files of any other type are ignored.

```
find / -user root -type f -perm -04000
```

Find any files that are SUID, and owned by root.

```
find / ! -type l -perm -21
```

Find any files that are writeable by others, not including symbolic link files.

```
find / -type l -ls
```

Find any symbolic links. This also prints a long listing of the files, so that the files the links point to are also listed.

```
find / -name "*core"
```

Find any core files, specifically, any files that end with the word "core."
If wildcards are used, you must use double quotes.

```
find / -nouser -nogroup
```

Find any files that do not belong to a known user or known group.

```
find / \( -flags uchg -or -flags schg \)
```

Find any files with the uchg or schg flags set.

The find command also can make use of regular expressions, which can make it possible to perform quite complex and customized searches.

netstat

The netstat command shows information about the status of your local network. Not every UNIX service on Mac OS X has a graphical configuration tool. Applications and services can open up local network ports and expose a system to attacks. Most services have well-known ports. If an open port is not recognized, reference the /etc/services file for a description of the service.

You quickly can see what ports your system is listening on with the following
netstat command:

```
bash-2.05a$ netstat -na | grep LISTEN
tcp4        0        0  127.0.0.1:631           *.*                     LISTEN
tcp4        0        0  *:22                    *.*                     LISTEN
```

This example shows two network ports listening for requests. The first port
(631) is the port used by the Common UNIX Printing System (CUPS). This can
be used to configure local printers. The column `127.0.0.1:631` means that
this port only accepts requests from the local machine. However, the next open
port is the SSH server. The * means this server is accepting requests from any
host. Detailed information about securing network services will be covered in
Chapter 6, "Internet Services."

Another useful feature of `netstat` is the capability to obtain network statistics
with the `-s` option. This shows information about connection attempts, packet
errors, current open connections, failed connections, and others. Information
about specific protocols can be obtained with the `-p` option. The application
Network Utility (`/Applications/Utilities/Network Utility.app`) is a
graphical version of `netstat`, but provides only a subset of the information
obtainable from `netstat`.

openssl

Mac OS X comes packaged with a version of OpenSSL, a popular cryptographic toolkit and secure transport library. The OpenSSL package also
includes a useful command line application. This application can be used to
create certificates and certificate requests, perform checksums, encrypt data,
and conduct SSL tests.

One simple, but handy feature of the `openssl` command line application is
the capability to calculate the *message digest* of a file. A message digest for a
file is a fingerprint. In theory, no two files that differ in content have the same
fingerprint. This concept can be applied to verify that certain files have not
been tampered with. Although Mac OS X also has a md5 application, the
`openssl` command includes many different message digest algorithms,
including MD5, SHA-1, and ripemd-160. The following is an example
of computing the SHA-1 checksum for the `ls` command:

```
bash-2.05a$ openssl sha1 /bin/ls
SHA1(/bin/ls)= fb1c94f7d2f552977be3d6d0b0315e7cc8a5b8ff
```

It is not uncommon for a checksum to be published alongside software available for download. The idea is that the integrity of the downloaded file or files can be verified before unpacking and installing them. The openssl command line makes it easy to perform such verification. However, there are a lot of things to consider when verifying the integrity of a file in this manner. We will discuss all these considerations in Chapter 12, "Forensics."

UNIX Security

This section covers some additional aspects of UNIX security. This includes SUID and SGID files, kernel security levels, and the management of the sudo command.

SUID and SGID Files

When dealing with UNIX file permissions, one of the most popular security concerns is with regard to SUID and SGID applications. SUID and SGID applications exist mainly to allow users to perform privileged operations or gain access to resources that require root privileges. As a result, most SUID applications are owned by root. This combination can be deadly to the integrity of a system.

The best way to deal with SUID or SGID files is to not have any of them. However, this is not realistic. Applications such as login and passwd are required to be SUID in order to function. One thing to consider with applications such as login and passwd is that they are somewhat tried and tested applications. Not all software is so fortunate. When installing applications, be mindful of file permissions. The installation of additional SUID root applications should not be done in haste. Many applications provide a means to drop in to a shell or execute a command. The vi command line text editor allows this. Even the less command allows commands to be executed by pressing the ! key. Reasonable assurance that a SUID application is benign can only be acquired by knowing all the ways in which that application can be used, misused, and abused.

THE DANGERS OF SUID ROOT

On a former project one of us (Brian) was involved in, one of the applications distributed was to be installed as SUID root. However, it was determined later that this program did not actually require root privileges to function. This did not present a problem until a buffer overflow was found in the code. The buffer overflow, combined with the elevated privileges, created a perfect environment for a malicious user to gain root access on any box running the software. The problem, in this case, was resolved by changing the permissions on the file such that it was no longer SUID root. However, it is not always that simple.

The moral here is that SUID root applications are a risk to a system. Know which ones exist, and why. To trust an SUID root executable is to trust that it cannot be exploited or misused in any way.

Mac OS X permits shell scripts to be SUID and/or SGID. For security purposes, some operating systems (such as Linux) do not allow them to exist. A shell script should *never* be SUID or SGID. There are far too many ways to exploit a shell script. A shell's environment, or the applications used in the script, can be exploited or abused. Never create SUID root shell scripts. Ever.

By default, removable media such as CDs, disk images, and network shares under Mac OS X do not permit the existence of SUID or SGID files. This includes disk images created with `hdiutil` or `Disk Copy.app`.

Finally, know all the applications that are installed as SUID or SGID, especially those owned by root. A quick examination using the `find` command can produce a listing of all applications currently on the system with such permissions. The following command produces a listing of all SUID or SGID files:

```
sudo find / -type f \( -perm -04000 -or -perm 02000 \) -ls
```

This is a quick way to perform a SUID audit on Mac OS X. A more robust method of doing so will be discussed in Chapter 12. Also, a complete list of the SUID and SGID applications installed with Mac OS X at the time of this writing can be found in Appendix A, "SUID and SGID Files."

Kernel Security Levels

The kernel on Mac OS X and Darwin can run at various security levels, similar to other versions of BSD. There are four levels of security ranging from –1 to 2, with 2 considered the most secure. The basic idea is that the kernel does not allow certain operations on the filesystem while running under higher security levels. The security levels are

- **–1 No Security.** Always run at security level 0.
- **0 Insecure.** Any filesystem can be written to provided the permissions allow it. The hidden `schg` and `sappnd` flags can be set or unset.

- **1 Secure.** The `schg` and `sappnd` flags cannot be removed from files.
- **2 Most Secure.** The `schg` and `sappnd` flags cannot be removed from files. Filesystems cannot be altered, and it is not possible to create new filesystems.

The root user can raise the security level, but only the init process can lower it. The init process is the master process. It creates all other processes and always has a process ID of one. By default, the Mac OS X kernel runs at security level one after booting. This is reasonable. Running at security level 0 renders the `schg` and `sappnd` file flags useless.

The following command shows the current kernel security level:

```
sysctl kern.securelevel
```

The root user can raise the security level with the following command:

```
sysctl -w kern.securelevel=2
```

In most cases, the default security level will suffice. However, if your security policy demands the kernel run at security level 2, there are basically two options:

1. Raise the security level during the last stages of the boot process. This involves adding the preceding command to the bottom of the `/etc/rc` file.
2. Recompile a new kernel after making a minor adjustment to the source. The man page for `init` describes this process.

The first option is obviously easier, but is also easier to circumvent. Building a new kernel is relatively involved, but is also slightly more resilient to being tampered with. To run the Mac OS X kernel at security level 0 (other than single user mode), it is necessary to recompile the kernel.

sudo

The `sudo` command is used to execute a command as another user. Usually `sudo` is used to execute a command as root, but it also can be used to execute a command as any other user. The following example shows the execution of the `id` command as a regular user, then as root:

```
bash-2.05a$ id
uid=501(brian) gid=20(staff) groups=20(staff), 80(admin)
bash-2.05a$ sudo id
```

continues

```
Password:
uid=0(root) gid=0(wheel) groups=0(wheel), 1(daemon), 2(kmem), 3(sys), \
->4(tty), 5(operator), 20(staff), 31(guest), 80(admin)
```

To execute a command as a non-root user, use the `-u` option and specify the username. For more information regarding the syntax of the `sudo` command, refer to the man page.

The `sudo` command can be useful for many reasons. First, let's look at some advantages associated with using `sudo`:

- Users are not left in a root shell. The dangers of using the root account as a regular account have previously been stressed. `sudo` enables administrators to obtain root privileges only when necessary. As soon as the command terminates, the privileges are dropped.

- The root password stays private. When a non-root user executes a command using `sudo`, it asks for that user's password, not the root password. Thus, it is possible to allow administrators to perform privileged operations without giving out the root password.

- The capability to perform privileged operations can easily be revoked. Because the root password is not disclosed to `sudo` users, removing their capabilities involves revoking `sudo` capabilities. The root password does not necessarily have to be changed.

- `sudo` commands are logged. With Mac OS X, all uses of `sudo` are logged to the system log, by default. This small audit trail includes the user who executed the command, their terminal port, the directory they were in, and the complete command that was executed.

- Finally, the use of `sudo` is conveniently quick compared to logging in as a different user. All that is required is to prefix a command with the `sudo` command.

Now that we have conducted a sales pitch for `sudo`, let's be realistic. `sudo` access is root access. The `sudo` command (unless configured otherwise) can be used to execute commands as root, or to spawn a root shell as follows:

```
sudo bash
```

The root password doesn't have to remain private. There is nothing to stop a user from changing the root password with:

```
sudo passwd root
```

The point here is that a user with sudo capabilities can do anything that the root user can do. In fact, he or she can become the root user. The greatest benefit of the sudo command is that it allows administrative tasks to be performed, without the need to login as root. sudo can protect the root user from themselves. Using a root shell, it is a lot easier to accidentally delete files, or whack a filesystem.

This being the case, it is critical that you not allow just any user the capability to use sudo. Granting uncontrolled sudo capabilities to a user is like handing them the root account, and doing so should only be done when deemed absolutely necessary. Also, the use of sudo must be accompanied by strict control over what those users can do. Fortunately, controlling which users can use sudo and what those users can do is quite easily configured. The next section describes how access to sudo can be controlled.

Managing sudo *Access*

After the installation of Mac OS X and Mac OS X Server, there is a single account capable of using sudo. This is the admin account, which is created during the installation process. Normal users created using the Accounts pane in the System Preferences application are not granted sudo capabilities.

The capability to use the sudo command is actually controlled by the contents of the file /etc/sudoers. This file specifies what users and groups have access, and what they can do with that access. For security reasons, this file is readable only by root and the wheel group. The initial contents of this file are

```
# User privilege specification
root       ALL=(ALL)  ALL
%admin     ALL=(ALL)  ALL
```

This configuration allows root and any member of the admin group the capability to run any command, as any user, on any host. The first word is the user or group. Groups are prefixed with a % character. A breakdown of the syntax used here is

```
user host=(user) command
```

The host, user, and command sections can be a list of comma separated items or aliases. There are four different alias types. If no user is specified, ALL is assumed. For example:

```
User_Alias        ADMINS=bob,sue,fred
Cmnd_Alias        ADMIN_CMDS=/bin/ls,/usr/bin/tar
ADMINS            ALL=ADMIN_CMDS
```

This allows the users bob, sue, and fred the capability to execute the ls and tar commands, on any host, as any user (including root).

With the default /etc/sudoers file on Mac OS X, the root user is allowed full access, as is every member of the admin group. After installation, there is only one admin user. However with the configuration, new admin users are automatically given sudo access because they are members of the admin group. One way to solve this is to comment out the admin line and individually add users to this file as necessary.

The actual syntax for the /etc/sudoers file is complex. There are many options that can be used in the /etc/sudoers file, and far too many to cover in this section. The amount of customization and effort that goes into configuring this file will vary depending on your security policy. For many, the default will work just fine. For more information, reference the sudoers man page for detailed information and options.

> **NOTE**
>
> The sudoers man page isn't installed with the base system. It is installed with the BSDSDK package, an optional part of the developer tools installation. Thus, it is possible your system may not have the man page for this file.

sudo *Versus the* su *Command*

The substitute user command (su) is yet another way to gain a root shell. Although sudo executes a command as another user, su actually brings up a shell as another user. The default is a root shell.

If the root account is disabled as described in Chapter 1, "Security Foundations," the su command will not bring up a root shell. However, this application can still be useful for an administrator to quickly assume the identity of a different user. As with sudo, the su command also leaves an audit trail in the system log.

The sudo command is generally considered a safer bet, for a couple of reasons. First, you can control exactly who can use the command, and what they can do with it. Second, the sudo configuration can specify a timeout value. This requires the user to authenticate after a certain amount of time passed. Thus, if a careless admin leaves his desk, his sudo abilities are not as easily exploitable once the timeout takes effect. A root shell obtained through the su command, however, would not be so lucky.

Summary

Mac OS X is a complex UNIX-based system. The security model includes users and groups and is largely based on the enforcement of file permissions. Although seemingly simple compared to operating systems such as Windows, Mac OS X file permissions have some dangerous elements to watch out for, such as hidden file flags and SUID files. Privilege elevation with sudo can be controlled, but an understanding of its configuration is essential.

Some users and administrators may find Mac OS X's UNIX foundation familiar, but for many it can be overwhelming. See Appendix C, "Further Reading," for some recommended reading material about UNIX security and UNIX in general. UNIX is a major part of Mac OS X and effective security begins with a solid understanding of this aspect of the operating system.

## CHAPTER 5

USER APPLICATIONS

"If you reveal your secrets to the wind you should not blame the wind for revealing them to the trees."
—*Kahlil Gibran*

This chapter is about general application security. An application's security features (if any) are often ignored, not understood, or not used properly. Sometimes, users do not even know that certain actions are risky, let alone why. Experienced users may not understand how security features work, or how to use them effectively. General application security is not just for administrators and computer security professionals. The average Mac OS X users can take steps to secure important information and protect their privacy.

This chapter discusses ways to ensure better security while engaged in the most common of user activities. This includes a few web browsers common to Mac OS X, including Safari, OmniWeb, and Internet Explorer. We will also discuss the many issues of email security with the use of `Mail.app`. Let's start by discussing the service that is the keystone of the security of many Mac OS X applications: the keychain.

Before we dive into some specific security issues with the previously mentioned applications, it makes sense to provide some background into what we mean by the term "application security."

General Application Security Considerations

First, you must realize that the risks surrounding the use of an application can vary in origin. The underlying design or behavior of the application can pose a threat to the security of the user and possibly the system. A lot of software today still suffers from bad design, careless programming, and an ignorance of required security considerations. Users cannot (realistically) audit each and every stage in the execution of all run applications; this would not be practical. Thus, the use of any application involves some degree of trust. Fortunately, more and more software is being scrutinized and audited as a result of an increasing awareness and concern over computer security. Not only that, the findings of such audits are also being given deserved attention. Security patches and updates to software are not uncommon. It is important to stay current with software security advisories and apply updates to software when necessary. Appendix C, "Further Reading," lists many online references for staying current with software security advisories. Another helpful tool for staying current with security updates on Mac OS X is the built-in software update application discussed in Chapter 3, "Mac OS X Client General Security Practices." Besides system updates, `Software Update.app` also provides updates to certain applications. For example, at the time of this writing Software Update has passed down three security-related patches specifically for Internet Explorer since the initial release of Mac OS X.

Misuse of an application as a result of ignorance on behalf of the user also can be an issue. It is not uncommon for users to be a threat to themselves by not understanding the consequences of their interactions with an application. This includes not understanding aspects of the technologies being used. A good example of this is the assumption that any use of SSL automatically secures the use of a web browser. Users may not understand how sensitive data is stored by an application, where that data is stored, or what constitutes secure storage. We will discuss such issues in more detail when we deal with web browser and email security later in this chapter.

Yet another aspect of application security has to do with intentional abuse or misuse. Good software does not only behave according to expectations, it prevents undesired functionality and takes measures to reduce side effects that can be abused or considered a threat to the security of the user or the system.

Secondly, it is important to understand what your risks are. Risks will vary depending on the type of application being used. For example, privacy is often an issue with web browsers, as is theft of important information such as credit card numbers. Other common risks include identity theft, denial of service, or hijacking of various login credentials or passwords. The degree of risk will vary depending on the sensitivity of the information involved.

Here are some general questions you might ask yourself when considering the security of an application:

- Is there any authentication involved?

  If so, consider what the consequences are if the credentials are compromised. Often mail server passwords are the same as a shell account, which could mean access to web pages and other private information.

- How is any network-based authentication process protected from eavesdropping or tampering?

  Applications such as web browsers and mail clients often can be made to use SSL, but usually they do not by default. A web page may require HTTP authentication, but does it use SSL to protect that authentication process? Also, an application is not automatically secured by the use of SSL. The SSL protocol can be used for authentication, integrity, and encryption, but all this effort is of no use if you do not make sure you are properly authenticating a remote host and that the intended recipient is the only one capable of decrypting the exchanged data.

- What does this application do with my password?

  Even if a password is not thrown onto a network, the application may be guilty of being careless with it. Some applications take care to remove passwords from memory as soon as they are no longer needed; some do not. Still others take steps to prevent sensitive data, such as passwords, from being written to disk by the virtual memory management system.

- How is confidential or sensitive data stored, and where?

  Some applications offer to permanently remember passwords or other private information. Consider what steps are taken to keep that information from getting into the hands of other users; in some cases there are none. We have even seen security applications that allow passwords to be stored in the clear without informing the user. In that case, you might as well write those passwords on sticky notes and pin them all over your monitor.

- Does the application require administrative privileges?

    If so, consider what the application does, what resources it has access to, and what the worst-case scenario is if the application goes berserk. Administrators should be wary of running unfamiliar applications that require super-user privileges. The integrity of the system is at the mercy of such applications. As an administrator, if you do not know what an application does, find out.

Keychain

Mac OS X supports what are known as *keychains*, a secure store for certificates, passwords, or any small bits of information to be kept private (known as secure "notes"). The primary purpose of a keychain is to facilitate the management of passwords for various applications and accounts such as mail and ftp servers, web sites, or encrypted disk images. The basic idea is that a single password, the keychain password, is used to unlock access to all passwords stored in that keychain. Whenever you use an application that is keychain-aware, that application can store and retrieve any needed password(s). Users can have multiple distinct keychains, but every user starts out with a single keychain, considered that user's default keychain. The name and password for this default keychain is the same as the user's login name and password. This allows for that keychain to be automatically unlocked upon login.

The keychain service found on Mac OS X is significant for two major reasons. First, it uses strong cryptography. Over time, many applications have provided the capability to store passwords but have failed to do so in a way that can be trusted or considered safe from compromise. Second, the storage and retrieval of all passwords is handled by a single service, not individual applications. After you have decided to trust this service, any time you are asked to store a password you don't have to worry about the means by which it is protected. What you do need to be careful of, though, is what applications you allow to make use of your keychain(s). When you unlock a keychain and allow an application to access a password, you open the door for that application to slip up and compromise the security of that password (more on this later). Although the keychain provides strong secure storage for passwords, any application can make use of the keychain API. Thus, be mindful of the applications for which you grant access to your keychain(s).

In this section we will discuss keychain management and configuration with `Keychain Access.app` and discuss some general security considerations regarding the use of keychains on Mac OS X.

Using the Keychain Access Application

Figure 5.1 shows the Keychain Access application (`/Applications/ Utilities/Keychain Access.app`) used to configure keychains. Keychain files are stored in each user's `~/Library/Keychains` directory—one file for each keychain. Initially, there is a single keychain known as the default keychain. New keychain files can be created by selecting File, New, New Keychain. To show all the keychains, select View, Show Keychains or use the Keychains icon on the far right of the toolbar. The toolbar of the Keychain Access application allows for the creation of new keychain items, including passwords and notes. The lock button on the toolbar can be used to lock or unlock the currently selected keychain.

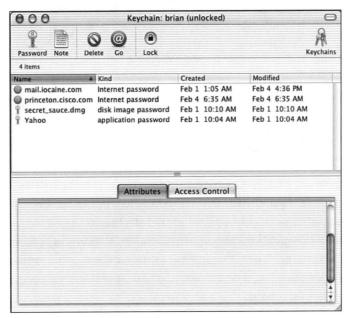

FIGURE 5.1 `Keychain Access.app` on Mac OS X for secure management of passwords.

The initial settings for the default keychain leave some room for improvement.

First, we recommend turning on the keychain menu bar icon. This icon allows you to quickly see if any of your keychains are unlocked. The locked icon means all keychains are locked, whereas the unlocked icon means at least one keychain is unlocked. The pull-down menu for this icon also allows for the locking and unlocking of each keychain, including an option to lock all keychains. Another nifty feature of this icon's menu is the capability to lock your screen if you have a password-protected screensaver setup. But be careful, this will only lock your screen if you have your screensaver configured to prompt for a password, otherwise it simply starts the screen-saver. To enable the keychain icon in the menu bar, choose the Show Status in Menu Bar option from the View menu of the Keychain Access application.

Second, we recommend some adjustments to the settings for the default keychain. With your default keychain selected, from the Edit menu, choose the Settings option. This brings up the Settings dialog similar to that shown in Figure 5.2.

FIGURE 5.2   Making improvements to the default keychain settings.

At the very least, be sure the Lock When Sleeping option is checked. Although it can be cumbersome to re-authenticate on waking up the machine, it means anyone else who has access to it in that state will also have to supply a password. Next, specify a reasonable idle timeout value for the keychain. After a certain number of minutes without use, the keychain will automatically become locked. This is a good idea in case you find yourself away from your machine for an extended period of time. Finally, if you do not want your default keychain to be unlocked automatically after logging in, change the password for that keychain. When logging in, you can then easily unlock the keychain through the menu bar icon or wait for an application to request a password stored in that keychain.

Creating a Secure Note

Besides passwords, the keychain also can be used to secure small amounts of important data, such as a PIN number or a password list. To create a secure note, choose the Note icon from the toolbar. Enter a name for the item and the text for the note as shown in Figure 5.3. Notes like this are useful, but we recommend creating a new keychain for items like this, as opposed to storing them in your default keychain. Keep that keychain locked and unlock it only when you need access to the items.

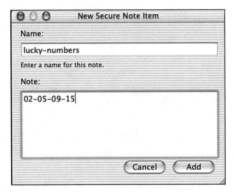

FIGURE 5.3 Creating a secure note with `Keychain Access.app`.

Managing Access to Keychain Items

Keychains can contain passwords and passphrases for web sites, mail servers, encrypted disk images, and many different third-party applications. Each item in your keychain can be configured differently to allow access only to certain applications. For example, there is probably no good reason for applications other than your email program to have access to your mail server password. This can all be configured through `Keychain Access.app`.

The bottom half of the Keychain Access window contains a tabbed view pane for configuring attributes and settings related to access control for each keychain item. The Attributes pane (see Figure 5.4) consists of metadata about the item, including the name, description, username, and URL associated with the keychain item. The Show passphrase check box allows you to view the passphrase for that item. Showing the password for an item requires you to enter the keychain password unless access is always allowed as described in the next section.

FIGURE 5.4   Configuring attributes of a keychain item.

The Access Control tab (see Figure 5.5) is where all the access control settings for the selected keychain items are configured.

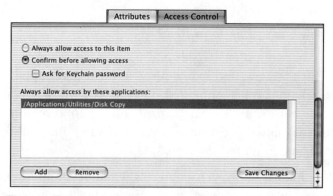

FIGURE 5.5   Configuring access control for a keychain item.

The Always Allow Access to This Item option still requires the keychain to be unlocked, but allows applications to access the passphrase without prompting the user. There are very few cases, if any, where this option is a good idea. One such example is for messaging or chat clients that have little risk attached to them.

The Confirm before Allowing Access option always prompts the user for permission before releasing a passphrase (unless that application is in the always-allowed list described here later). If the Ask for Keychain password box is checked, not only is the user informed upon each access request, but the user is also required to enter the keychain password before the passphrase is released.

Underneath the access options is a list of applications that are always authorized to retrieve the passphrase from the keychain. That is, any application found in this list has access to the passphrase without having to inform the user or ask for approval (provided the keychain is unlocked). When applications add passwords to the keychain they sometimes add themselves to this list. If you have a passphrase you want to keep tight tabs on, it is a good idea to keep this list empty so that you are aware of every request for that passphrase.

The Keychain Access Dialog

Many applications can store passwords in the keychain; sometimes this is the only interaction users ever have with their keychain. Depending on how the access control for a passphrase is configured, you may see a dialog similar to the one shown in Figure 5.6. A passphrase that requires confirmation with each access is presented with three options: Deny, Allow Once, or Always Allow.

FIGURE 5.6 Authorization dialog requesting access to a keychain item.

To Deny access means that the user must then specify the passphrase for the application and the keychain is ignored.

To Allow Once grants the requesting application access to the password. Subsequent requests display this same dialog.

To Always Allow changes the configuration for this keychain item by adding the requesting application to the always-allow list.

This dialog also may request the keychain's password if the Ask for Keychain password option is set. It is a good idea to show the details on this dialog to verify the application path of the application that is requesting access to the passphrase; by default these details are hidden.

Is the Keychain Safe?

Generally, yes. The main password used to unlock a keychain is not stored on disk, and is never available to any other application, ever.

However, if there is any part of the keychain that warrants concern it is the handing off of passwords to other applications. After an application takes possession of a passphrase the keychain no longer has any control over the security of that passphrase. An application can compromise the security provided by the keychain by storing the passphrase unencrypted on disk, sending it across a network in the clear, or allowing it to be paged to disk by the virtual memory manager. Obviously, there is a need for trust on behalf of the applications that make use of any keychain(s).

As a user, don't assume that because an application makes use of a keychain that any involved passwords are automatically safe. Also, periodically audit the access lists of each item in your keychain file to be sure that only the necessary applications are allowed access.

Mail.app Security

There are many facets of security involved with the practice of sending and receiving email. First, you need to consider the communications between the client application and the mail server. Allowing the authentication process to be conducted without strong encryption can result in a variety of evils, including the compromise of mail account credentials, tampering with the contents of mail messages, or invasions of privacy. Email can be encrypted so that only the recipient can decrypt it. It can be digitally signed to determine the authenticity of mail content.

This section covers using SSL or SSH with `Mail.app` to secure communications to a mail server. We will discuss methods to secure how `Mail.app` stores mail data with Mac OS X's built-in support for encrypted disk images. Finally, tools such as PGP and GnuPG can be used to provide powerful longstanding security to email messages.

Using SSL to Send and Receive Mail

`Mail.app` has built-in support for both the secure sending and receiving of email using SSL. This provides for the confidentiality of any exchanged information to the mail server, including any sent or received email messages. However, we would like to point out that this confidentiality is only between `Mail.app` and your mail server; additional measures must be taken to ensure confidentiality between the sender and receiver of any email transaction. This will be covered later in this chapter when we discuss the use of GnuPG and PGP.

Two benefits of SSL are authentication and confidentiality. `Mail.app` can be made to use the SSL protocol; however, it does not perform any certificate validation. The mail server's SSL certificate can be changed or not signed by a trusted root and `Mail.app` will still silently trust and use it. The bottom line is that `Mail.app` does not perform any real authentication of the remote host. This is not to say that using SSL with `Mail.app` is worthless. It is not. Using SSL still provides a reasonable amount of security and is certainly better than talking to the mail server in the clear. If you are ultra-paranoid about this issue, we recommend using SSH port forwarding described in the next section.

Setting up `Mail.app` to use SSL is a quick and simple process. The underlying issue is whether your mail server supports the use of SSL, and if so, for which mail services. If you receive your mail via IMAP or POP, that server must support SSL connections. Likewise, any SMTP server used to send mail must support SSL connections.

To set up `Mail.app` to use SSL when sending mail, do the following:

1. Locate the SMTP configuration dialog. First, choose the Preferences option from the Mail menu. From the Accounts pane, select your account and choose the Edit button. Next, locate the Outgoing Mail Server section at the bottom of the Account Information tab. Be sure your SMTP server is selected and click the Options button. This brings up the SMTP Server Options dialog shown in Figure 5.7.

FIGURE 5.7   Configuring `Mail.app` to use SSL to secure SMTP traffic.

2. To enable SSL, be sure the Use Secure Sockets Layer (SSL) check box is checked. Set the port correctly if your secure SMTP port is different from the default.

3. To set up `Mail.app` to use SSL when receiving mail, navigate to the Advanced tab of your account settings (see Figure 5.8). Near the bottom of the dialog be sure the Use SSL check box is checked. Set the port correctly if your server port is different than the default.

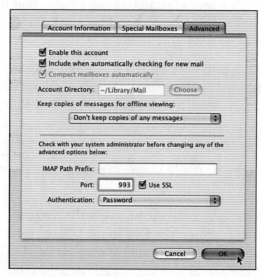

FIGURE 5.8   Configuring `Mail.app` to use SSL to secure received mail.

Using SSH to Send and Receive Mail

If SSL is not an option, SSH can be used to secure connections to your mail server (provided the mail server supports SSH logins). The basic idea is that a SSH tunnel is established to your mail server and local ports are forwarded through the tunnel to the appropriate ports on the mail server. Instead of having Mail.app connect to the remote mail server, it connects to designated ports on the local machine. The downfall to this approach is that it requires some additional setup measures. The benefit is that it provides authentication for the remote host, something not provided with the SSL feature described in the previous section.

1. First, set up the SSH tunnel to the remote mail host. For example, to secure SMTP and a POP account on the host example.com, make a SSH connection on the command line as follows:

```
ssh example.com -L2020:example.com:25 -L2021:example.com:110
```

This forwards the local port 2020 to the SMTP port on example.com. Likewise, the local port 2021 is forwarded to the POP server port on example.com. You will need to replace example.com with the hostname for your mail server and your choice of local ports. The local port numbers are arbitrary, as long as they are not being used and are not privileged ports; only root can forward privileged ports (ports less than 1024). The concept is the same if you use IMAP, differing only by the value used for the remote port (usually 143).

The first time you connect to a host using SSH, it will present the remote host's public key and allow you to trust this key or not. We recommend verifying the public key over a different trusted path before accepting the initially offered key. This is because SSH saves that key locally (in the file ~/.ssh/known_hosts) and checks against it with every subsequent connection to that host. If the host changes its key, or if the verification of the remote key fails for any reason, SSH will (by default) fail to connect and print a harsh warning message. If you encounter such a message do not connect to the mail server until you find out why the key verification failed. Once again, the use of SSH in this manner is good because it not only encrypts all the traffic, but it provides an acceptable way to ensure that you are talking to the intended mail server and encrypting the data such that only that host is able to decrypt it.

Setting up this SSH connection each time you log in can be cumbersome. There are ways to make this process easier, such as creating a shell script that is executed each time you log in. There are also different methods of SSH authentication that can be used. That being the case, we will leave any efforts to automate the setup of the SSH tunnel as an exercise for the reader.

2. Now that the SSH tunnel has been established, `Mail.app` needs to be configured to make use of it. First, open your mail account settings dialog; locate the Incoming Mail Server field under the Account Information tab. Enter `localhost` followed by a colon and the local port specified when the SSH tunnel was setup. Following this example, you would enter:

```
localhost:2021
```

3. Next, locate the Outgoing Mail Server section at the bottom of the dialog, select your SMTP server, and then click Options to bring up the SMTP Server Options dialog. Change the hostname to `localhost` and enter the local port specified when the SSH tunnel was setup (see Figure 5.9).

FIGURE 5.9   Configuring `Mail.app` to make use of SSH port forwarding.

Keeping Mail Off the Server

For users that read their mail via POP, Mail.app can be configured such that all mail is deleted from the server immediately after it has been retrieved. This might be an issue in the case where the mail server is not trusted as a permanent storage location for mail data.

To configure Mail.app so that mail is not retained on the server, open your mail account settings dialog and select the Advanced tab; be sure the Remove Copy from Server After Retrieving a Message check box is checked. Right under this check box is a combo box of options related to when mail will be deleted from the server; select the option named Right Away as shown in Figure 5.10.

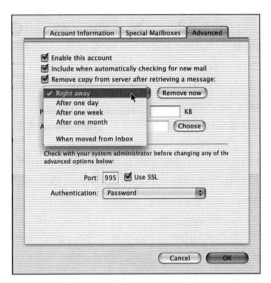

FIGURE 5.10   Configuring Mail.app so that mail is not left on the remote server.

NOTE

For those readers who use IMAP, we would like to point out that the default IMAP settings in Mail.app include storing all downloaded email messages (including attachments) locally. It is reasonable to assume that users who use IMAP may not want any mail data stored locally, and Mail.app can be configured not to do so.

Storing Mail on an Encrypted Disk

Whether you use IMAP or POP, it is a good idea to encrypt any locally stored email. In the unfortunate event that an attacker gains access to your machine, including physical access, your email will remain protected.

1. Create an AES encrypted disk image with `Disk Copy.app`. This process was described in Chapter 3. The size of this image will vary depending on the volume of mail received. If it turns out the created volume becomes too small, it is possible to transfer your data to a bigger volume.

2. Next, configure `Mail.app` to store any downloaded mail data on this encrypted volume. By default, `Mail.app` stores all mail data in your `~/Library/Mail/` directory. If you are setting up an account for the first time, the storage location can be specified on the Advanced tab of the account settings dialog. Locate the field named Account Directory and enter the appropriate path to your encrypted volume.

3. If you have already setup your mail account(s), `Mail.app` will not allow you to change the path found in the Account Directory field. However, there is way to move your mail data without having to re-create and configure any accounts. First, copy the entire contents of `~/Library/Mail/` directory to the desired location on your encrypted disk volume; be sure to close `Mail.app` before doing this. Next, create a symbolic link from `~/Library/Mail` to the path where you moved your Mail directory. For example, if you moved your Mail directory to `/Volumes/mail-safe/Mail`, then you would create the link as follows:

```
ln -s /Volumes/mail-safe/Mail/ ~/Library/Mail
```

Although Mail is still configured to use `~/Library/Mail/`, all the data will actually be stored on the encrypted volume.

4. Finally, verify the permissions on the directory used to store the mail data; other users should not have access to these files.

Using PGP to Encrypt Email

PGP is a collection of products that use public key cryptography to provide secure messaging and data storage capabilities on a variety of platforms. It provides a mechanism to encrypt messages for confidentiality and sign messages for authenticity and integrity verification.

Philip Zimmermann originally authored PGP; however, the current suite of PGP products is now owned by PGP Corporation. The source code for PGP is still available for review. There is a freeware version of the product available for Mac OS X from `http://www.pgp.com`. This includes a graphical key management interface, integrated mail facilities for `Mail.app`, and a PGP Service that allows for PGP operations on any selected text or files.

With PGP, the basic idea is that messages can be encrypted such that only the intended recipient or recipients can decrypt them. PGP makes use of public key cryptography. Each participating user has at least one keypair consisting of a public key and a private key. The public key is made available to anyone who wants to participate in encrypted communications, whereas the private key is kept private, disclosed only to the owner. To send an encrypted message to someone, all that is needed is his or her public key. Data encrypted using the public key can only be decrypted with the private key. Also with PGP comes the capability to digitally sign email messages. This is useful for two reasons: to guarantee the original sender, and to guarantee that the message has not been tampered with. For more information about PGP and public key cryptography, see the references listed in Appendix C.

On Mac OS X, PGP is generally more usable than the GNU alternative GnuPG discussed in the next section. First, PGP is far easier to set up and use on Mac OS X than GnuPG. Often security tools such as PGP do not find themselves in widespread use because the installation and configuration is so cumbersome. Encrypting email should not be made to be a difficult process for the average user. Second, PGP benefits from a uniform suite of integrated applications and graphical tools. GnuPG is basically a command line application with independent development efforts providing add-on modules for various graphical environments. Finally, PGP integration into `Mail.app` is user friendly as opposed to the GnuPG bundle, which is basically a wrapper around the command line interface.

Using PGP with Mail.app

One distinction between the free version of PGP (PGP Freeware) and the licensed version is that the free version does not include the plug-in for `Mail.app`. The noticeable difference is that the licensed version contains toolbar icons for quick access to PGP operations on selected mail messages. However, PGP Freeware works just as well with `Mail.app`.

To adjust how PGP behaves in `Mail.app`, open `PGP.app` and select Preferences from the PGP menu. On the left side select Email to reveal the options shown in Figure 5.11.

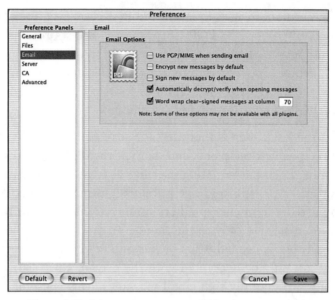

FIGURE 5.11   Adjusting email preferences for PGP.

If you plan on making regular use of PGP, we recommend placing the icon in the dock. The PGP dock icon context menu can open the preferences dialog, purge the passphrase cache, perform PGP file and mail operations for Mail.app, and perform PGP operations on the contents of the Clipboard.

To encrypt and/or sign a message while using Mail.app, compose the desired message and select all text with the Command-A keyboard shortcut. Next, from the Mail menu, navigate to the Service submenu and select the desired operation from the list of PGP menu items. If you are encrypting a message, the PGP Recipients dialog will appear so that you can adjust which keys will be incorporated into creating the outgoing ciphertext. When complete, the selected text in Mail.app will be replaced with the resulting encrypted and/or signed data. This procedure also can be used outside of Mail.app because it makes use of the PGP Service. Services are a handy feature of Mac OS X that allow for specific functionality of an application to be made available to all other applications.

To decrypt or verify a PGP message from within Mail.app, select the PGP block of the message and use the PGP service similar to the process described previously. It is also possible to set the PGP preferences to automatically decrypt and verify received messages. The only drawback with this option is that the preferences for PGP do not allow automatic decryption and verification to be specified independently.

Storing PGP Keys on an Encrypted Volume

By default, both the public and private keyrings created by PGP are protected by file permissions. However, in the unfortunate case that our host is compromised, we would like to prevent an attacker from gaining access to our private keyring; an almost perfect solution is to place both keyrings on an encrypted volume. We consider this almost perfect because if the host is compromised while the volume is mounted, it is still possible for an attacker to obtain the key files. This is why it is important to understand the concepts of physical security covered in Chapter 3. Locking your screen will go a long way toward prevent unauthorized access in this case.

1. Copy the PGP keyring files to the desired location on your encrypted disk volume. By default, PGP stores the public keyring file in `~/Documents/PGP/PGP Public Keyring.pkr`, and the private keyring file in `~/Documents/PGP/PGP Private Keyring.skr`.

2. Next, change where PGP will look for your keyring files. Open `PGP.app` and select the Preferences option from the PGP menu. Select the Files option from the Preferences panel on the left, and then use the Browse buttons to locate and specify the path for each keyring. If the volume where the keys are stored is not mounted when PGP tries to read these files, it will ask you to locate them. If this happens, you can quit PGP, mount the disk image, and try the operation again.

USING PGP TO EFFECTIVELY DELETE FILES

While we are covering PGP, one of the features that we would like to point out is the capability to "wipe" files. When a file is deleted, or moved to the trash, the operating system frees up the disk space but does not always purge the contents of the file from disk. If a disk is stolen or seized and examined, those files can easily be resurrected.

PGP freeware comes with a utility called PGPmail. Open `PGP.app` and from the Window menu, choose PGPmail to bring up the toolbar shown in Figure 5.12.

FIGURE 5.12   Use PGPmail's Wipe to effectively erase files.

The last toolbar item named Wipe can be used to more effectively delete files. When selected, this button brings up a standard file-open dialog that allows you to select multiple files for deletion. There is a confirmation before the files are wiped; however, there is no confirmation that the operation was successful.

The basic idea is that the contents of the files are zeroed out, and then deleted. Although this is not a foolproof means of removing any trace of data, it's certainly better than dragging files to the trash, or even removing them with the `rm` command. However, if you do not have PGP, the `-P` option to the `rm` command is better than nothing. This option wipes the contents of the file three times, alternating between 0x00 and 0xff, before actually deleting the file.

Using GnuPG to Encrypt Email

GnuPG is essentially the same kind of animal as PGP but it is licensed under the GNU Public License. GnuPG is just a command line application. Additional front-ends have been created to work with GnuPG to provide for key management, preferences (options) management, GnuPG related services, and Mail integration. Most of these front-ends can be found at the Mac GnuGP SourceForge project site (`http://macgpg.sourceforge.net`). Stéphane Corthésy maintains a bundle designed specifically to bring GnuPG functionality to `Mail.app`. This bundle (and source code) is available for download at `http://www.sente.ch/software/GPGMail/English.lproj/GPGMail.html` and is free for personal use.

Download, Build, and Install GnuPG

To use GnuPG with `Mail.app`, all that is required is GnuPG and the GPGMail bundle mentioned previously. If you have the developer tools installed and would prefer to build GnuPG from source, the source distribution from `http://www.gnupg.org` compiles just fine on Mac OS X. Otherwise, there are prebuilt Mac OS X installer packages available from `http://macgpg.sourceforge.net`.

1. To build from source, download and verify the distribution file.

```
bash-2.05a$ openssl sha1 gnupg-1.2.1.tar.gz
SHA1(gnupg-1.2.1.tar.gz)= 27b94f42fbc5a620a51e124ad4244f708addcb1a
bash-2.05a$ curl https://knowngoods.org/search.php \
->?release=gnupg-1.2.1.tar.gz\&item=sha1
27b94f42fbc5a620a51e124ad4244f708addcb1a
```

2. Next, unpack, configure, build, and install the application with the following commands:

```
tar xvfz gnupg-1.2.1.tar.gz
cd gnupg-1.2.1
./configure --disable-asm
make
sudo make install
```

3. Now that GnuPG is installed, you need to install the `Mail.app` bundle. Create a bundle directory if it does not already exist.

```
bash-2.05a$ mkdir ~/Library/Mail/Bundles
```

4. Next, mount the downloaded GPGMail disk image and copy `GPGMail.mailbundle` from that image into the newly created Bundles directory; be sure `Mail.app` is not running at the time.

5. Finally, enable `Mail.app` to use bundles.

```
bash-2.05a$ defaults write com.apple.mail EnableBundles YES
```

The next time `Mail.app` starts, an additional icon will appear in the account settings dialog. Figure 5.13 shows the settings dialog for the GPGMail bundle. These settings are for how GnuPG is handled from within `Mail.app` and have nothing to do with the GnuPG options file or the behavior of the GnuPG command line application.

FIGURE 5.13   Adjusting email preferences for GnuPG.

Using GnuPG with Mail.app

The installed GPGMail bundle makes use of the command line installation of GnuPG; the bundle itself does not perform any of the cryptographic operations. As a result, any existing GnuPG keyrings will automatically be used, but there are some limitations to how GnuPG can be used from within `Mail.app`. First, only a single private key can be used. If multiple private keys exist in the private keyring, then the default key is automatically used to sign and decrypt messages. Second, if a recipient does not match any IDs in the keyring, the send operation fails. This is unlike PGP where the user is allowed to choose from a list of public keys from the public keyring.

GnuPG operations can be performed within `Mail.app` from the PGP submenu found under `Mail.app`'s Message menu. There are four options:

- The Decrypt option attempts to use the default key in your secret keyring to decrypt the currently selected message.

- The Authenticate option attempts to verify any digital signature attached to the currently selected message against a corresponding public key from the public keyring.

- When composing a new message, the Encrypt New Message option flags that message for encryption to all recipients. GnuPG does not actually encrypt the message until the user attempts to send the message. The public keyring must have a corresponding public key for each recipient, otherwise a warning dialog appears and no message is sent.

- Likewise, when composing a new message, the Sign New Message option flags that message to be signed using the default key in the secret keyring.

Besides these menu options, the toolbar for the various message composition dialogs can be customized to add icons for encrypting and signing outgoing messages. To add these icons to the toolbar, select Customize Toolbar from the View menu and drag the appropriate GnuPG icons to the toolbar.

Storing GnuPG Keys On an Encrypted Volume

As with PGP, GnuPG can be configured to use keyring files stored at a more secure location, such as an encrypted volume.

1. To set up GnuPG to use key files located someplace other than the `~/.gnupg/` directory, edit the GnuGP options file and specify the full path to each file. For example, suppose you want to store the keyrings in a directory keys on a mounted volume name named secret-sauce. Add the following two lines to the `~/.gnupg/gpg.conf` file:

```
keyring /Volumes/secret-sauce/keys/pubring.gpg
secret-keyring /Volumes/secret-sauce/keys/secring.gpg
```

2. Next, copy the keyrings to the locations specified previously:

```
cp ~/.gnupg/pubring.gpg /Volumes/secret-sauce/keys/
cp ~/.gnupg/secring.gpg /Volumes/secret-sauce/keys/
```

Now, when gpg is run on the command line, or through `Mail.app`, it reads the options file and makes use of the specified keyring files.

Web Browser Security Issues

Web browsing is easily one of the most common of day-to-day computer activities. In this section, we will cover security issues related to the use of some well-known web browsers for Mac OS X including OmniWeb, Safari, and Internet Explorer. Although these browsers differ considerably, there are some common changes to their default settings that can make their use more secure.

Web Browsing and SSL

SSL is the primary means of securing browser-based transactions over the Internet. Many users are comforted by seeing a little lock icon somewhere on their browsers and assume that they have a secure connection, and often this is the case. However, there is more to a web browser's use of SSL than the lock icon.

The goal of using SSL with a web browser (in most cases) is to provide authentication of a remote host, and confidentiality of any communication to that host. The authentication serves to protect the user from being duped into conversing with an imposter and potentially disclosing private information, whereas the confidentiality aspect serves to protect against eavesdropping or the invasion of privacy.

At the time of this writing, Safari is still somewhat of a new browser on Mac OS X and lacks a lot of the needed security features for dealing with SSL certificates. However, there is a relatively hidden debug menu that can be turned on to allow for the configuration of certificate checks. Use the following command to turn on the Safari debug menu:

```
defaults write com.apple.Safari IncludeDebugMenu 1
```

Use the same command and specify 0 to turn it off again. The settings for certificates are located under the Security menu. Choosing Strict Checks will inform you when you encounter a SSL-enabled site that makes use of an unknown root certificate.

Internet Explorer has a list of trusted root authorities for SSL certificates. Choose the Preferences option from the Explorer menu. Next, select the Security bullet from the Web Browser menu on the left to show the trusted root certificates.

Out of the three browsers, OmniWeb is the only browser that gives considerable control over how it conducts SSL transactions. For example, some users may not feel comfortable making use of SSLv2 because it is susceptible to truncation and downgrade attacks. Among other things, with OmniWeb, you can adjust the preferences so that the browser will only negotiate the more trusted SSLv3 or TLSv1 connections. Figure 5.14 shows the SSL configuration dialog for OmniWeb.

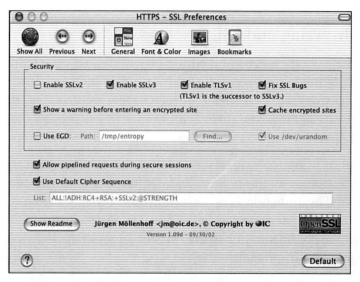

FIGURE 5.14   Adjusting SSL settings in OmniWeb.

Cookie and Cache Management

In this section we will discuss security issues related to web browser cache and cookie management, but first some background information on both.

Web browser cache is a collection of previously viewed web page content, including text and images stored on the local disk by the web browser. The idea is that frequently viewed sites will load quicker because the unchanged elements of the site can be loaded from the cache instead of downloaded from the remote web server. Another piece of information these three browsers store is a list of recently visited URLs. This is the list that is used to help complete URLs as you enter them. Our concern here is that most browsers are set up to store this information by default, thus leaving a trail of surfing habits on your hard disk. The issue in both cases is one of privacy.

Cookies are small pieces of information originating from a web server that the web browser allows to be stored in a local file, part of this information being the URL from which the cookie originated. When the browser is directed to a URL that is found in the cookie file, that cookie is then returned to the web server. Cookies are a result of the stateless aspect of HTTP. By its nature, HTTP is a stateless protocol, meaning that there is no built-in mechanism for HTTP to maintain data about a browsing session between the many individual requests that may occur during that session. By using cookies, the idea is that a user's interaction with a web site can be maintained across multiple requests without the need for obscenely long URLs, JavaScript, or tricks with form values. There are essentially two uses for cookies: practical web site session management and fueling the evils of advertising.

The security issue with web cache data is simply one of privacy; you either disable the cache or store it on an encrypted volume. With cookies, however, there is often confusion about whether they constitute a security risk. We will explore that issue in the next section.

Is Accepting Cookies from Strangers Dangerous?

No. Initially cookies were given a bad reputation. Web users were often told that cookies constituted a serious security threat and, unless disabled, would lead to one's bank accounts being drained within seconds. If this ever happens, it is probably not the result of enabling cookies on your web browser. The reality is that cookies can be abused, but they also can be put to practical use.

The practical use of cookies is for session management as described in the previous section. It is important to understand that all the data in a cookie originates from the web server. When a web browser returns a cookie, the remote site has access to the same information it originally sent to the browser, and nothing more. Thus, cookies cannot be used to steal information from a browser or other cookies; they can only be used to deposit information that you have already provided to the remote host. However, still be mindful of sensitive information you send to hosts that you know make use of cookies, for example, an online banking site. Web browsers have had bugs in the past that allowed unauthorized access to cookie information.

The abuse of cookies has to do with the invasion of privacy. Basically the way this works is that certain Internet advertising companies (that do not deserve to be named) use cookies to collect and correlate the browsing habits of Internet users. All this collected data is then used to display advertisements that might appeal more to the user than, for example, a randomly chosen advertisement.

An HTTP cookie consists of six elements:

- Name
- Value
- Expiration date
- Path
- Domain
- Secure

The name and value elements are mandatory but the other four are optional. The name and value are arbitrary data supplied by the remote site and will vary depending on the purpose of the cookie. The expiration date is a time-stamp specifying when the cookie *should* expire. The path is used to designate in what subset of a site the cookie is considered valid. Likewise, the domain is used to specify for which hosts the cookie is valid. The secure element is a Boolean value; when set this means that the cookie *should* only be transferred across a secure connection. The "secure" element is not really defined, but you might think this means SSL. For detailed information about cookies, see the Request For Comments document, *HTTP State Management Mechanism* (RFC 2109).

At this point in time, you might be wondering how some of these constraints are enforced, such as the domain and secure elements. If there is any element to worry about in this system, it is the browser. The browser is supposed to delete expired cookies, the browser is supposed to respect the secure element of a cookie, the browser is supposed to deal with parsing the cookie data and writing it to disk, the browser is responsible for limiting how much cookie data can be written to disk, and the list goes on. As mentioned earlier, be mindful of what data is being stored in your cookies file. The browser is supposed to enforce this security, but that doesn't mean it actually does. The location of cookie files for the various browsers is specified in the next section.

The bottom line is that cookies are useful and can be invasive, but they don't have to be. OmniWeb, and Internet Explorer (like many browsers) allow you to audit all cookie requests. Cookies can be seen before accepted. They can be rejected on a per-domain basis and put in black lists so that you are never bothered by their requests again. And for those that simply do not want to deal with cookies at all, most browsers allow you to reject all cookies.

Web Browser Cookie Configuration

There is no best way to configure and manage cookies. There are those that are paranoid about them, and those that could care less. In reality, the only real concern is that of privacy. Cookies can and are being used to anonymously track web browsing habits. Here we will point out where to configure cookie settings in the previously mentioned browsers and leave the configuration choices to the reader.

To configure how cookies are handled in Internet Explorer, choose the Preferences option from the Explorer menu. Next, select the Cookies bullet from the Receiving Files menu on the left to show the cookies configuration dialog. Internet Explorer stores cookie data in the plist file `~/Library/Preferences/com.apple.internetconfig.plist` as a base-64 encoded block of data. The key to look for in the plist file begins with HTTP Cookies. Notice that this is also the same file that holds all the preferences. The only way to easily view and edit the cookies is through the Preferences dialog.

To configure how cookies are handled in Safari, choose the Preferences option from the Safari menu and select the Security pane. At the time of this writing, Safari stores cookie data in the file in the `~/Library/Application Support/WebFoundation/Cookies.plist`.

Of all three browsers, OmniWeb has the most configurable and user-friendly interface for managing cookies. To configure how OmniWeb handles cookies, choose the Preferences option from the OmniWeb menu and select the Cookies pane (see Figure 5.15).

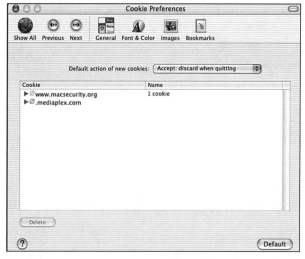

FIGURE 5.15 Adjusting cookie settings in OmniWeb.

OmniWeb stores all cookie information in the file `~/Library/Application Support/OmniWeb/Cookies.xml`.

Web Browser Cache Configuration

The main concern over stored web browser cache is one of privacy. Whether you are using a corporate laptop, a shared computer, or whether you are paranoid that the FBI is going to break in and seize your equipment at any second, this issue can be dealt with by either disabling web cache altogether or storing it on an encrypted volume.

Unfortunately, of the three browsers we are concerned with here, Internet Explorer is the only browser that will allow the user to specify the location for web cache data. Both OmniWeb and Safari have a cache, but the location of that cache cannot be configured.

By default, Internet Explorer stores its cache in the `~/Library/Preferences/ MS Internet Cache/` directory. To configure Internet Explorer to store cache files somewhere more secure do the following:

1. Choose Preferences from the Explorer menu.
2. Next, select the Advanced bullet from the Web Browser menu on the left. In the middle of the dialog is the cache configuration (see Figure 5.16). Click the Change Location button and select an appropriate directory on your encrypted volume.
3. To disable the cache altogether, clear the cache by clicking the Empty Now button, then set the size to be zero megabytes.

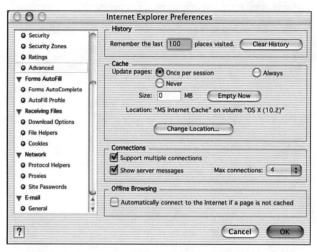

FIGURE 5.16 Adjusting Internet Explorer cache settings.

While this dialog is open, notice that the history list can also be configured, but not where it is stored. Internet Explorer's history list data is stored in the file, `~/Library/Preferences/Explorer/History.html`. One solution for securing this file is to move it to an encrypted location and create a symbolic link to it, similar to the method used to secure email files in the previous section. As with the cache, set the size to zero to completely disable the storing of this information.

At the time of this writing, Apple's Safari web browser does not allow cache or history settings to be configured. The cache files are stored in the `~/Library/Caches/Safari` directory, as is the history information. To clear the current cache, choose the Empty Cache option from the Safari menu.

Likewise, the OmniWeb browser does not allow the location of cache and history information to be configured. OmniWeb stores cache information in the `/tmp` directory; history information is stored in the file `~/Library/Application Support/OmniWeb/PersistentHistory.plist`. To clear the current cache in OmniWeb, choose the Flush Cache option from the Tools menu.

With Mac OS X being a widely accepted and useful desktop environment, web browsing and email are not uncommon activities. Mac OS X now comes with both a built-in web browser, as well as a feature rich email client. However, the default settings for these applications are not desirable from a security standpoint.

Summary

In this chapter we have discussed some concepts related to general application security. We have seen some of the security issues surrounding the use of common web browsers and Mac OS X's `Mail.app`. We have also shown that steps can be taken to secure the privacy and confidentiality of personal data involved in the use of these applications. Although these steps are effective, they are not always obvious. Security in an application requires effort on the part of the user as well as the developer.

PART III
NETWORK SECURITY

## CHAPTER 6

INTERNET SERVICES

*"Now that we have all this useful information, it would be nice to do something with it.
(Actually, it can be emotionally fulfilling just to get the information.
This is usually only true, however, if you have the social life of a kumquat.)"*
—Unix Programmer's Manual

Modern industrial society is all about information. Modern computing is all about sharing this information. To do this, we connect our lonely individual computers together into networked communities of computers. Once connected into networks, we set about sharing our bits of data, sometimes for pleasure; other times for business or education. Life would be simple if we wanted to share all of our information with everyone, and everyone played nice, but reality and human nature creep in and dictate otherwise. Sometimes we find that only certain people should have access to certain information, and that not all people play nice. So into our perfect little IT world the specter of malicious attack falls. The very network services we rely upon to share information with our friends and associates become the points of attack against our data and systems. The brief history of networked computing is riddled with vulnerability after vulnerability, exploit after exploit, attack after attack, and patch after patch.

We have made this point earlier, but it bears repeating. Past versions of the Mac OS have been less susceptible to attack than most other operating systems of the era. Whether one considers this to be due to inherent security in the operating system or an inherent inability to network depends on whether one considers an inherent inability to network to be inherent security. Previous versions of the Mac OS simply were not capable of many of the networking feats we attribute to most modern general-purpose operating systems. Such claims of inherent security are specious logic. It is like saying an old fashion hand drill is inherently more reliable than my 24V cordless drill because the hand drill does not require a battery. It is true in a sense, but that cordless drill is capable of so much more work (especially with me, Preston, behind the hand drill) that it makes the conclusion invalid. In the same way, older versions of the Mac OS are often thought of as being more secure against network attacks because they do not have the wealth of network services provided by other operating systems.

Mac OS X has changed this thinking. The operating system now has the infrastructure to support any number of network services. Out of the box, Mac OS X can share files with other Macs and UNIX systems as well as Windows-based PCs. With little work and no additional installation, a Mac OS X can be a full-fledged web server, email server, or DNS server. This is a far cry from the older operating system line, in which most of these services required third-party applications to be installed.

But with our new-found capabilities comes new risk. Now that our Macs are full-fledged systems on the networks of the world, our Macs are also full-fledged targets on those same networks. Fortunately, Apple has chosen to disable all these services by default, helping us to ensure that "out-of-the-box" security is reasonably sound. This chapter will introduce readers to these new network services and provide details on how to configure and secure them so that these new capabilities do not become holes to be exploited by those who do not play nice.

Web Services

Mac OS X is not the first Apple operating system to ship with a web server built in. In early 1997, Apple released Personal Web Sharing as a 20-dollar add-on to System 7.5.3 (it would later be integrated into Mac OS 8, released later that year). It provided basic HTTP serving capabilities as well as some capability to handle CGI applications (it was mostly compatible with MacHTTP and WebSTAR CGI applications, two popular Mac OS-compatible HTTP servers of the day).

Instead of shipping its own Personal Web Sharing software, Apple now ships the venerable Apache HTTP Server with Mac OS X. More Internet web servers run Apache than all others combined, with about 64% of all active sites according the Netcraft survey (see `http://www.netcraft.com/survey`). In both Mac OS X Server and Client the default http server is Apache version 1.3.x. In addition, Mac OS X Server also includes version 2 of the HTTP server, although version 1.3.x is the default when the web service is enabled. Like most other services under Mac OS X, Apache is not enabled in a default configuration of Mac OS X.

In this section, we will discuss various security considerations for the Apache HTTP Server, including potential modifications to the default configuration. Apache has a rich configuration language—far too rich for us to go into in any depth in this book; there are entire books dedicated solely to configuring and managing Apache. As we indicate in Appendix C, "Further Reading," one of the best books available is O'Reilly & Associates' *Apache: The Definitive Guide*. For any administrator serious about managing an Apache web server, we suggest obtaining and digesting this tome. Because of this, we will be assuming that readers have familiarity with the Apache configuration syntax and should be able to apply general concepts involving various configuration directives to their own specific configurations and needs.

Mac OS X Configuration Oddities

Before we get too far into the security discussion, we feel it is necessary to discuss some of the differences between Mac OS X's Apache configuration and that of a "standard" installation. We also want to point out the differences between the configuration of Mac OS X and Mac OS X Server. In each of the two editions of the operating system, Apple has made different assumptions about the end use of the web server. These differences in configuration cause issues that will have bearing upon a number of the following discussions.

Of the two editions of Mac OS X, the client edition has the most "standard" install of Apache. In the client edition, the binaries, scripts, headers, modules, and log files are located within the traditional UNIX directory structure; binaries and shell scripts are kept in the `/usr/bin` and `/usr/sbin` directories, modules are kept in `/usr/libexec/httpd`, and log files are kept in

/var/log/httpd. There are only a few ways in which Mac OS X differs from a normal Apache installation. The first and probably most quickly noticeable difference is the addition of a simple graphical interface for stopping and starting Apache, aka Personal Web Sharing. This simple GUI is available from the Sharing pane of the System Preferences application (see Figure 6.1). On the Services tab, the web service (and the rest of the more common of Mac OS X's services) can be stopped or started by selecting the service and clicking the Start button just to the right of the list of services. This is as far as the UI goes; any configuration changes must be completed manually by editing the configuration files. It is likely that Apple considers the client edition to be only a light-duty web server that requires no advanced features and thus no advanced user interface. It also helps to differentiate the service from that found in Mac OS X Server (more on this in a moment).

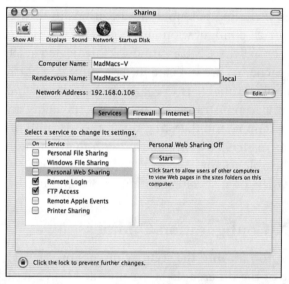

FIGURE 6.1   The Mac OS X Sharing Preference pane.

Another aspect of Mac OS X that is different from the usual configuration is the way it deals with user directories. Typically, Apache configurations use the UserDir directive to specify directories to be used for individual users' sections of a website, and Mac OS X is no different. However, it does differ in the way the user directories themselves are specified. Most often, user directories are specified with a directory directive that includes a wildcard for user directory names (such as <Directory /home/*/Sites>). Mac OS X instead has a directory within the configuration directory, which is where it stores individual users' configuration files. These configuration files get added to the main

Apache configuration by an `Include` directive. When a user is created, a file of the form `username.conf` is created in the users subdirectory (`/etc/httpd/users`), which explicitly adds the Sites subdirectory of the user's home directory to the Apache configuration. The other major difference in a Mac OS X Apache installation is the inclusion of an additional module, `mod_hfs_apple`, which enables Apache to properly handle the case-insensitivity of HFS+ filesystems. As of Mac OS X v10.2.4, Apple also includes `mod_rendezvous_apple`, which publishes the web server via the Rendezvous protocol.

Although Mac OS X clients contain only minor differences from a standard Apache configuration, the server edition of Mac OS X is different in several ways. Here again, one of the major differences is the addition of a graphical interface for managing Apache. Mac OS X Server's GUI goes far beyond that of the client edition of Mac OS X. The graphical interface, which is available via the Server Settings utility application, permits much more than simply stopping and starting the daemon, such as configuration of SSL, WebDAV, and Tomcat support. The default Apache web site listens on port 9010, but does not offer up any web pages. Actual web sites are individually configured as virtual hosts via the user interface. Most of the common settings for a site are available through this interface (see Figure 6.2).

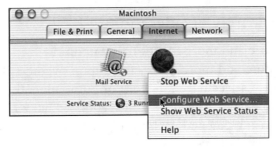

FIGURE 6.2   The Mac OS X Server configuration interface.

All of this gooey GUI goodness creates some interesting issues when it comes to the configuration files. Mac OS X Server moves most of an Apache configuration from the usual `/etc/httpd/httpd.conf` file into another file: `/etc/httpd/httpd_macosxserver.conf`. Apple's UI uses comments through-out the file to provide their application points of reference for modifying the configuration. The file is well-documented in the comments, including various admonishments not to futz with any of the pseudo-directives placed throughout the file. Technically, this configuration file is as modifiable by hand as the one in the client edition of Mac OS X, but one gets the distinct feeling that the gates of hell may open beneath one's chair should one do so. In fact, Apple states in the Mac OS X Server Administrator's Guide: "However, Apple does not provide technical support for modifying Apache configuration files." We have been warned. Unlike the configuration in the Mac OS X client edition, Mac OS X Server's version of Apache does not support user directories for web sites. As in the client edition, Apple includes the modules `mod_hfs_apple` and `mod_rendezvous_apple`, as well as a few other modules to provide additional functionality to the web server. Among these modules are `mod_macbinary_apple` (used to convert some web files to macbinary on-the-fly), `mod_sherlock_apple` (used to give administrators an easy way to interface their web site with the Sherlock application), and `mod_auth_apple` (used to provide additional user authentication capabilities to Apache).

All these configuration oddities will affect the way any configuration suggestions we may have will be applied. In the case of Mac OS X Server in particular, some of what we speak will not apply, at least to the preinstalled instance of Apache. It is certainly possible to download and compile one's own copy of Apache if one wants to avoid the existing install at all, and in some cases, it may be the preferable choice. Whatever the path, most of the following discussion will apply just the same.

General Security Considerations

As we push more and more functionality upon the http protocol, web servers have more and more of an effect upon overall system security. Web servers themselves have a history of both vulnerabilities and commonly available exploits, and Apache is no exception. Lucky for us, Apple has been prompt in releasing patched versions of Apache for its customers in the few instances where they have been needed.

Security issues with Apache tend to derive from one of a few different sources: poor permissions management, misconfiguration, insecure modules and CGIs, and bugs within Apache itself. Because software bugs are generally beyond the control of us mere mortals, what we need to do is concentrate on configuration and maintenance.

Typically, one of the first things to do to secure an Apache install is to ensure that permissions are set appropriately—as is the default behavior, only root has write permission to the log files (located in the `/var/log/httpd/` directory), the executables (which are in the `/usr/bin` and `/usr/sbin` directories), the directory in which the pid file is located (`/var/run/`), and the modules directory (`/usr/libexec/httpd/`).

For the sake of usability, Apple has chosen to give the group `admin` write permissions to the document tree's root (`/Library/WebServer/Documents/`), to which only root is given write permissions by default. This allows any member of the admin group to create, modify, delete, and execute any document in the web server's document tree. These permissions also extend to the CGI directory (`/Library/WebServer/CGI-Executables/`). If this is unacceptable for a system, permissions can be tightened by changing the group ownership and write permissions on the directory and its contents:

```
bash-2.05a$ sudo chown -R root:wheel /Library/WebServer
bash-2.05a$ sudo chmod -R g-w /Library/WebServer
```

SECURITY AND MODULES AND CGI APPLICATIONS

The relationship between Apache and its modules and CGIs is similar to the relationship between an operating system and its applications. Much as applications provide computers with additional functionality beyond the operating system (otherwise, they would not be of much use to ordinary users), modules and CGIs both provide additional information processing capabilities and other features to Apache, and by extension its users (people with web browsers).

The added functionality can vary wildly; from additional language support (such as PHP, a popular language for creating dynamic content), to an application that manages banner ads for a site, to something that simply counts hits on a page. And like applications on operating systems, some modules and CGIs are written with security in mind, and the majority of others are not. Wherever the code runs, as a module on an Apache server or an application on a PC, the emphasis is generally on functionality, reliability, and stability; anything specifically dealing with security tends to be down the list a ways. An insecurely written bit of code might ruin our day in either case if it is exploited. In the case of a network application such as Apache, because the insecure code can be executed from anywhere on the network (maybe even the Internet), the likelihood that a vulnerability will be exploited is that much greater. It is because of this that it is important that not just any user be able to install a module or CGI application in Apache. It is hard enough trying to gauge the security of the modules we administrators knowingly install ourselves, let alone those that less-particular users place on the system.

By default, Apache appends a line containing its version and virtual hostname to some of the pages it generates (error pages, directory listings and a few others). This can sometimes give would-be attackers information that is useful in tailoring an attack on the server. Changing the value of the `ServerSignature` to `Off` in httpd.conf will turn this off. Unfortunately, this does not provide much protection from attack these days. Most attacks on the Internet these days do not involve checking server versions (or vendors, even); the chosen exploit is attempted regardless because it is generally faster to attempt and fail than to check the version, and then attempt, and then possibly still fail. It is the much rarer (and typically more dangerous) targeted attack that takes the time to figure out which version of which web server is running. For those administrators who want to take no chances, this little change will make the server leak a little less information.

Server Side Includes (SSI) tends to be a hot topic when it comes to web site security. SSI is a mechanism (in its basic form) that allows the contents of one file to be included inline in another file and it is enabled with the Includes option (intuitively an argument for the Options directive). This is often used by webmasters to create single instances of commonly used HTML elements in their web sites, such as page headers, footers, or navigation bars. One of the other things SSI can do is to "include" the output of a CGI. This is not necessarily a problem in those situations where the system's administrator is also its webmaster, but it becomes one when there are many webmasters on a system (such as when an ISP hosts many of their users' web sites). Allowing CGIs to be executed from any directory provides the same potential issues we have previously discussed. The best thing to do is to use ScriptAlias directives to provide set directories in which CGI applications are to be stored and then use the IncludesNoExec option instead of the more permissive Includes option. Users can still use SSI with CGI applications, but only those in the ScriptAlias directories.

While we are on the topic of CGI applications, we should note that they are all executed as the same user (www by default; we will discuss this user more in a moment). Again, this is not much of a concern in single-web site shops, but gets to be a problem when multiple sites are hosted on a single server. If one of the hosted users does not play nice, it may be possible for the bad user to use shared access to a CGI application to affect other users' use of the CGI, perhaps even overwriting data generated thereby. An Apache add-on commonly used to avoid this is suexec, which is a special wrapper program that allows CGIs to be executed as specific users rather than global default. Combined with judicious use of the ScriptAlias directive, it can allow CGIs with differing permissions to reside on the same server. This feature, however, is not enabled in the default distribution, and although the man pages are shipped with Mac OS X, it is not enabled with Apple's configuration, either. Enabling suexec requires it to be done at make (compile) time, so enabling this under Mac OS X would require administrators to compile their own installation from downloaded source code.

Several of the options (including access control) in the Apache configuration file can be overridden on a directory-by-directory basis with .htaccess files. This is yet another situation waiting to be abused in a multiuser, multisite situation. In general, administrators do not want their users overriding their configuration settings, so Apple's Apache configuration (mostly by default) includes several `AllowOverride` directives with their values set to `None`. This value should not be changed unless there is a very good reason, and the administrator promises not to whine if he or she gets bitten by the modification.

There is another issue for Apache, and it pertains equally to a server hosting a single site as well as one serving many. Because it listens on a privileged TCP port by default (the standard for the HTTP protocol: 80), Apache's httpd daemon starts as root. This is a cause for some concern. Web servers are commonplace on both local area networks and the Internet as a means of distributing data to the masses. This commonality makes http servers prime targets. No code is perfect: Vulnerabilities are found and exploits are released. Apache is no exception to this rule. When exploits are successful, it is common for the malicious code to attempt to execute further commands on the exploited host. Such exploits perform actions as the user that started the web server. Because this would be the user `root` (and `root` has the permissions to do anything), this is obviously a bad thing.

To combat this, Apache starts as root and then creates child processes as the user and group defined by the `User` and `Group` directives in its configuration file (located at `/etc/httpd/httpd.conf` on Mac OS X and at `/etc/httpd/httpd_macosxserver.conf` on Mac OS X Server) to perform the actual serving. This user and group have fewer privileges than root, so they protect the system from some of the effects of a successful exploit. In Mac OS X, the user and group are www. They should never be given write permissions to any part of the system without good reason, especially anything the user `root` may execute. Doing so could allow even a minor configuration mistake or vulnerability to allow a user (bad guy or not) to damage the system. One notable exception is when utilizing Web-based Distributed Authoring and Versioning (WebDAV, which we will discuss in more detail in Chapter 7, "File Sharing"), which requires additional write privileges for the www user and group, but only on items that root should not be executing.

And, just in case it is not obvious, never ever run Apache fully as root. Ever.

For many sites, this is as far as they need to go with securing Apache—other than keeping up with the odd patch now and then. There are many Apache-based web sites on the Internet that do no more than this and remain free of compromise. But, as we shall soon see, for those who have the necessity and the ability to create still more secure configurations, it is certainly possible, but with added complexity of administration and maintenance. Whether this added complexity is too much to bear or whether the added level of security is necessary will depend both upon the administrators and security policy involved.

Running Apache on a Non-privileged Port

Due to extra doses of paranoia or because of security policy, some sites disallow any network processes from running as the root user. In these cases, even Apache's user switching is not good enough because the parent process continues to run as root, allowing it to listen on TCP port 80.

NETWORK SERVICES AND PRIVILEGED PORTS

Most UNIX-based operating systems, including Mac OS X, restrict the creation of processes that bind to privileged ports (TCP and UDP ports from 0 to 1023) to the root user account. This is not done simply to make our lives more difficult. Historically, these ports are used by the most common TCP and UDP protocols on our networks.

Here again, commonness breeds attack. There have been numerous documented cases of malicious code impersonating these common daemons and protocols for their own nefarious purpose. So, in an attempt to mitigate the problem, we are required to create any processes requiring privileged ports with the root user account. Without this protection, imagine a scenario in which a user on a multiuser system is able to crash the Secure Shell process (TCP port 22) allowing her to start her own deviant process (on the same port), which does nothing more than gather passwords as her fellow users attempt to log on to the system. With the added protection, the user would not only have to crash the process, but then elevate her privileges to such a degree as to be able to start the impostor process on the privileged port. This is certainly a more difficult task.

There is a way to combat the issue of running Apache's httpd as root, and that is to run the daemon on a non-privileged port as a non-privileged user. If httpd is compromised while running as this non-privileged user, the exploit will not likely be able to further damage the system because the user simply does not have the permissions required to do so.

This may sound like a great solution, but it may not be the panacea it appears to be; there are some definite caveats. Top of the list is that it makes the Apache install non-standard in Apple's eyes. When the changes are complete, the GUI can no longer be used to manage the daemon; for this reason, we will not be using the GUI to make most of the modifications for this configuration. Chances are also high that some part of the configuration may be overwritten the next time Apple releases an OS update or security update for Apache. This means that an administrator would be faced with redoing some of the steps listed here if the configuration were overwritten.

The other major downside to running httpd on a non-standard port is that URLs such as http://www.example.com/ no longer work for web site visitors. Web browsers assume the standard port is to be used. This means clients must manually specify the port on which they wish to communicate when attempting to browse at a non-standard port (that is, `http://www.example.com:8080/` where `8080` is the non-privileged port the server is configured to communicate with). This anomaly can often be sidestepped at sites in which firewalls are in use. It is generally possible for firewalls to accept connections on one port and redirect them to another. In other words, the firewall could accept http requests on TCP port 80 (the standard port) and redirect these requests to the server's http port (TCP port 8080). This allows users to use an unmodified URL (`http://www.example.com`) to access the web server.

Finally, the Apache's user switch has been time-tested to be safe for all but the most stringent of security regimes, so this change may not be worth the effort involved.

To run Apache on a non-privileged port, one must modify a few configuration files, some files' permissions and a user account, all of which must be done as root (either directly or by using `sudo` appropriately). Before making any of the following configuration changes, we want to take a moment to remind the reader to make backups of any files prior to making modifications to them. Additionally, for reasons we discussed earlier in this chapter, this entire process is not suggested for use with the default Apache installation on Mac OS X Server. Finally, ensure that Personal Web Sharing is not running. Apache can be turned off by opening the Sharing pane of the System Preferences application, selecting Personal Web Sharing on the Services tab, and clicking the Stop button.

The first file we will modify is Apache's main configuration file: `/etc/httpd/httpd.conf`. Open the file in an editor and locate the PidFile directive. The root user is the only one with write permissions to the `/private/var/run` directory (where the pid file is usually stored). We do not wish to change the default permissions to such an important directory, so we must change the location of the pid file to a more suitable location. Once located, change the `PidFile` directive's value to `"/private/var/run/httpd/httpd.pid"`.

```
#
# PidFile: The file in which the server should record its process
# identification number when it starts.
#
PidFile "/private/var/run/httpd/httpd.pid"
```

Next, we must change the port on which the httpd daemon listens. To do this, locate the Port directive in the configuration file and change it from 80 to a non-privileged port, such as 8080. After this is completed, save and exit the file.

```
#
# Port: The port to which the standalone server listens. For
# ports < 1023, you will need httpd to be run as root initially.
#
Port 8080
```

Typically, the www user should not have a valid shell with which to log in, but in this configuration, it is necessary so that the account may execute Apache's startup script. To do this, we must modify the user's account information with the NetInfo Manager application (/Applications/Utilities/Netinfo Manager.app). Authenticate NetInfo Manager; then locate /users/www. Next, locate the shell property and set its value to /bin/sh (see Figure 6.3); then save the changes and exit the application.

FIGURE 6.3 Setting the shell with NetInfo Manager.app.

Now we need to create the directory for the pid file we referenced previously (/var/run/httpd), as well as grant the necessary permissions to it. Do so by executing the following commands in a terminal window:

```
bash-2.05a$ sudo mkdir /var/run/httpd
bash-2.05a$ sudo chown www:www /var/run/httpd
```

We also need to give the www user permissions to write to the directory and files where Apache keeps its logs.

```
bash-2.05a$ sudo chown -R www:www /var/log/httpd
```

The management script (/usr/sbin/apachectl) for Apache must also be updated with the new location of the pid file. This change is one that is most likely to be undone by an Apple update to Apache. Open the file for editing, locate the line that begins with the string PIDFILE, modify the path that follows accordingly, and then save the changes and exit. It should look like the following snippet when changed.

```
# |||||||||||||||||| START CONFIGURATION SECTION  ||||||||||||||||||||
# ------------------                              ------------------
#
# the path to your PID file
PIDFILE=/private/var/run/httpd/httpd.pid
```

We next need to modify the startup scripts so that Apache can start automatically when the system starts. Locate the /System/Library/StartupItems/Apache and copy it to /Library/StartupItems. Then, rename the directory to **NonRootApache**. Next, locate the file named Apache within the NonRootApache directory and change its name to **NonRootApache** as well.

```
bash-2.05a$ sudo cp -R /System/Library/StartupItems/Apache
/Library/StartupItems /Library/StartupItems/NonRootApache
bash-2.05a$ sudo mv /Library/StartupItems/NonRootApache/Apache
/Library/StartupItems/NonRootApache/NonRootApache
```

Now we need modify the `NonRootApache` file in the `NonRootApache` directory to start Apache as the www user. Locate and replace the line containing `apachectl start` with su - www -c "/usr/sbin/apachectl start". Then locate the line containing `apachectl restart` and replace the text with su - www -c "/usr/sbin/apachectl stop". Finally, replace the two instances of the string WEBSERVER with NONROOTWEBSERVER. The completed file should look like the following:

```sh
#!/bin/sh

##
# Apache HTTP Server
##

. /etc/rc.common

StartService ()
{
    if [ "${NONROOTWEBSERVER:=-NO-}" = "-YES-" ]; then
        ConsoleMessage "Starting Apache web server"
        su - www -c "/usr/sbin/apachectl start"
    fi
}

StopService ()
{
    ConsoleMessage "Stopping Apache web server"
    apachectl stop
}

RestartService ()
{
    if [ "${NONROOTWEBSERVER:=-NO-}" = "-YES-" ]; then
        ConsoleMessage "Restarting Apache web server"
        su - www -c "/usr/sbin/apachectl restart"
    else
        StopService
    fi
}

RunService "$1"
```

When the modifications are complete, save the changes and close the file.

Finally, we need to edit /etc/hostconfig to tell the system to start the Apache httpd server when it boots. Add a line containing the string NONROOTWEBSERVER=-YES- after the last line in this file; then save and close the file.

That should be all that is required to start Apache on the non-privileged port the next time the system starts. To test the configuration without rebooting, type **sudo /Library/StartupItems/NonRootApache/NonRootApache start** in a terminal window. If the following output is displayed, Apache is probably up and running as its new, less-privileged self.

```
bash-2.05a$ sudo /Library/StartupItems/NonRootApache/NonRootApache \
->start
Starting Apache web server
Processing config directory: /private/etc/httpd/users
 Processing config file: /private/etc/httpd/users/curator.conf
/usr/sbin/apachectl start: httpd started
```

To double-check, one can use ps to make sure that the httpd process is running (and that it's running as the www user) and use netstat to make sure it is listening on the designated port (8080 in our example).

```
bash-2.05a$ ps -auxww | grep httpd
www           860    0.0   0.1     2776     1236  ??  Ss   11:04PM    0:00.01 \
->/usr/sbin/httpd
www           861    0.0   0.0     2776      276  ??  S    11:04PM    0:00.00 \
->/usr/sbin/httpd
curator       863    0.0   0.0     1828       76 std  R+   11:04PM    0:00.00 \
->grep httpd
bash-2.05a$ netstat -an | grep LISTEN | grep 8080
tcp4          0       0   *.8080                   *.*                        \
->LISTEN
```

If this is not the case, check the error logs (/var/log/httpd/error_log) for messages and retrace the preceding steps to determine if any errors were made. Otherwise, the web server should be fully functional in its new configuration and reachable in a browser at http://www.example:8080 (where www.example.com is the hostname of the server, and 8080 is the port Apache is listening on).

As we shall see in the next section, simply forcing Apache to listen on an un-privileged port is not the ultimate in security.

Putting Apache in a Jail

There is an additional method that administrators can use to provide further security for an Apache installation and that is to put it in a jail, otherwise known as chroot'ing. In Mac OS X, like other UNIX-based operating systems, / is considered the root file system, below which all other directories exist and file systems are mounted. What chroot'ing does is to force Apache to see a different directory (`/usr/local/jail`, for instance) assigned by the administrator as its root directory. Once jailed, Apache would not be able to access any directory not beneath the new root directory (in other words, it would not be able to escape the jail). In a situation in which Apache is compromised, this would theoretically disallow the exploit from damaging anything outside the jail hierarchy.

JAILING OTHER APPLICATIONS

Jailing is not specific to Apache, but an application (wrapped around a system call) in and of itself (see `man 8 chroot`); neither is `chroot` specific to Mac OS X, but it is an inheritance from its UNIX parentage. As such, it can be used with just about any application running on the operating system, including most of the services discussed in this chapter. The processes used in determining how to jail Apache will work with any application that an administrator wishes to jail. Some applications are relatively easily jailed; others are not so simple. Some daemons can even be made to jail themselves without using the `chroot` command (such as Bind's `named`).

There are some caveats to chroot'ing applications, though. First, putting things in jails tends to make them more difficult to manage. Among other things, it means that because the application is in a non-standard location, patches will not automatically apply themselves properly and thus must be applied manually. This is not so difficult for one or two services on a single host, but does not necessarily scale to many services or many hosts. Making things more difficult to manage can often make things less secure when human factors are weighed in.

Secondly, the harder it is to chroot an application, the less a good idea it is to do so. At some point, there are diminishing returns. If an administrator ends up having to put nearly an entire functional operating system in the jail, she has not really gained that much. At that point, it is better, easier, and probably more secure to simply devote an entire host to whatever complicated service is in question or to find a different method of mitigating the risk.

Also it is generally a bad idea to put multiple services in the same jail. If the point of jailing is to keep daemons from hurting each other, it does not make much sense to put them in the same jail, where they can do just that. Sometimes it would seem necessary to keep them all in the same jail, particularly when they must communicate with or modify each other. In these situations, it is perhaps a waste of time to jail the processes, and time is better spent working on other aspects of the system's security.

Finally, using `chroot` is not a panacea for securing network services. It does not mean that other aspects of the configuration, as well as regular maintenance and monitoring, can be neglected. It also does not mean that a daemon might not be able to damage itself (that is, Apache might still be able to deface its own web pages). Also there have been instances where an executable can escape the jail.

This section will cover how to perform a basic jailing of the preinstalled version of Apache httpd. Like the previous section on running Apache on a non-privileged port, this section does not attempt to provide details on how to perform this action on Mac OS X Server. Mac OS X Server is complicated enough that if an administrator is considering creating a jailed installation of Apache, it is probably easier to do so with a separate installation from source (see Appendix C). Also, like the previous section, this configuration cannot be managed by the standard Mac OS X GUI tools, as should be apparent. Root user permissions will also be required.

The steps for creating a jailed installation of Apache (or any daemon really) are as follows:

1. Create the jail directory hierarchy.
2. Copy files into the jail (includes any necessary executables, configuration files, and libraries).
3. Modify or create startup scripts to start the daemon in the jail.

The first item of step 1 is to create the root of the jail. This can be anywhere the system has adequate space; for our purposes, it will be `/usr/local/jail`.

```
bash-2.05a$ sudo mkdir -p /usr/local/jail
```

Next, we need to make the directories that we know Apache will need. These include the configuration directories, the document tree, the log file directory, the built-in icons, and the directories for the executables and modules.

```
bash-2.05a$ sudo mkdir -p /usr/local/jail/private/etc/httpd/users
bash-2.05a$ sudo mkdir -p /usr/local/jail/Library/WebServer/ \
->CGI-Executables
bash-2.05a$ sudo mkdir -p /usr/local/jail/Library/WebServer/Documents
bash-2.05a$ sudo mkdir -p /usr/local/jail/usr/sbin
bash-2.05a$ sudo mkdir -p /usr/local/jail/usr/bin
bash-2.05a$ sudo mkdir -p /usr/local/jail/usr/libexec/httpd
bash-2.05a$ sudo mkdir -p /usr/local/jail/usr/share/httpd/icons
bash-2.05a$ sudo mkdir -p /usr/local/jail/private/var/log/httpd
bash-2.05a$ sudo mkdir -p /usr/local/jail/private/var/root
bash-2.05a$ sudo mkdir -p /usr/local/jail/private/var/run
bash-2.05a$ sudo mkdir -p /System/Library/Frameworks
```

Experience tells us that there are a few other directories that will be needed (and tend to be common whenever jailing any daemon). Among these are the directories for the time zone files and character set, the base binary directory (/bin), the directory /dev (for /dev/null and /dev/zero), and /usr/lib and /usr/lib/system, which contain system libraries.

```
bash-2.05a$ sudo mkdir -p /usr/local/jail/bin
bash-2.05a$ sudo mkdir -p /usr/local/jail/dev
bash-2.05a$ sudo mkdir -p /usr/local/jail/usr/lib/system
bash-2.05a$ sudo mkdir -p /usr/local/jail/usr/share/locale
bash-2.05a$ sudo mkdir -p /usr/local/jail/usr/share/zoneinfo
```

Now we need to make a few symlinks within the tree to simulate those in the original directory structure.

```
bash-2.05a$ cd /usr/local/jail
bash-2.05a$ sudo ln -s private/etc etc
bash-2.05a$ sudo ln -s private/var var
```

When finished, the basic tree is in place and it's time to move on to copying the necessary files. We will start with the Apache executables in /usr/sbin and /usr/bin.

```
bash-2.05a$ sudo cp /usr/sbin/ab /usr/local/jail/usr/sbin
bash-2.05a$ sudo cp /usr/sbin/apachectl /usr/local/jail/usr/sbin
bash-2.05a$ sudo cp /usr/sbin/apxs /usr/local/jail/usr/sbin
bash-2.05a$ sudo cp /usr/sbin/httpd /usr/local/jail/usr/sbin
bash-2.05a$ sudo cp /usr/sbin/logresolve /usr/local/jail/usr/sbin
bash-2.05a$ sudo cp /usr/sbin/rotatelogs /usr/local/jail/usr/sbin
bash-2.05a$ sudo cp /usr/bin/checkgid /usr/local/jail/usr/bin
bash-2.05a$ sudo cp /usr/bin/dbmmanage /usr/local/jail/usr/bin
bash-2.05a$ sudo cp /usr/bin/htdigest /usr/local/jail/usr/bin
bash-2.05a$ sudo cp /usr/bin/htpasswd /usr/local/jail/usr/bin
```

Next, we need to copy the configuration files, icons, modules and the document trees.

```
bash-2.05a$ sudo cp -R /etc/httpd /usr/local/jail/etc
bash-2.05a$ sudo cp -R /usr/share/httpd/icons \
->/usr/local/jail/usr/share/httpd
bash-2.05a$ sudo cp -R /usr/libexec/httpd /usr/local/jail/usr/libexec
bash-2.05a$ sudo cp -R /Library/WebServer /usr/local/jail/Library
```

Rather than copying the log files, we will simply create them.

```
bash-2.05a$ sudo touch /usr/local/jail/var/log/httpd/access_log
bash-2.05a$ sudo touch /usr/local/jail/var/log/httpd/error_log
```

Beyond copying these files, Apache needs some additional files that are not readily apparent. Two of these are files in the jail's /dev directory: /dev/null and /dev/zero. These files cannot be copied, but must be created and given the proper permissions.

```
bash-2.05a$ sudo mknod /usr/local/jail/dev/zero c 3 3
bash-2.05a$ sudo mknod /usr/local/jail/dev/null c 3 2
bash-2.05a$ sudo chmod 666 /usr/local/jail/dev/zero
bash-2.05a$ sudo chmod 666 /usr/local/jail/dev/null
```

Most binaries on Mac OS X require at least one shared library, /usr/lib/ libSystem.B.dylib, but some may require more. To determine the libraries an application uses, we use the application otool (from the Developer Tools).

```
bash-2.05a$ otool -L /usr/sbin/ab
/usr/sbin/ab:
        /usr/lib/libSystem.B.dylib (compatibility version 1.0.0, \
        ->current version 60.2.0)
```

This shows us that we need the shared library for ab, Apache's standard benchmarking tool. Now we must see what other libraries are required by the libSystem.B.dylib library.

```
bash-2.05a$ otool -L          /usr/lib/libSystem.B.dylib
/usr/lib/libSystem.B.dylib:
        /usr/lib/libSystem.B.dylib (compatibility version 1.0.0, \
        ->current version 62.0.0)
        /usr/lib/system/libmathCommon.A.dylib (compatibility \
        ->version 1.0.0, current version 40.1.0)
```

It appears that libSystem.B.dylib needs the library libmathCommon.A.dylib to work. A further check reveals that libmathCommon.A.dylib does not require any further libraries.

```
bash-2.05a$ otool -L  /usr/lib/system/libmathCommon.A.dylib
/usr/lib/system/libmathCommon.A.dylib:
        /usr/lib/system/libmathCommon.A.dylib (compatibility \
        ->version 1.0.0, current version 40.1.0)
```

We then must repeat this process for each of Apache's binaries and modules, compiling a list of libraries that need to be copied into the jail. This list includes the two libraries we have already determined that we need, as well as a few others.

```
bash-2.05a$ sudo cp /usr/lib/libSystem.B.dylib /usr/local/jail/usr/lib/
bash-2.05a$ sudo cp /usr/lib/system/libmathCommon.A.dylib /usr/local/ \
->jail/usr/lib/system/
bash-2.05a$ sudo mkdir -p /usr/local/jail/System/Library/Perl/darwin/ \
->CORE
bash-2.05a$ sudo cp /System/Library/Perl/darwin/CORE/libperl.dylib \
->/usr/local/jail/System/Library/Perl/darwin/CORE/
bash-2.05a$ sudo cp /usr/lib/libpam.dylib /usr/local/jail/usr/lib
bash-2.05a$ sudo cp /usr/lib/libssl.0.9.dylib /usr/local/jail/usr/lib
bash-2.05a$ sudo cp /usr/lib/libcrypto.0.9.dylib /usr/local/jail/usr/ \
->lib
bash-2.05a$ sudo cp /usr/lib/libz.1.1.3.dylib /usr/local/jail/usr/lib
bash-2.05a$ sudo cp -R /System/Library/Frameworks/ \
->DirectoryService.framework /usr/local/jail/System/Library/Frameworks
bash-2.05a$ sudo cp -R /System/Library/Frameworks/Security.framework \
->/usr/local/jail/System/Library/Frameworks
bash-2.05a$ sudo cp -R /System/Library/Frameworks/ \
->CoreFoundation.framework /usr/local/jail/System/Library/Frameworks
bash-2.05a$ sudo cp -R /System/Library/Frameworks/IOKit.framework/ \
->usr/local/jail/System/Library/Frameworks
bash-2.05a$ sudo cp -R /System/Library/Frameworks/ \
->SystemConfiguration.framework /usr/local/ jail/System/Library/ \
->Frameworks
```

Some of the executables used by Apache are simply shell scripts, which reference other scripts and binaries. These executables are /usr/sbin/apachectl, /usr/sbin/apxs, and /usr/bin/dbmmanage. A quick perusal through these files shows that they need /bin/sh and /usr/bin/perl (for the scripts themselves) and a handful of other executables. After we have gathered the list of need files, we can copy them in place.

```
bash-2.05a$ sudo cp /bin/sh /usr/local/jail/bin
bash-2.05a$ sudo cp /usr/bin/perl /usr/local/jail/usr/bin
bash-2.05a$ sudo cp -R /System/Library/Perl /usr/local/jail/System/ \
->Library
bash-2.05a$ sudo cp /usr/lib/libncurses.5.dylib /usr/local/jail/usr/lib
bash-2.05a$ sudo cp /bin/cat /usr/local/jail/bin
bash-2.05a$ sudo cp /bin/kill /usr/local/jail/bin
```

```
bash-2.05a$ sudo cp /usr/bin/awk /usr/local/jail/usr/bin
bash-2.05a$ sudo cp /bin/stty /usr/local/jail/bin
bash-2.05a$ sudo cp /bin/ps /usr/local/jail/bin
bash-2.05a$ sudo cp /usr/bin/gzip /usr/local/jail/usr/bin
```

Experience has also shown that there are a few additional files that most jailed applications require. These files include character sets, time zones, the dynamic link editor (dyld), and /etc/resolv.conf and /etc/hosts files for DNS resolution.

```
bash-2.05a$ sudo cp /var/run/resolv.conf /usr/local/jail/etc
bash-2.05a$ sudo cp /usr/lib/dyld /usr/local/jail/usr/lib
bash-2.05a$ nidump hosts . / > /tmp/hosts
bash-2.05a$ sudo cp /tmp/hosts /usr/local/jail/etc
bash-2.05a$ sudo cp -R /usr/share/locale /usr/local/jail/usr/share
bash-2.05a$ sudo cp -R /usr/share/zoneinfo /usr/local/jail/usr/share
```

There are two items remaining to be copied for the jail. By default, Mac OS X creates user subdirectories for the website (that is, /Users/sally/Sites becomes http://www.example.com/~jane), which are added to the configuration with files in the /etc/httpd/users directory. These user directories are meant to give users of a system a place to put their own web pages, without requiring permissions to the parent web site's files and directories. This gets a little disturbed in a jailed installation because user directories are not in the jail. What to do about this is left up to the administrators. Possible solutions include periodically copying the user's Sites directory into the jail in the appropriate location or (what we think will be more common for chroot environments) just eliminating support for user directories in the web site. To do the latter, one must only comment out the line containing Include /private/etc/httpd/users in the configuration file. The other remaining item is the web-based Apache documentation. In a default configuration, these are symlinked into the document tree (/Library/WebServer/Documents/manual) from a location outside the normal tree (/Library/Documentation/Services/apache). The method we used to copy the document tree into the jail does not follow the symlinks to also copy the files and directories located therein, but instead simply copies the symlink itself. After the web server is in the chroot environment, the symlink will point to a nonexistent directory within the jail. The fix for this is simple: Either delete the symlink (if is unneeded) or copy the necessary directory structure into the jail so the symlink references a valid location.

After these final two issues are cleared up, the chrooted environment is complete, and we can progress to the final step in the process—modifying the startup configuration. As before, this begins with creating our own StartupItem, which we will do by copying the existing one for Apache to a new location.

```
bash-2.05a$ sudo cp -R /System/Library/StartupItems/Apache /Library/ \
->StartupItems/ChrootApache
bash-2.05a$ sudo mv /Library/StartupItems/ChrootApache/Apache /Library/ \
->StartupItems/ChrootApache/ChrootApache
```

Next, open the /Library/StartupItems/ChrootApache/ChrootApache file in the directory for editing. Locate the line containing apachectl start and replace it with /usr/sbin/chroot /usr/local/jail /usr/sbin/apachectl start. Then find the line containing apachectl stop and replace it with /usr/sbin/chroot /usr/local/jail /usr/sbin/apachectl stop. Next do the same, replacing apachectl restart with /usr/sbin/chroot /usr/local/jail /usr/sbin/apachectl restart. Finally, replace the two instances of the string WEBSERVER with CHROOTWEBSERVER; then save the file and exit the application. When completed, the file should appear as follows:

```
#!/bin/sh

##
# Apache HTTP Server
##

. /etc/rc.common

StartService ()
{
    if [ "${CHROOTWEBSERVER:=-NO-}" = "-YES-" ]; then
        ConsoleMessage "Starting Apache web server"
        /usr/sbin/chroot /usr/local/jail /usr/sbin/apachectl start
    fi
}

StopService ()
{
    ConsoleMessage "Stopping Apache web server"
    /usr/sbin/chroot /usr/local/jail /usr/sbin/apachectl stop
}

RestartService ()
{
```

```
if [ "${CHROOTWEBSERVER:=-NO-}" = "-YES-" ]; then
    ConsoleMessage "Restarting Apache web server"
    /usr/sbin/chroot /usr/local/jail /usr/sbin/apachectl restart
else
    StopService
fi
}

RunService "$1"
```

Finally, open /etc/hostconfig for editing and append a line with the text CHROOTWEBSERVER=-YES- to the end of the file; then exit, saving the changes.

This concludes the configuration for the jailed Apache. Now that we have done all this work, we should state that most of the preceding is scriptable, especially after one knows all of the subsidiary libraries and miscellaneous files the daemon needs. In fact, a shell script to create the simple jail is available on the book's website (http://www.macsecurity.org/macosx10.2security). One can test the configuration by typing **sudo /Library/StartupItems/ ChrootApache/ChrootApache start** in a terminal window.

```
bash-2.05a$ sudo /Library/StartupItems/ChrootApache/ChrootApache start
Starting Apache web server
/usr/sbin/apachectl start: httpd started
```

If the web server does not start for some reason, the Apache error logs (remember, they are located in /usr/local/jail/var/log/httpd now) may provide some helpful hints, and a review of the above steps is probably in order.

If Apache does start without error, we have succeeded in our goal and can go take a nap knowing that our Apache is secure in its jail, but only for a little while. Inevitably, either the users or the administrator will want to add more services to the Apache install, such as MySQL access or Tomcat for Java servlets. Each of these will require their own integration into the jail, following much the same process used here for Apache. Apache and the rest of the applications within the jail will continue to need patches and updates, and a method must be devised for this (whether it is manually copying the files or creating a shell script to do the refreshing automatically). Also, for added security, one might want to combine this section with the previous and have Apache run in the jail on a non-privileged port. The steps required to do so are easily adapted from this material, and thus are left as an exercise for the reader.

Configuring Authenticated Access

Sometimes, administrators find it necessary to share information over the Internet via their web servers but do not wish to share the information with everyone on the Internet. The most intuitive way to do this is to require some form of authentication to access the site.

One of the most basic methods of controlling access to a web site is host-based authentication or host-based access control. This method uses some aspect of a client computer's hostname or address to determine whether the client is allowed access to the web site. Configuring host-based authentication involves three directives: `Order`, `Allow`, and `Deny`. The `Order` directive specifies the order in which the `Allow` and `Deny` directives are applied. A configuration of `Order Allow,Deny` means that `Allow` directives are processed before the `Deny` directives and that access is denied by default; `Order Deny,Allow` enforces the opposite situation. The `Allow` and `Deny` directives take space-delimited lists of fully qualified hostnames, partial hostnames, addresses, or partial addresses and intuitively determine whether a certain host is to be allowed or denied.

```
<Directory "/foo/bar">
    Order Allow,Deny
    Allow from 127.0.0.1 good.example.com
</Directory>
```

This example explicitly allows access to the localhost (`127.0.0.1`) and the host `good.example.com`, and denies access to all other hosts implicitly.

```
<Directory "/foo/bar">
    Order Deny,Allow
    Deny from .mil .gov
    Allow from nsa.gov
</Directory>
```

In this example, the .mil and .gov TLDs are denied access explicitly (except the nsa.gov domain, which is explicitly granted access). All other hosts are implicitly allowed access.

This is a useful mechanism for access control, but only to a point. It should not be used as the sole means for controlling access to a sensitive area of a web site; hostnames and IP addresses are too easily faked or subverted.

User authentication comes in a couple of different flavors in the typical Apache configuration. The first and most basic type is Basic authentication (go figure).

Basic authentication uses a flat file containing username and encrypted password pairs. When a user attempts to access a directory protected with Basic authentication, the user is presented with a dialog box, displaying the name of the protected area of the web site they are trying to access (known as the "realm") and a request for their username and password. Assuming that the user types in a username and password, these credentials are sent to the server, which attempts to validate them against its password file. If the username and password are valid, the request continues through the authorization phase to determine whether the authenticated user is allowed to view the particular page they have requested. If the authentication fails, access is denied and an appropriate error returned to the browser.

Basic authentication is relatively easy to configure. As an example, we will configure Apache to require authentication for users accessing its online manual. The first step is to create the password file. This is done in a terminal window, using the htpasswd application. To create the password file we pass htpasswd the -c flag (which tells the application to create the file), followed by the location in which we want the password file created and the first user to be stored in the file.

```
bash-2.05a$ sudo htpasswd -c /etc/httpd/htpasswd alice
New password:
Re-type new password:
Adding password for user alice
```

> **NOTE**
>
> If the sudo password has timed out, administrators will be prompted for that password prior to being queried for the htpasswd password, which can be a bit confusing, but is recognizable as a `Password:` prompt before the `New password:` prompt.

Because this password file has encrypted passwords in it, it is a good idea to restrict access to this file accordingly. The root user needs to write to the file to modify the database, and the www user needs to read the file to perform the authentication. Other than that, no other users should need access to the file, so we will remove all permissions for others and give the www group read access. We should also mention that the password files should not be placed anywhere in Apache's document tree; doing so is an unnecessary risk that can only lead to trouble.

```
bash-2.05a$ sudo chgrp www /etc/httpd/.htpasswd
bash-2.05a$ sudo chmod 640 /etc/httpd/.htpasswd
```

Additional accounts added to the file are also created with the `htpasswd` application.

```
bash-2.05a$ sudo htpasswd /etc/httpd/.htpasswd bob
New password:
Re-type new password:
Adding password for user bob
```

Notice the lack of the -c flag. Issuing the `htpasswd` command with the -c flag and the path of an existing database will overwrite the database and cause a bad day to spontaneously occur.

With the password file created and populated, we must now modify the configuration to require authentication for access. Open the Apache configuration file for modification and locate a `Directory` directive for `/Library/WebServer/Documents/manual`. Insert a line before the `</Directory>` with the text `AuthName "restricted manual"`. This configures the realm for this section of the site. Inserting another line with the text `AuthType Basic` sets the authentication method to basic. On the next line, we will tell Apache where to find the authentication database, with the text `AuthUserFile /etc/httpd/.htpasswd`. Finally, we must let Apache know who is authorized to view the manual, and this is done with the phrase `require valid-user`. When complete, the `Directory` directive should appear as follows:

```
<Directory "/Library/WebServer/Documents/manual">
        Options Indexes FollowSymlinks MultiViews
        AllowOverride None
        Order allow,deny
        Allow from all
        AuthName "restricted manual"
        AuthType Basic
        AuthUserFile /etc/httpd/.htpasswd
        Require valid-user
    </Directory>
```

After the configuration file is saved, Apache must be restarted for the configuration to take effect:

```
bash-2.05a$ sudo apachectl restart
/usr/sbin/apachectl restart: httpd restarted
```

With the configuration complete and Apache restarted, any attempt to browse to the manual pages (`http://localhost/manual`) should be greeted with a login page with the realm set to "restricted manual." Any user with a valid username and password should be able to type in her credentials and get access to the manual, any user without should be forbidden.

Basic authentication can also be configured to provide group-based user access.

```
<Directory "/Library/WebServer/Documents/manual">
        Options Indexes FollowSymlinks MultiViews
        AllowOverride None
        Order allow,deny
        Allow from all
        AuthName "restricted manual"
        AuthType Basic
        AuthUserFile /etc/httpd/htpasswd
        AuthGroupFile /etc/httpd/htgroups
        Require group theone
    </Directory>
```

Here, the `AuthGroupFile` directive determines the file Apache will use for looking up groups. `Require group theone` tells Apache to allow access by users that are members of the group `theone`. The group file can be created with a simple text editor and has the format of a group name followed by a colon, followed by a comma-separated list of users to include in that group. Thus, the following would put Alice in the group `theone`, Bob in `theotherone`, and both in `yetanotherone`.

```
theone:   alice
theotherone:   bob
yetanotherone:   alice,bob
```

Now not just any user with a valid username and password is authorized to access the site, but only those that have valid credentials that are members of the group `theone`.

Mac OS X Server provides a slightly different method of authentication—configured completely via a graphical interface, but which remains based upon Basic authentication. It uses an Apple-specific module (`mod_auth_apple`), which allows Apache to use Mac OS X Server's password database for authenticating users. To configure a web site on Mac OS X Server to require users to authenticate, first select Configure Web Service from the Web icon on the Internet tab of the Server Settings application (`/Applications/Utilities/ Server Settings.app`). From the Sites tab of the resulting dialog box, select the target web site to be modified and click the Edit button. Next, select

the Access tab from the web site configuration dialog box; then click the
Add button.

FIGURE 6.4   Adding a realm to Web Service under Mac OS X Server.

In the new dialog box (see Figure 6.4), enter a descriptive name into the Realm
Name text box. Next, select the directory that comprises the realm with the
Select button. By default, everyone is allowed to access this realm. To change
this, deselect the Everyone check box, which expands the dialog box to include
an area for specifying the users and groups that are allowed access. Users and
groups can be dragged from the Accounts pane of the Workgroup Manager
(/Applications/Utilities/Workgroup Manager.app). Simply open the
Workgroup Manager application and select the User tab (the single-user icon
on the left side) of the Accounts pane; then drag the chosen users into the
Users and Groups who can Browse and Author box in the Realm dialog
(see Figure 6.5). To include groups in the realm, select the Group tab (the
multiple-user icon on the left side) in Workgroup Manager and drag the group
into the same box in the Realm dialog.

When finished selecting users and groups, click the Save button. If the Web
Service is already running, a dialog box will appear, reminding us that the
web server needs to be restarted for the changes to take affect. To do so, select
Stop Web Service from the Web icon menu, followed by Start Web Service
from the same menu. User authentication is now enabled for specified directory
in the web site.

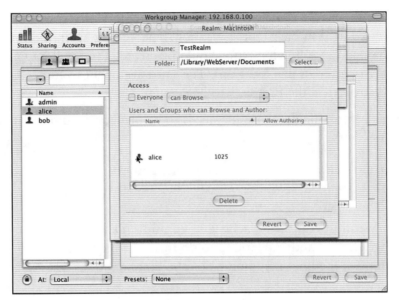

FIGURE 6.5   Adding users to a Web Service realm.

Though it seems to provide a web site with some measure of security, Basic authentication has a major security issue. Basic authentication is a plain-text authentication method, meaning that the credentials are sent to the server unencrypted. This means that anyone sniffing packets off the wire on any network between the user and the server would be able to recover the username and password. And because the credentials are sent with every request to the server, it would be obscenely easy. Because of this, anyone really seeking to provide a secured realm within their web site should not use Basic authentication.

Digest authentication provides a more secure alternative to Basic authentication by not sending passwords in the clear; instead, it sends passwords back to the server as MD5 hashes. Digest authentication like Basic is relatively simple to implement. Here too, the first step is to create a password database, which is done with the `htdigest` application.

```
bash-2.05a$ sudo htdigest -c /etc/httpd/htpasswd "restricted manual" \
->alice
Adding password for alice in realm restricted manual.
New password:
Re-type new password:
```

As we can see, the syntax for the htdigest command is similar to that of htpasswd used in Basic authentication. The -c flag again indicates that the database at the following path should be created (and will happily overwrite any existing file in this location). The third argument to htdigest is the realm, and the fourth is the first user to be created.

Just as before, the database file needs to be protected from prying eyes and reckless deletes.

```
bash-2.05a$ sudo chgrp www /etc/httpd/htpasswd
bash-2.05a$ sudo chmod 640 /etc/httpd/htpasswd
```

Next, we must edit the Apache configuration file to enable the module that manages Digest authentication. To do this, edit the file and then locate and uncomment the lines containing LoadModule digest_module and AddModule mod_digest.c.

As with Basic authentication, we must modify the Directory directive for the manual to require digested authentication.

```
<Directory "/Library/WebServer/Documents/manual">
        Options Indexes FollowSymlinks MultiViews
        AllowOverride None
        Order allow,deny
        Allow from all
        AuthName "restricted manual"
        AuthType Digest
        AuthDigestFile /etc/httpd/htpasswd
        Require user alice bob
</Directory>
```

As in the Basic authentication example, AuthName specifies the realm. Apache is told to require Digest authentication with the AuthType directive, and the password database location is specified with the AuthDigestFile directive. The last line (Require alice, bob), allows access to Alice or Bob by username rather than group (although Digest authentication will gladly perform group-based access using the same syntax as Basic authentication). Like any other changes to Apache's configuration files, the new authentication method will take effect when Apache is restarted.

Like Basic authentication, Digest authentication is not without its own security issue. The problem is that although the passwords are now hashed when sent to the server, someone could still sniff the hashes off an intervening network and, with a little HTTP protocol `fu`, use them to log into the web site. This is definitely more difficult than compromising Basic authentication, but certainly not any great impediment to entry. Apache does provide additional alternate methods of authentication, but they are concerned with improving scalability of the authentication, not with improving its security. Also neither Basic nor Digest authentication encrypts the content as it is being sent between the server and the client. Presumably, if sites contain data worth restricting access to, they also probably contain data beyond the username and password that should not be sent in the clear where a malefactor can sniff it. The best way to do this is to encrypt all the data sent between the client and the server.

SSL

The most common method of encrypting traffic on the Internet is through the use of Secure Sockets Layer, otherwise known as SSL. There is also a protocol based on (and the successor to) SSL, named TLS (Transport Layer Security), which provides the same features, but which currently has less software support. SSL is commonly used with the HTTP protocol, referred to as HTTPS, as well as numerous other common application layer protocols, such as IMAP, POP3, SMTP, and LDAP. SSL sits between the TCP/IP layer and the higher layer application protocol, making the use of SSL essentially transparent to the upper layer protocols. In addition to encrypting all session traffic, SSL can also provide for client-based authentication of the server and server-based authentication of the client. This section will cover the basics of enabling SSL encryption for Apache with the `mod_ssl` module.

For us, the process of enabling SSL under Apache begins with the certificate. During the initial negotiation of an SSL session, the server sends its certificate to the client, which supposedly uses it to verify that the server is who it claims to be. I say "supposedly" because it is up to the individual client applications to take care of this validation, and more than a few do not or at least do not do it well. The certificate contains a number of pieces of information including a valid date range, the name and signature of the certificate authority (CA) that issued the certificate, and the hostname of the system that the certificate was issued to.

Certificates are given a finite range of dates when they are valid, not just to give commercial CAs ongoing revenue streams, but to ensure that even if a certificate has been silently compromised, the compromise will have a limited lifetime. This is a bit analogous to changing locks every so often just to ensure that no one that may have copied a key can access a property indefinitely. If a client determines that the current date is outside the valid range, it should return an appropriate error. Some clients will flat-out deny access to web sites with expired certificates; others will simply warn the user, and still others (thankfully a dwindling few) will completely ignore it.

Client applications use the issuing CA's name and signature to determine whether they should really trust the certificate that the server is sending them. Client applications have a store of "trusted signers": certificate authorities that they trust to sign and issue certificates. If a server sends a certificate that is signed by a CA not in this list or whose signature does not match the one in the store, a client is generally warned. Again, some clients will deny, others will either warn or simply ignore the issue.

One of the final pieces of the certificate a client uses to authenticate a server is the hostname off the server sending the certificate. Clients do this to ensure that the server at www.example.com is not sending out a certificate that indicates it came from evilwww.example.com in an attempt to keep the session from being subject to man-in-the-middle attacks. Perhaps surprisingly, this is not a mandatory feature of SSL communications, but it is widely used nonetheless.

Certificates can be issued in a number of different ways, each with its own advantages. The cheapest and easiest method is to create a self-signed certificate. This means that a host issues itself a certificate for use by the server. Although cheap and fast, this method is really only good for internal systems that do not need rigorous security. Because the issuing CA (the host itself) is not in the list of trusted certificate issuers on any client, the server cannot be adequately verified, and the client will likely generate warnings to that effect. It also opens the communications up to easier man-in-the-middle attacks. Still, it can be useful for test purposes or for situations in which encryption is necessary but server validation is not, and the risks of man-in-the-middle attacks are extremely low.

For production systems in which real security is required, certificates should be purchased from a commercial vendor. Commercial certificates can be purchased from a number of different vendors (VeriSign, GeoTrust, and Comodo among others), each of which competes with the others on price, service, and "trust." The first two items are straightforward and should be evaluated as they would in any business purchase. The final aspect of this competition, trust, is a bit more slippery to grasp. There are essentially two components to this trust: browser penetration and reputation. Each web browser has a list of trusted certificate authorities; if the browser is sent a certificate that is not in the list, an error is generally generated for the user. The more web browsers supporting a CA as a trusted signer, the greater is that signer's browser penetration. If a company buys a certificate from a vendor, it behooves them to use a vendor that has a sizeable browser penetration; otherwise, the company must teach its users how to get their browsers to trust the issuing certificate authority, if it is even possible. Reputability is a more subjective aspect of trust. If people do not trust the entity that issued a business' certificate, they may not trust any transactions that are to be secured by that certificate. In practice, however, this has not been much of an issue.

The most notable example of this is the when VeriSign issued a couple certificates to an individual who had fraudulently represented himself as a Microsoft employee. This made a fair amount of news, but caused no real impact on VeriSign's business, nor Microsoft's. For the most part, consumers with browsers do not pay much attention to SSL. The more knowledgeable among them know to look for their browsers' indications that they are using SSL when it is warranted, but nothing more. So, why should an administrator use a commercial certificate if most users ignore SSL, anyway? For one, not all customers ignore SSL. Also, web browsers tend to care very much about SSL, so much so that if everything is not just right, they will not let users access the malfunctioning site. It is also incumbent upon administrators to do the right thing, even though it is a thankless job.

Some companies may (instead of or in addition to purchasing commercial certificates) establish their own certificate authorities. This is usually done as part of a larger public key infrastructure (PKI) initiative designed to provide larger enterprises with a method enhancing corporate-wide security. This includes the use of single sign-on mechanisms in which client (users and systems) are given certificates with which to authenticate themselves to all systems within the enterprise.

Enabling SSL with Apache

The process for enabling SSL under Mac OS X is essentially the same whether using a commercial certificate or one that is self-signed. The first step in either case is to determine the fully qualified hostname that web browsers will be using to access the site. This information will be used in the remaining steps to properly generate a certificate for the specified host.

The second step is to create a key file, which is an RSA key pair that is used by SSL to encrypt the key exchange for the symmetric algorithm that will actually be used to encrypt a browsing session's data. To create a key file, open a terminal window and create a directory to store the key file in; we suggest /etc/httpd/ssl.key (it may already exist in Mac OS X Server):

```
bash-2.05a$ sudo mkdir /etc/httpd/ssl.key
bash-2.05a$ sudo chmod go-rwx /etc/httpd/ssl.key
```

Next, we will use the openssl application to generate the key file using this random data (replacing www.example.com for the fully qualified domain name of the host the certificate is being created for):

```
bash-2.05a$ sudo /usr/bin/openssl genrsa -des3 -out /etc/httpd/ \
->ssl.key/www.example.com.key 1024
Generating RSA private key, 1024 bit long modulus
............++++++
..++++++
e is 65537 (0x10001)
Enter PEM pass phrase:
Verifying password - Enter PEM pass phrase:
```

The genrsa command tells the openssl application to generate a 1024-bit RSA key with random data from the default source (/dev/random) for the Triple-DES symmetric algorithm (-des3), and to output it to a file (-out /etc/httpd/ssl.key/www.example.com.key).

As part of the process of generating the key file, openssl requests a pass phrase. This password will be required to start up the SSL-enabled web server, which among other things means that the web server cannot be started at boot time. Some administrators will be tempted to use a blank password, and we strongly discourage this. If someone should compromise a host and gain access to this file, the password is the only barrier that would keep that someone from using the certificate themselves in an attempt to impersonate the original web site.

Before we move on to the next major step, we need to lock down the permissions on the key file.

```
bash-2.05a$ sudo chmod go-rwx /etc/httpd/ssl.key/www.example.com.key
```

The third step is to generate a certificate signing request (CSR). Intuitively, this is a file used by an issuing certificate authority to generate a certificate for the requested host. Like generating the key file, generation of the CSR is completed with the openssl application. For administrative purposes, we will create a directory to store the request file first, then use openssl to create the actual request:

```
bash-2.05a$ sudo mkdir /etc/httpd/ssl.csr
bash-2.05a$ sudo openssl req -new -key /etc/httpd/ssl.key/ \
->www.example.com.key -out /etc/httpd/ssl.csr/www.example.com.csr
Using configuration from /System/Library/OpenSSL/openssl.cnf
Enter PEM pass phrase:
```

This pass phrase is the one we used in the previous step when we created the key file. Following the request for the pass phrase is a series of questions that will be used in creating the certificate. These questions include the following:

- **Country Name.** A two-letter code indicating the country in which the organization which owns the server is based (US for the United States).
- **State or Province.** The full name of the state or province in which the organization that owns the server is based.
- **Locality Name.** (Optional) The city in which in which the organization that owns the server is based.
- **Organization Name.** The name of the organization that owns the server.
- **Organizational Unit Name.** (Optional) If it exists, the specific department or division that maintains the server.
- **Common Name.** The fully qualified domain name of the web server.
- **Email Address.** A valid administrative address to which the certificate can be sent.

After these questions are answered, two more questions will be asked (about a challenge password, and an optional company name); leave these items blank. The CSR has now been created at the specified location.

At this point, the paths of a self-signed certificate and one obtained from a commercial certificate authority diverge for a step. With a commercial CA, this request would be sent, along with proof that the request is valid. Some time later, the CA would be in contact with information on how to properly download the new certificate. Once obtained, the certificate needs to be copied to the server and protected appropriately. The directory may already exist in Mac OS X Server installs.

```
bash-2.05a$ sudo mkdir /etc/httpd/ssl.crt
bash-2.05a$ sudo chmod go-rwx /etc/httpd/ssl.crt
bash-2.05a$ sudo cp acertfromca.crt \
->/etc/httpd/ssl.crt/www.example.com.crt
bash-2.05a$ sudo chown root:wheel \
->/etc/httpd/ssl.crt/www.example.com.crt
bash-2.05a$ sudo chmod go-rwx /etc/httpd/ssl.crt/www.example.com.crt
```

With a self-signed certificate, we have to take the role of the certificate authority upon ourselves. As readers may have already guessed, this is done with the openssl application. First, we will create a directory (which may already exist in Mac OS X Server) to hold the certificate and then use openssl to generate the certificate.

```
bash-2.05a$ sudo mkdir /etc/httpd/ssl.crt
bash-2.05a$ sudo chmod go-rwx /etc/httpd/ssl.crt
bash-2.05a$ sudo openssl x509 -req -days 30 -in /etc/httpd/ssl.csr/ \
->www.example.com.csr -signkey /etc/httpd/ssl.key/www.example.com.key -out / \
->etc/httpd/ssl.crt/www.example.com.crt
Signature ok
subject=/C=US/ST=Alaska/L=Anchorage/O=Example Company/CN=madmacs-v.local/ \
->Email=alice@example.com
Getting Private key
Enter PEM pass phrase:
```

The preceding command indicates that we will be performing a certificate function (x509), generating a self-signed certificate (-signkey /etc/httpd/ ssl.key/www.example.com.key) whose request will be read from a file (-in /etc/httpd/ssl.csr/www.example.com.csr). It also indicates that the certificate will be valid for 30 days from the creation date (-days 30) and be output to a file (-out /etc/httpd/ssl.crt/www.example.com.crt). The requested pass phrase is the same one used to create the key file earlier in this section. Now that the certificate file has been created, it must be properly secured.

```
bash-2.05a$ sudo chmod go-rwx /etc/httpd/ssl.crt/www.example.com.crt
```

The final step in the process is to configure Apache to enable its use. Though SSL support in Apache is enabled through the mod_ssl module in both Mac OS X and Mac OS X Server, enabling it differs between the two.

In Mac OS X Server, enabling SSL for a web site can be done completely via the GUI. To add SSL support for a web site under Mac OS X Server, open the /Applications/Utilities/Server Settings.app application, select the Internet tab, and then select Configure Web Service from the Web icon menu, which will spawn another dialog box (intuitively enough), allowing one to configure the Web Service.

Before an individual site can be configured for SSL, it must be enabled for the entire server. On the General tab, ensure that the Enable SSL Support check box is checked (see Figure 6.6), and then click the Save button to save the configuration.

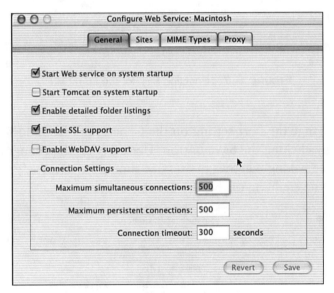

FIGURE 6.6   Enabling SSL for Web Service.

Next, select a target web site on which to enable SSL from the Sites tab, and click the Edit button. On the Security tab of the resulting dialog box (see Figure 6.7), check the Enable Secure Sockets Layer (SSL) check box. Click the Edit Certificate File button and paste the contents of the certificate for the web site (in our example, this is /etc/httpd/ssl.crt/www.example.com.crt). Next, click the Edit Key File button and paste the key file's content into the resulting dialog box (/etc/httpd/ssl.key/www.example.com.key in our example).

The pass phrase for the key file can also be set here. Doing so causes Mac OS X Server to place the password in plain text in its configuration file (/etc/httpd/httpd_macosxserver.conf).

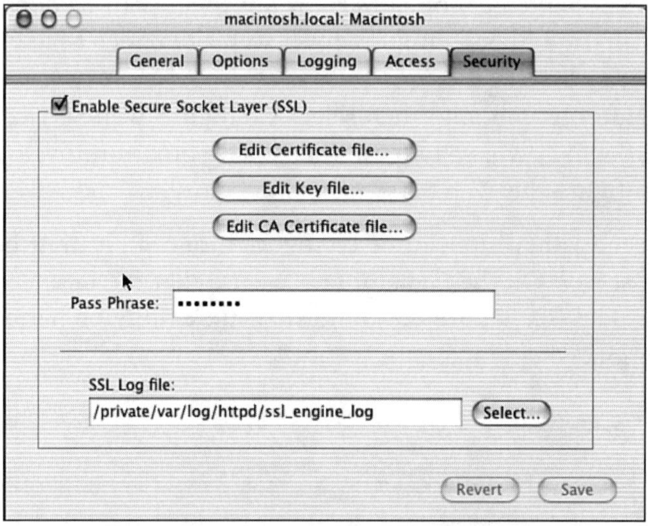

FIGURE 6.7   Enabling SSL for the target site.

Finally, change the Port setting on the General tab from 80 to **443** and save the changes by clicking the Save button. Upon saving the changes, a dialog box will appear, asking whether the service should be restarted; doing so will complete the enabling of the SSL for the target site.

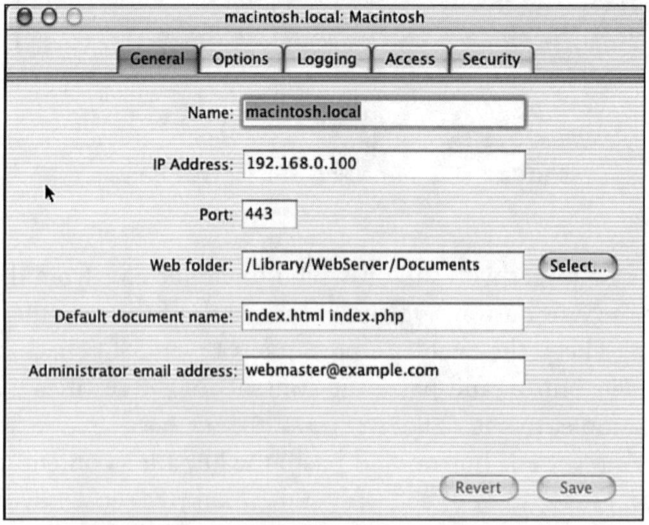

FIGURE 6.8   Enabling SSL for Web Service.

Mac OS X lacks Mac OS X Server's easy graphical configuration of SSL, but still supports it via manual modification of the Apache configuration file. To enable SSL support in Apache, open the configuration file (`/etc/httpd/httpd.conf`), locate and uncomment the line containing the text `#LoadModule ssl_module libexec/httpd/libssl.so`, and then locate and uncomment the line containing `#AddModule mod_ssl.c`. Next, append the following lines to the end of the configuration file:

```
<IfModule mod_ssl.c>

    Listen 80
    Listen 443

    <VirtualHost _default_:443>
        SSLEngine on
    </VirtualHost>

    SSLCertificateFile /etc/httpd/ssl.crt/www.example.com.crt
    SSLCertificateKeyFile /etc/httpd/ssl.key/www.example.com.key

    SSLRandomSeed startup builtin
    SSLRandomSeed connect builtin

</IfModule>
```

This process enables SSL on the default web site. Virtual hosts can be individually configured to require SSL as well. A typical `VirtualHost` directive would look as follows:

```
<VirtualHost 192.168.1.1:443>
    ServerName       www.example.com
    DocumentRoot     /Library/WebServer/www.example.com
    ErrorLog         /var/log/httpd/www.example.com.error.log
    CustomLog        /var/log/httpd/www.example.com.access.log combined
    <Directory "/Library/WebServer/www.example.com">
        Options      None
        Override     None
        Order        allow,deny
        Allow from all
    </Directory>
    SSLEngine On
    SSLCertificateFile /etc/httpd/ssl.crt/www.example.com.crt
    SSLCertificateKeyFile /etc/httpd/ssl.key/www.example.com.key
    SSLRandomSeed    startup     builtin
    SSLRandomSeed    connect     builtin
</VirtualHost>
```

These are obviously fairly basic configurations of mod_ssl and Apache. Like Apache in general, there are many other possible aspects to an SSL deployment that an administrator may need to configure, and mod_ssl provides a wealth of directives to do so. In fact, there are far too many directives configurable in far too many combinations to explain in the book that is not entirely about Apache. Appendix C contains additional suggested reading on configuring all of the aspects of mod_ssl as well as Apache as a whole.

And Apache is not the only Internet service that Mac OS X is capable of running, of course, and therefore not the only Internet service that may need to be secured. We will discuss the most common of these in the following sections, starting with mail services.

Email Services

Email has been a backbone service on the Internet since well before web browsers were browsing. As such, it has often been the target of much abuse. Whether it is Sendmail buffer overflows common in days of yore, worms, hoaxes, scams, or spam, the history of email is full of nasty problems. For sites using email services, making sure that these services are secured is an important aspect of not only the server's security, but of the security of all the server's email users.

Mac OS X and Mac OS X Server ship with different applications to handle email. In Mac OS X, there is only an MTA, Sendmail, which is the most common SMTP server on the Internet. It is not enabled by default and requires some work to even get the daemon to run. Mac OS X Server ships with a different default mail server called MailService (Mac OS X Server also includes Sendmail, but it is not enabled). Each of these different email services has different capabilities and methods for securing them.

Sendmail

Apple has actually helped administrators by not enabling Sendmail by default in Mac OS X. Given its history of issues and the unlikelihood of an average user being able to properly manage the daemon, this can be seen only as a good thing. Apple does not provide a GUI with which to manage Sendmail, and most of the niceties of a typical Sendmail installation are missing (such as scripts to compile the configuration files when the service starts). There are few reasons for a client operating system to ever have its own SMTP server, and Apple seems cognizant of this fact with the hoops one must jump through to make the client version of Mac OS X a full-fledged email server. Sendmail is like a redheaded stepchild to Apple; they would rather it didn't exist, but it is family, so they include it anyway. Just barely. In other words, Apple seems to include it simply because it is a "standard" in many UNIX-based operating systems, and for no other reason.

If Sendmail is enabled, one of the most important aspects of its security is simply maintaining patches. Apple is pretty good about releasing patches in a timely manner, so judicious use of the Software Update application is probably all that is needed. Relaying is another consistent problem with any SMTP server. True to form, Apple has disabled relaying by default. If relaying is enabled by hand, it must be done with care.

An unfortunate downside of Apple's treatment of Sendmail is that those wishing to use it in a serious manner are forced to make up a lot of the features of a typical OEM install themselves. For instance, Sendmail was not compiled to allow for SSL-encrypted sessions, so administrators who want to provide secure authenticated relaying would be forced to compile and install their own version of Sendmail.

The bottom line is that there are few reasons to enable Sendmail on a client. If there is a genuine need, administrators should be aware of the risk and read a book or two on proper Sendmail configuration before proceeding. In general, one should not consider using Sendmail unless forced to do so with threats of bodily harm, eternal damnation, or unemployment. There are easier MTAs to use that do not have the lengthy history of vulnerabilities that Sendmail does.

MailService

In contrast with Sendmail, which is only an MTA, Mac OS X Server's MailService is a full-featured server that supports not only SMTP, but also IMAP and POP3. In addition, MailService also supports encrypted transports for all these services, as well as basic anti-SPAM measures.

MailService is not a redheaded stepchild. It sports a comprehensive GUI to manage its configuration, which is stored in the NetInfo database. Like most Mac OS X Server services, MailService is configured through the Server Settings application (see Figure 6.9). With this interface, it is possible to stop and start the service, as well as configure the server's settings. The Configure Host Settings dialog modifies DNS usage, relay settings, and other parameters.

The specifics of how the various email protocols are used are governed by the Configure Mail Services dialog box. Both dialog boxes contain settings affecting the security of both the service itself and its use by users.

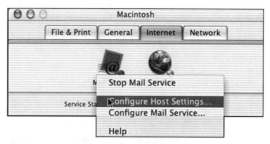

FIGURE 6.9   Configuring the Mac OS X Server Mail Server.

The Configure Host Settings dialog box contains three tabs: Incoming Mail, Outgoing Mail, and Network Setting. On the Incoming Mail tab, administrators can set the hosts that are allowed to relay through the server. Clicking the Add button brings up a simple dialog box with a text box that accepts a hostname, domain name, IP address, range of IP addresses (192.168.1.1-254), or a subnet (192.168.1.0/255.255.255.240). The dialog box does not perform rigorous sanitizing of the input text, so administrators must be extra careful to type correctly. The Outgoing Mail tab allows administrators to decide whether to even allow the server to send mail outside the organization (see Figure 6.10). By default, outgoing mail is limited to local users and hosts (those hosts identified in the Configure Mail Service dialog box's Local Hostnames box). Setting the top pop-up menu to Allow outgoing mail allows the server to deliver mail to servers outside the organization (that is, those on the Internet). The final tab specifies how the server should handle hostname lookups for outgoing email and the outgoing TCP port it should use. The defaults are reasonable and should be changed only if truly necessary.

The Configure Mail Service dialog box configures more of the protocol-specific aspects of MailService and consists of four tabs: General, Messages, Filter, Protocols. The General tab contains the previously discussed Local Hostnames box (which contains the hostnames of other email servers within the organization). This tab also allows administrators to move the mail store. Extra care should be taken to preserve the permissions (allowing only root read and write permissions; everyone else is denied access) on the files and directories if the mail store is moved. Among other things, there are privacy concerns involved with the storage of an organization's email, so making sure that only root has access to the mail database is important. The mechanism that clients are allowed to authenticate with can be set with the pop-up list in the middle of the panel. Administrators can choose Kerberos, standard SMTP, or Any Method (see Figure 6.11).

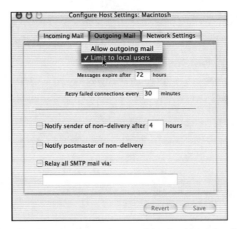

FIGURE 6.10 Configuring outgoing mail in the Host Settings dialog box.

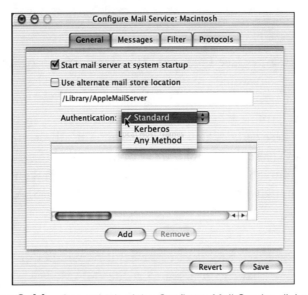

FIGURE 6.11 General tab of the Configure Mail Service dialog box.

Setting a message size limit on the Messages tab (see Figure 6.12) can keep someone from maliciously consuming the server's resource (disk and network bandwidth) by sending numerous large files to users. However, it may also anger those users who routinely use email as their primary file-sharing protocol (engineers with giant AutoCAD drawings seem especially prone to this disease).

For those sites with concerns about email retention for legal reasons (such as Microsoft), the Message tab also allows administrators to configure the retention of both read and unread mail messages.

FIGURE 6.12   The Messages tab of the Configure Mail Service dialog box.

The third tab, Filter (see Figure 6.13), permits administrators to cut down on the amount of unwanted email their users process. The top option specifies the address of an ORBS (Open-Relay Behavioral modification System) server to be queried to determine whether a sending host is an open relay that can be used for SPAM. These servers generally require paid subscriptions for access, but can markedly decrease the load of junk mail transiting a server. ORBS are not bullet proof, however, because some servers are mistakenly added to the lists. Also, even though a server may be an open relay for SPAM, it probably has legitimate users as well that may be trying to conduct important business via email.

Clicking in the check box next to Reject if name does not match address is another method that can be used to reduce SPAM. It is a common tactic for some junk mailers to make their messages appear to come from one location when they really come from another; thus, MailService will check to ensure that the address and hostname are appropriate for each other. This also is not foolproof because there are occasionally valid reasons why a server may appear to have a different address than its name would indicate. The final box on the Filter tab lets administrators specify specific servers to be disallowed from sending their server email.

FIGURE 6.13   The Filter tab of the Configure Mail Service dialog box.

The fourth and final tab, Protocols (see Figure 6.14), contains options for each of the three major protocols supported by MailService (SMTP, POP3, and IMAP), as well as an oddment named NotifyMail (which is a proprietary protocol for notifying users when they have new mail without having the client's email client poll for new messages). Each of the three major protocols has an option for a secure mode of authentication (CRAM-MD5 for SMTP and IMAP; APOP for POP3). Rather than enabling these kinds of authentication—which attempt to secure only the authentication phase, not the entirety of the session—we suggest using SSL to encrypt the entire sessions.

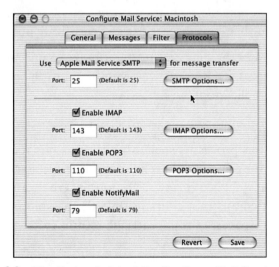

FIGURE 6.14   The Protocols tab of the Configure Mail Service dialog box.

Enabling SSL Encryption for MailService

Like the configuration of most SSL-enabled services, enabling SSL for
MailService consists of four basic steps:

1. Generate a Certificate Signing Request (CSR).

2. Obtain a certificate using the CSR.

3. Insert the new certificate into the certificate store.

4. Configure MailService to use the certificate.

The CSR for MailService must be created as root (logged into the console, not
via a terminal session) with the `certtool` command-line application. We must
also create a certificate store in which to put the certificate (otherwise known
as a *keychain*).

```
bash-2.05a# cd /var/root/Library/Keychains/
bash-2.05a# /usr/bin/certtool r csr.txt k=certkc c
```

This listing creates a keychain for root named certkc and starts the certificate
request process. The application will prompt for a passphrase in the GUI to
use for the new keychain; then return to the terminal session to continue the
certificate request process. The first question asked when generating the CSR
is for a key and certificate label (which must be separated by spaces). A good
choice here is the domain name of the organization for the key and MailService
for the label. The rest of the questions asked are standard to any CSR process
and should be answered accordingly (see "Enabling SSL with Apache"
previously in this chapter). After all questions have been answered, a CSR will
be generated in a text file named csr.txt in /var/root/Library/Keychains.
This text should then be submitted to the certificate authority (CA) of choice.

After the CA issues the new certificate, it must be injected into the keychain so
that it may be used. To do this, we again log in to the console as root and use
the `certtool` application.

```
bash-2.05a# /usr/bin/certtool i example.crt k=certkc
```

Assuming that this process is successful, there is one remaining step: to put
the passphrase for the certkc keychain in a text file so that MailService can
read the passphrase when it starts. To do this, create a text file with vi (or any
other plain text editor) that contains only the passphrase. Be sure not to include
any whitespace (spaces, tabs, or carriage returns) after the passphrase. Save
this file as certkc.pass in /var/root/Library/Keychains and change the

permissions so that only root has read and write permission (everyone else has no access). Apple's knowledge base contains a useful document providing more detail on setting up SSL for MailServer (Article ID 75335).

A quick restart of MailService, and that's all it takes to enable SSL for all three of MailService's protocols. There is no further configuration needed (or possible). It is not, for instance, possible to require users to use IMAP-SSL from within MailService (though it is certainly possible using a firewall). Regardless, using SSL is probably the best way to secure email sessions without diving into IPSec, and is one of the biggest ways to improve security when using MailService.

FTP

FTP is one of the older and more cantankerous (due to its dual-channel nature) protocols on the Internet. Mac OS X and Mac OS X Server ship with different FTP servers, much like they ship with different mail servers. The FTP server that ships with the client version of Mac OS X (lukemftpd) is a typical basic ftp daemon. Apple chose not to provide any configuration utility for it beyond the start and stop in the Sharing Preference pane. For the Mac OS X Server FTP server (xftpd, based upon Washington University's wu-FTPd), Apple created a simple user interface in the Server Settings application. Apple also added a number of capabilities, including Kerberos integration, on-the-fly conversion of compressed files, and the capability to export sharepoints into the FTP server's filesystem root (the FTProot).

Its use of clear-text authentication and data transmission makes FTP an obsolete protocol for anything more than anonymous downloads. Additionally, the software basis for xftpd, wu-FTPd, has a lengthy history of vulnerabilities and readily available exploits. We highly suggest that no one use FTP for anything but anonymous downloads, even with all of Apple's additions. Even this concession is a bit of a stretch; for such situations, it often makes more sense from both the client and server sides to set up a small web server (or section of a website) to allow people to browse for and download files. The http protocol allows for all the needs of anonymous downloads without all the hassle of the ftp protocol and the vulnerabilities typical in the servers used to implement it. The http protocol can even provide for authentication and encryption, if needed.

For those wanting FTP-style access with authentication, SFTP clients, which use a much more secure protocol (see the following section on Remote Login), are readily available for most platforms while providing a similar user interface to FTP. SFTP is also easier to manage at the firewall because it uses a single channel for both commands and data transfer.

Remote Login (SSH)

What Apple calls Remote Login in its control panel (refer to Figure 6.1), the rest of the world calls OpenSSH. OpenSSH is an open-source suite of network tools implementing the Secure Shell protocol and providing encrypted communications between networked hosts. Among its various utilities are replacements for common unencrypted protocols such as RCP, TELNET, and FTP. OpenSSH can also automatically forward X11 connections over an established tunnel, compress data as it is transmitted (for slow connections or inefficient protocols such as X11), and perform RSA-based client and server authentication. With all its features and the wide availability of clients, there is quickly becoming no reason to use the less-secure applications SSH was meant to replace. Table 6.1 presents a rundown of OpenSSH applications and what they do.

TABLE 6.1   OpenSSH Applications and Their Usages

APPLICATION	USAGE
/usr/sbin/sshd	SSH server
/usr/libexec/sftp-server	SFTP subsystem server
/usr/libexec/ssh-keysign	Part of the SSH client, used for managing SSH2's host-based authentication
/usr/bin/sftp	SFTP client
/usr/bin/scp	Secure network file copying utility
/usr/bin/ssh	SSH client
/usr/bin/ssh-add	Adds identities to ssh-agent
/usr/bin/ssh-agent	Client-side authentication agent
/usr/bin/ssh-keygen	Manages authentication keys
/usr/bin/ssh-keyscan	Key gatherer for public keys
/usr/bin/slogin	A symlink to /usr/bin/ssh

Security Considerations

As with all network services, Mac OS X ships with Remote Login disabled by default. Disabling Remote Login means that only access to Mac OS X as an SSH server (/usr/sbin/sshd) is disabled; it does not disable the command-line client applications. SSH will likely be useful only to those users who utilize the command line on occasion and should only be enabled in such situations.

As it ships, Mac OS X includes a mostly default configuration for both the SSH server (/etc/sshd_config) and the client utilities (/etc/ssh_config). The good news is that Apple's default configuration is reasonably sane. The only non-default setting it has applied is the enabling of the SFTP subsystem for sshd. Even though the default configurations are sound, there are a few items that administrators may want to consider for their own systems.

Server Configuration

Access to the SSH server can be controlled in a few different ways by using various keywords in the configuration file. User-based access control is managed with the keywords AllowUsers and DenyUsers. Both parameters accept a space-delimited list of users that are either allowed or denied login. Asterisks or question marks can be used as wildcards for multiple characters and single characters, respectively. Usernames can also take the form of username@host, which allows administrators to permit access from certain users originating from certain hosts. Group-based access is controlled in a similar fashion to user-based with the keywords AllowGroups and DenyGroups. Similar to user-based access control, the group-based access control keywords accept space-separated lists of groups that explicitly allowed or disallowed the right to login. By default, all users and groups are allowed to log in to the SSH server.

The following is a snippet of an example configuration that allows access by users whose usernames start with the letter a, denies access by users whose name ends with the letter z from the host evil.example.com, and allows access to any member of the group admin while denying access to members of the group enemy.

```
AllowUsers      a*
AllowGroups     admin
DenyUsers       *z@evil.example.com
DenyGroups      enemy
```

Another area of concern for a server configuration is the protocol with which it communicates to clients. By default, sshd speaks either version 1 or version 2, preferring the latter. There are known issues with the version 1 protocol that allows for some man-in-the-middle attacks. Beyond this, various implementations and versions of SSH1 are prone to a host of different vulnerabilities. There is a tool called dsniff (see http://naughty.monkey.org/~dugsong/dsniff/) that will even automate an attack. For this reason, we suggest disabling the version 1 protocol if at all possible. This can be done by using the Protocol keyword and setting it to a value of 2 (as opposed to 2,1, which is the default).

Properly maintaining the security of the server's key file is another important aspect of securing Remote Login. This aspect is configured properly out of the box, but it must be maintained throughout the lifetime of the server. A simple directory listing shows the proper permissions that should be maintained:

```
-rw-------  1 root   wheel   668 Nov 26 15:21 /etc/ssh_host_dsa_key
-rw-r--r--  1 root   wheel   599 Nov 26 15:21 /etc/ssh_host_dsa_key.pub
-rw-------  1 root   wheel   524 Nov 26 15:20 /etc/ssh_host_key
-rw-r--r--  1 root   wheel   328 Nov 26 15:20 /etc/ssh_host_key.pub
-rw-------  1 root   wheel   883 Nov 26 15:20 /etc/ssh_host_rsa_key
-rw-r--r--  1 root   wheel   219 Nov 26 15:20 /etc/ssh_host_rsa_key.pub
```

Of note here are the files that end with the .key extension. These are the server's private keys and thus need the most protection. They should never be readable or writeable by any user other than root to prevent modification or theft.

For those sites whose policy dictates it (and the account is enabled), it is possible for administrators to disallow direct logins by the root user. This is accomplished by modifying the configuration to set the PermitRootLogins to no.

Although there are a lot of other keywords available in the SSH server configuration file (54 by our count), few are worthy of modification unless there is an overriding need. Many will serve only to decrease the overall security of the conservative default configuration.

Client Configuration

Client configuration can come from three different sources and is gathered in this order: command-line flags, a user-specific configuration file (~/.ssh/config), and the system-wide configuration file. If an option is specified in multiple configuration sources, the first instance is used.

Client security is less exciting than security for the server. By default, all the user-specific files are stored in the .ssh hidden directory at the root of each user's home directory. This directory holds the user's known_hosts file; any public and private keys the user may be using; and a user-specific configuration file, if the user has one. As with the server key files, any private keys a user may have should be protected, allowing only read and write permissions to the owning user. This goes for configuration files as well. Also, like the server configuration, we suggest not changing the defaults in the ssh client configuration unless there is a clear and well thought-out reason to do so.

Some readers may be wondering why we are not talking about protocol versions for the client. The unfortunate reality is that though SSH use is widespread, many implementations rely upon the older version 1 protocol. A lot of the systems we deal with are manufactured by Cisco, which supports SSH. However, Cisco supports only version 1 of the protocol, which it has stated is the only version that it will ever support. It is because of this stance that we have a hard time restricting clients from using it if necessary; the default for the client is to prefer version 2 of the protocol, but use the older protocol, if necessary. It's a case of the alternate being telnet, which makes version 1 "secure enough" for our purposes.

SSH Tunnels

Another nice feature of SSH is its capability to create tunnels for other protocols. For instance, I do some work for a university museum, which has a firewall that wisely blocks external access to an Oracle database. My work requires me to have access to this database from remote locations, which presents me with a problem. Here is where SSH can come to the rescue. With the following command, I can create a tunnel to the remote oracle server through SSH.

```
bash-2.05a$ ssh -C -L 1521:museum.example.com:1521 museum.example.com
```

This command sets up a socket to listen on TCP port 1521 on the loopback interface. To connect my computer to the museum's database, I configure the database client software to connect to the database via the localhost address, which is all that is required to give me the access I need in a reasonably secure and efficient manner.

This method can be used to secure all manner of TCP-based communications. SSH tunnels are a great way to secure many unencrypted protocols. For awhile, before Mail.app was able to do IMAP-SSL, the easiest way for my associates and I to securely use our IMAP server was to use SSH tunnels to the mail server. Tunnels can be used with POP3, AFP, and NFS.

There are other aspects to using SSH that we have not broached here. Additional documentation on SSH usage can be found in Appendix C.

Remote Apple Events

Remote Apple Events (RAE) allows Macintosh's applications to be driven by any other workstations on the network. Under Mac OS 9.x and its predecessors, this was called Program Linking. This is a very handy feature for those who need it. For instance, if an administrator runs a horde of Adobe Photoshop workstations, she can instruct all of the machines to perform rendering operations on graphics files, all from a centralized location. Applications must be coded by their developers in order to take advantage of Remote Apple Events. Developers can even leverage the technology to create quasi-clustering or Beowulf solutions.

Security Considerations

Just don't. In all seriousness, this is definitely a service that should not be enabled unless there is a very good reason to. At the very least, this service should never ever be accessible through the Internet, and access to its service port (TCP port 3031) should be strictly controlled. Authentication is required for remote access to a machine's applications, but this is not foolproof because it is still possible to cause problems on a host by consuming resources just by connecting to the host. To allow access to a Mac OS X host by a Mac OS 9 host, the preference pane requires a password. Mac OS X stores a hash of this password in a world-readable file (`/Library/Preferences/com.apple.AEServer.plist`). It is a good idea to change the permissions on this file:

```
bash-2.05a$ sudo chmod go-r \
->/Library/Preferences/com.apple.AEServer.plist
```

Also never set the Mac OS 9 compatibility password to the same password used for other trusted operations or accounts.

Xinetd

Since the early days of UNIX-based operating systems, they have shipped with applications called super-servers. In its most basic form, a super-server acts as a network listener for the services for which it is configured. Upon executing, a super-server parses its configuration file(s) and determines the network services it is responsible for. It then begins listening on the ports or sockets on which its servers communicate. When the server receives a request on the port, it starts the configured server to further handle the service request. There are exceptions to this scheme, mostly for single-threaded servers, wherein the super-server starts the single-threaded server. The single-threaded server then takes care of service requests until the server itself dies. This tactic can be more efficient than having each server (of which there may be many) start and patiently wait for requests themselves.

As of version 10.2, Mac OS X ships with xinetd, a secure replacement for the inetd super-server (which Jaguar also includes for backward-compatibility). xinetd has several features to recommend it as a replacement for inetd. These features include access control (based on source address, destination address, and time), extensive logging, and the capability to bind services to specific interfaces. In this section, we will attempt to illustrate several of most common features of xinetd, as well as how to manage its configuration in Mac OS X.

Configuring xinetd in Mac OS X

Under Mac OS X, xinetd's configuration consists of a main configuration file (located at /etc/xinetd.conf) and a configuration directory (/etc/xinetd.d/). In general, a complete xinetd configuration consists of a defaults entry that establishes default values for specified parameters to be used throughout the configuration. The defaults entry is followed by one or more services entries, which specify the configuration for individual services. Mac OS X's main configuration file specifies only the defaults entry, which leaves individual services to be defined in the configuration directory. Any modification of an xinetd configuration file requires xinetd to be restarted for it to take effect (that is, killall xinetd). Also, if xinetd is started (or restarted) and it is not configured to listen for any connection (as is the default), xinetd will terminate itself peacefully.

The defaults *Entry*

This is Mac OS X's default main configuration file for xinetd:

```
# man xinetd.conf for more information

defaults
{
        instances               = 60
        log_type                = SYSLOG daemon
        log_on_success          = HOST PID
        log_on_failure          = HOST
        cps                     = 25 30
}


includedir /etc/xinetd.d
```

In any xinetd configuration file, lines beginning with a pound sign (such as the first line of xinetd.conf) or containing only whitespace (the second line) are ignored. The defaults entry begins on the third line of the configuration file with the keyword defaults. A typical defaults entry consists of the defaults keyword, a left curly brace, one or more parameters, and then a right curly brace. Each parameter in the defaults entry (as well as any service entry) is of the following general form:

```
<parameter_name> <assignment_operator> <value1> <value2>...<valueN>
```

In the preceding example, the first <parameter_name> would be instances, the <assignment_operator> would be the equals sign, and <value1> would be 60. Some parameters (such as log_type, log_on_success, and cps in this example) accept or require multiple values, which are separated by spaces after the equals sign. The defaults entry accepts only the equals sign as an assignment operator, but the service entries support additional assignment operators (-= and +=), which we will discuss a little bit later.

The first parameter (instances = 60) specifies the maximum number of requests or connections any service may handle at one time. This can provide some sanity-checking that helps guard against Denial-of-Service attacks against a host. Unless specified, instance defaults to the value UNLIMITED, which means that xinetd will place no limits upon the number of connections.

The second setting (log_type = SYSLOG daemon) configures xinetd services to log to the syslog daemon using the daemon facility (for more information on logging in Mac OS X see Chapter 11, "Auditing"). A third value can be added to this line, specifying the log-level (from `debug` to `emerg`) to be logged; otherwise, the log-level defaults to `info`. Logging can also configured to use a file instead of the syslog daemon by modifying the line accordingly:

```
log_type = FILE /var/log/xinetd.log
```

File-based logging is enabled with the value `FILE`, and the path to the log file is set with the second value (`/var/log/xinetd.log` (in this example, however, it can be any valid filename).

The second and third parameters in the `defaults` entry (`log_on_success` and `log_on_failure`) determine what is to be logged upon successful or failed connections to a service. For `log_on_success`, these include the following:

- **PID**. Logs the process id of the responding server.
- **HOST**. Logs the IP address of the remote host.
- **USERID**. Logs the userid of a connecting user, provided that the host is running identd, and the requested server is a multi-threaded server.
- **EXIT**. Logs exit events from the responding server.
- **DURATION**. Logs the duration of a connected session.

`log_on_failure` accepts a slightly smaller list of values: HOST, USERID, and ATTEMPT (which logs each failed attempt and is implicitly included by the other two options). Both `log_on_failure` and `log_on_success` accept multiple values.

The final value in the defaults entry (`cps = 25 30`), which stands for "connections per second," provides a way to rate limit connections to a particular service. The first value (`25`) defines the rate at which clients can connect. If the connections exceed this rate, further connections are disallowed for the number of seconds indicated by the second value (`30`). Unless otherwise specified, xinetd's default is to limit connections to 50 in a 10-second interval.

xinetd's `defaults` entry allows an administrator to provide default values for some but not all the configuration parameters available for individual services. In addition to those already discussed, the defaults entry supports `no_access`, `only_from`, `per_source`, `passenv`, `groups`, `umask`, `disabled`, and `enabled`.

Both the `disabled` and `enabled` attributes accept lists of services that will be explicitly disabled or enabled and are unique to the defaults entry. If the `disabled` parameter is used, any service not listed will be considered enabled. The same is true of the `enabled` parameter, except that anything not listed is implicitly disabled. If a service is listed as being both enabled and disabled, the service is considered disabled.

The `passenv` parameter provides a list of environment variables that xinetd will pass from its own environment to any server it starts. The number of connections from individual IP addresses can be limited with the `per_source` parameter, which accepts an integer specifying the maximum number of connections allowed from any one IP address.

Sometimes it is necessary for xinetd to start servers with access to the groups that their effective UID is a member of, which is configured through the `groups` parameter. Most BSD-based operating systems such as Mac OS X require this, so they set `groups` equal to `yes`. In Mac OS X's configuration, each individual service definition specifies this setting, although Apple could have included it in the `defaults` entry.

For those services that may need to create files on the server, xinetd allows an inherited umask to be set with the `umask` parameter. This umask allows an administrator to specify the default permissions on any files created by xinetd's services. Like the command-line application of the same name, the `umask` parameter expects an octal value (such as `002`). If `umask` is not specified, the umask will default to xinetd's own `umask` OR'd with `022`.

The remaining two parameters, `only_from` and `no_access`, form the basis of xinetd's address-based access control. These parameters are also of the most interest to those wishing to add security to any of the services that xinetd can provide. Values for both parameters are lists of host addresses or ranges of addresses, and can be specified in a number of different formats, including CIDR notation (`192.168.1.0/24`), dotted-decimal quads (`192.168.1.2`), factorized quads (`192.168.1.{1,2,3,5}`), and hostnames (`www.example.com`). If either parameter is left blank, it is the equivalent of saying "none." That is, an empty value for `no_access` translates into "allow from any address," and the converse for `only_from`. If both `no_access` and `only_from` are specified, the best match wins. This means that if a connection were attempted from the host `192.168.0.1`, and `only_from` were set to `192.168.0.0/24` and `no_access` to `192.168.0.1`, access would be denied. In cases of a tie, `no_access` takes precedence. As with all parameters, any access control specified in the defaults entry applies to all defined services, but can be overridden individually by those services. Any settings established in individual service entries apply only to the entry in which they are defined.

The final line of `xinetd.conf` (`includedir /etc/xinetd.d`) tells xinetd to parse and process any files in the directory `/etc/xinetd.d` (except those either containing a period character or ending with a tilde character) as part of its configuration. It is in this directory where we find the entries for all the services xinetd is configured to manage.

Service Entries

Out of the box, xinetd is configured to manage 19 different services (20 for Mac OS X Server), although none of them are enabled by default. Of these 19, only one has a GUI with which to manage it: ftp. Management and configuration of all other services are done through editing the text files. To make management of each service easy, Apple has created a single file for each service that is defined, with each of these files being the name of the service that is configured therein.

For our first example, we will use the tftp service definition (`/etc/xinetd.d/tftp`):

```
service tftp
{
        disable             = yes
        socket_type         = dgram
        wait                = yes
        user                = nobody
        server              = /usr/libexec/tftpd
        server_args         = /private/tftpboot
        groups              = yes
        flags               = REUSE
}
```

In this example, we can see the major aspects of a service entry. An entry begins with the keyword `service` followed by the service name, which is the name defined in `/etc/services` (`tftp` in this case). Next comes a left curly brace, the list of parameters and their values, and finally the right curly brace. As with the `defaults` entry, any whitespace line is ignored, as is any line beginning with a pound sign.

Minimally, most services entries require six parameters to be defined: `socket_type`, `wait`, `user`, `server`, `server_args`, and (because Mac OS X is a BSD-derived operating system) `groups`. RPC-based services (which are generally not managed by xinetd due to performance issues) additionally require the `parameters protocol` and `rpc_version`.

The first parameter in the example service entry is `disable`, which accepts the strings `yes` or `no` and dictates whether xinetd should start listening for connection attempts for the tftp service. The GUI management tools for ftp simply set the value of `disable` to `no`, and start (or restart) xinetd. The parameter `socket_type` defines the type of network socket to create for connections. Most TCP-based services should set the value to `stream`; most UDP services are dgram. The parameter wait tells xinetd whether a server is multithreaded or not; most of the servers that are commonly started by xinetd are not and would set the value to yes. The user with which to start the server is set by the value of the parameter user.

The server parameter is used to set the path to the application or daemon xinetd should use to respond to connection attempts. Sometimes it is desirable to start the server with additional arguments, which may specify an alternative configuration file, modify the logging configuration and location, or use some other runtime option. To do this, administrators can use the server_args parameter; the setting indicated in the example tells tftpd to restrict access to files in the indicated directory (/private/tftpboot, which does not exist). The final parameter in the example, flags, is used to pass a number of different configuration options to xinetd itself, most of which tell xinetd about special requirements for the server or its connections.

As with the defaults entry, xinetd provides additional parameters to allow administrators to provide access control for their services: only_from, no_access, and access_times. The first two parameters, only_from and no_access, are configured in the same manner as the corresponding parameters in the defaults entry. The last parameter, access_times, allows administrators to specify periods of a 24-hour day in which a service is accessible. The values are a range of times formatted as HH:MM-HH:MM, where HH is the two-digit hour using a 24-hour clock, and MM is the two-digit minutes after the hour. The load and connection-limiting parameters available in the defaults entry (per_source and cps) are also available in individual service entries and are configured in the same way.

As discussed previously, the service entries support more than one assignment operator for some parameters. These parameters are only_from, no_access, log_on_success, log_on_failure, passenv, and env. All of these parameters accept the equals sign as well as += and -= (except env, which does not support -=). A += means that values listed thereafter are added to an already established list (such as one defined in the defaults entry) rather than simply replacing a list, which is the default behavior. Items are subtracted from a set value using the -= operator. All these parameters may also be specified multiple times in a single service entry.

To configure xinetd to listen for tftp connections, explicitly denying access from a few troublesome hosts (192.168.0.1, 192.168.0.23, 192.168.0.24), and allowing access only during business hours (8 a.m. to 5 p.m.), one would modify the tftp service to appear as follows. We will also chroot tftpd to the

/tmp/ folder just for safety's sake (with the argument, -s /tmp/) and log additional information for successful connections.

```
service tftp
{
        disable             = no
        socket_type         = dgram
        wait                = yes
        user                = nobody
        server              = /usr/libexec/tftpd
        server_args         = -s /tmp/
        groups              = yes
        flags               = REUSE
        no_access           = 192.168.0.{1,23,24}
        access_times        = 08:00-17:00
        log_on_success      += EXIT DURATION
}
```

...And one more thing...

Before we move on, there is one more trick that xinetd can do that we would like to share. Among its other attributes, xinetd has the capability to redirect TCP streams from one address to another. This means, for instance, that xinetd can accept connections on the port a web server typically listens on and forward it to another computer, which has the actual web server running on it. This can be especially handy when the machine running xinetd is acting as a firewall for a network. Using port redirection, one could easily allow connections from an external host to an internal host. This is probably not the best way of handling this kind of redirection (one should generally use the firewall software itself for that because the firewall can perform many more sanity checks upon the connections, providing better security overall), but there may be valid reasons to do so.

Redirection is initiated using the redirect parameter, which accepts a destination IP address and TCP port. It is also possible to use a hostname in place of the IP address, but we would advise against this because the lookup for the name is done only once, when xinetd is started, an aspect that could be abused. When redirecting, the server parameter is not a required parameter.

An example of redirecting http connections (TCP port 80) from the host running xinetd to another would appear as follows:

```
service http
{
        disable             = no
        socket_type         = stream
        wait                = no
        user                = root
        groups              = yes
        bind                = 192.168.1.1
        redirect            = 10.11.12.13 80
}
```

Observant readers will notice the bind parameter in this example. It is used to force xinetd to monitor for connections on a single IP address, as opposed to all IP addresses the host may have (which is the default).

xinetd has several other parameters that we have not described here and has features that are beyond discussion in a book of this type. We urge readers to read the man pages for xinetd (see man xinetd and man xinetd.conf), which provide a lot of useful information, including examples of sample configurations.

Summary

Mac OS X ships with a number of services never before seen in an Apple operating system, providing capabilities once only dreamed of by Macintosh administrators. The Mac OS now has the capability to coexist on the Internet on the same terms and at the same level of interaction as any other modern operating system. This also means that Mac OS X is subject to same risks as every other modern operating system. Fortunately, Apple has chosen wisely in disabling all of the services we have discussed here. Hopefully, we have provided readers with enough incentive to better understand the powerful tools that they have been given and to internalize the fact that (as the cliché goes) just because one can do a thing does not necessarily mean that one must do that thing. None of the preceding services should be enabled without reason; any one of them can negatively affect the security of the system. Even OpenSSH, with its very essence being security, has seen its share of vulnerabilities, and its support of an older protocol could be dangerous in the wrong environment.

Mac OS X's newfound capabilities extend beyond just these Internet services, however. As we shall see in the following chapters, these new capabilities reach a little closer to home with new file-sharing capabilities and outward again with enterprise directory integration.

## CHAPTER 7

FILE SHARING

"I think sharing is overrated too. And helping others."
—*Bart Simpson*

Out of the box, Mac OS X Server supports many common file-sharing services. WebDAV allows Apache locations to be used as a repository for the collaborative file-editing activities. The AppleTalk Filing Protocol (AFP) serves to accommodate legacy Apple file sharing over AppleTalk or TCP/IP. Samba is used to provide SMB/CIFS shares for Windows clients. NFS shares provide familiar file-sharing services for UNIX and Linux users.

All these file-sharing services are disabled by default. Ideally, we would leave them this way; each one poses a security risk to your system. This is a perfect example for a security versus usability discussion. Given motive and enough time, a malicious user can eventually exploit one of these services to gain unauthorized access to a system. The truly paranoid would be advised to leave these services disabled. However, this is not always a realistic option. Only enable the services that are needed, and understand their function, keeping in mind the administration time needed to maintain them. None of these file-sharing protocols were designed with security in mind and some are completely devoid of any real security.

This chapter highlights the risks involved with each of the file-sharing services native to Mac OS X. Here, we will shed some light on what can be done to reduce those risks. In this chapter, we assume you have knowledge of any service being deployed. The material presented is not an exhaustive reference for these services, but rather a dissection of the security implications of each.

WebDAV Services

WebDAV is an extension to HTTP/1.1, the primary protocol for the web. It stands for Web-based Distributed Authoring and Versioning. WebDAV extends the HTTP protocol with an additional set of methods and headers. The primary goal behind the development of the WebDAV protocol is to allow for the collaborative editing of files over the web. A few common examples include

- Distributed web site authoring and maintenance
- Remote collaboration of documents
- A network file system

The WebDAV protocol is still a work in progress. At the time of this writing, the completed aspects of the protocol include file properties (meta-data), concurrency control (locking), and namespace management (moving, copying, and creation of files). Aspects such as search management and version control are still being developed.

Because it is an extension to HTTP, WebDAV is commonly implemented as an add-on module to a web server. For the Apache web server, this module is called mod_dav. This module is included with the installation of Mac OS X, but is disabled by default.

Mac OS X has the capability to communicate with WebDAV-enabled servers through a built-in WebDAV client. Connections can be made directly from the Finder or on the command line. However, as of the Jaguar release this built-in client does not support SSL, so its use is quite limited. We suggest using Goliath, a WebDAV client that supports Mac OS X. Goliath is still being developed, but is quite usable. It supports SSL and the use of client certificates. Goliath is released under the GNU General Public License. Source code and binaries for Goliath can be found at: http://www.webdav.org/goliath/.

WebDAV can be used for a variety of reasons, but if not configured correctly, this service can be a security risk. Unauthorized access can lead to the denial of service, loss or theft of data, or the defacement of important web content.

This section discusses the process of securely setting up WebDAV on Mac OS X, beginning with some security considerations. Even if you are not planning to deploy WebDAV, it may be helpful to know some of the risks involved.

Security Considerations

Obviously, it does not make sense to say that a network service is perfectly secure. When we refer to a secure deployment of any network service, what is meant is that steps were taken to reduce known risks. Over time, new vulnerabilities are exposed, and measures must be taken to address them. Although Apple does a fine job of keeping up with security patches, adding another service such as WebDAV still requires more attention on behalf of an administrator.

We advise you to strongly consider whether enabling WebDAV is necessary. Setting up a secure Apache installation is not a trivial thing. If Apache is not yet enabled, enabling it for the sole purpose of providing WebDAV access is probably not worth the risk. There may be other ways to address your requirements. For example, collaborative editing of files can be managed with Concurrent Versions System (CVS). CVS comes installed on Mac OS X and can be secured with SSH—an easier service to manage.

NOTE

Before we get too involved with the configuration of WebDAV, we would like to bring to your attention that WebDAV only provides access to files that reside under the web server document root directory. WebDAV users will not have access to the files in their home directories. Likewise, when users log in through some other means, such as SSH, they will be unable to access their files that reside in the WebDAV repository. This should be taken into consideration before setting up WebDAV. It could lead to an administrative mess, or at least an inconvenience for users.

Only enable the locations that require WebDAV access. WebDAV can be enabled for an entire directory tree, or just a specific location in the Apache configuration. When possible, create special locations to be used specifically for WebDAV access. Allowing write access to an Apache location has some implications that may not be obvious. For example, a WebDAV user with write privileges can possibly alter the web server configuration by uploading an .htaccess file. Make wise use of Apache realms. If multiple distinct projects exist, segregate them so that users have access to only the files they need to access.

WebDAV access can be controlled on a per-user basis with the Apache Limit directive. Thus, you can limit which users can have write privileges to the location(s). WebDAV-enabled locations allow the web server to write to files under the document root. A compromised account would have obvious consequences, but malicious or ignorant users also can be problematic. Only grant authorship privileges to trusted users.

Another thing to consider with WebDAV locations is file permissions. As a result of the Apache process being a proxy for file operations, files must be read/write by the www user. There is no per-user–based access control as far as the WebDAV module is concerned. As a result, there is no quota system built into the WebDAV module. Later in this chapter we will cover some options that can be used to limit write operations, but the fact is, a malicious user with write privileges can cause problems.

Always use SSL with WebDAV-enabled sites. Always. SSL not only provides for the transport security of data, it also protects the authentication process. The process of setting up a SSL-enabled web server is covered in Chapter 6, "Internet Services."

Setting Up Secure WebDAV Services on Mac OS X

This section walks through the process of securely setting up WebDAV on Mac OS X and Mac OS X Server. The application Server Settings.app found on Mac OS X Server provides a graphical interface for enabling and configuring WebDAV locations. Our examples don't use that tool because it does not allow for fine-grained control over the configuration. With a service such as WebDAV, it is important that you know exactly what the configuration specifies, and what operations it will allow.

The Apache module, `mod_dav`, enables Apache to provide WebDAV services. Any directory under the web server can be made available to WebDAV clients. As mentioned earlier, it is recommended that only those directories that require WebDAV access be given such.

Setting up Apache to provide WebDAV services on Mac OS X is a four-step process:

1. Modify the Apache configuration file.
2. Set up and secure passwords to restrict access to files.
3. Create a location for the WebDAV module to store a lock database.
4. Set up and secure the location where files will be stored.

Note, before setting up and enabling WebDAV, it is critical that SSL be configured and enabled for that server. *WebDAV services should only be accessed through a SSL-enabled server.* Given the nature of the service, access must be restricted, and thus the authentication process must be protected from eavesdropping. Setting up a secure Apache configuration with SSL is covered in Chapter 6.

Modifying the Apache Config

The first step in enabling WebDAV access is to modify the main configuration file for apache, /etc/httpd/httpd.conf. For Mac OS X Server, the main configuration file is, /etc/httpd/httpd_macosxserver.conf. In this file, we will enable the web_dav module, set some WebDAV options, set up access control, and specify which locations will be WebDAV-enabled. We recommend creating a backup copy of the Apache configuration file before making any changes.

As mentioned earlier, the WebDAV module for Apache is disabled by default. To have the WebDAV module loaded into Apache's address space, uncomment the following line:

```
LoadModule dav_module            libexec/httpd/libdav.so
```

Next, enable the web_dav module. Uncomment the following line:

```
AddModule mod_dav.c
```

Locking information for the WebDAV module is stored in a database file. For security reasons, this file should always be kept outside the document root of the web server. The path to the lock file must be specified using the DavLockDB directive. The WebDAV module will create the file specified, if it does not already exist. WebDAV clients can specify a period of time (in seconds) that the server will wait before automatically removing a lock. This timeout value can be overridden with the DAVMinTimeout directive. The lock database directive must be placed in a global section of your Apache configuration file. The lock timeout directive can be placed in the global section, or in a container directive. In this example, we will create a directory, WebDAV, in the directory /Library/WebServer to be used to store the lock database. We also set a minimum lock timeout of 10 minutes (600 seconds).

```
DAVLockDB    /Library/WebServer/WebDAV/locks
DAVMinTimeout 600
```

Now that the WebDAV module is loaded, we need to specify which locations under the web server document root will be WebDAV-enabled, and establish access control for those locations.

Before making any of the following configuration changes, remember that WebDAV should only be enabled for SSL-enabled sites, and only for those locations that absolutely require it.

To enable WebDAV, specify the following under any container in the configuration file:

```
DAV on
```

If placed in a `<Directory>` directive, WebDAV is enabled for any subdirectories that may exist. If placed in a `<Location>` directive, WebDAV is enabled only for that location.

For this example, we will create a directory under the web server document root, specifically for WebDAV access. Access will be limited to three users, all of whom will have write privileges.

Create a new `<Directory>` directive. Set `Options` to None, and set `AllowOverrides` to None. Set the name of the realm; in our example, we set the realm to be "authors." Set the authentication type to be basic. Digest authentication can be used, but basic authentication will be sufficient assuming this site is SSL-enabled.

Next, we need to set up access control for the users. Access to any location can be restricted with the user of an Apache `Limit` or `LimitExcept` directive. Because the WebDAV protocol extends HTTP, there are additional methods that can be specified in the limit directives. Table 7.1 lists the additional methods that are handled by the WebDAV module.

TABLE 7.1 Additional HTTP Methods for WebDAV

METHOD	DESCRIPTION
PROPFIND	Fetch properties for a resource, or group of resources
PROPPATCH	Set, edit, or remove the properties of a resource
MKCOL	Create a new collection
COPY	Copy files or resources
MOVE	Move or rename files or resources
LOCK	Set a lock on a file or resource
UNLOCK	Remove a lock on a file or resource

We allow all these methods in our example because these users will be allowed authorship privileges. When complete, the `Directory` directive should appear as such:

```
<Directory "/Library/WebServer/Documents/webdav">
    DAV on
    Options None
    AllowOverride None
    AuthName "authors"
    AuthType Basic
    AuthUserFile /etc/http/.webdav.passwords

    <Limit GET HEAD OPTIONS CONNECT PUT POST DELETE PROPFIND PROPPATCH
    MKCOL COPY MOVE LOCK UNLOCK>
            Require user preston brian bruce
    </Limit>
</Directory>
```

This `Limit` statement allows authorship privileges. To add another user read access to this location, we would use an additional `Limit` statement. For example, the following gives Bob read access to this WebDAV location.

```
<Limit GET HEAD OPTIONS CONNECT>
    Require user bob
</Limit>
```

Creating the Lock File

The lock file we specified earlier in the configuration file does not need to exist, but the path to this file should. Remember, this file must be outside the directory root, otherwise it runs the risk of being tampered with, or possibly deleted. In our example, we specified the lock database to be located in the file `/Library/WebServer/WebDAV/locks`. Create this directory:

```
bash-2.05a$ sudo mkdir /Library/WebServer/WebDAV
```

We need to give the www user ownership of this directory:

```
bash-2.05a$ sudo chown www:www /Library/WebServer/WebDAV
```

Only the www user needs access to this file, so we will change permissions on the directory:

```
bash-2.05a$ sudo chmod o-rwx /Library/WebServer/WebDAV
```

When the lock file is actually created, it will inherit these same permissions and ownership.

Setting Up and Securing Locations

Any location that is WebDAV-enabled must be readable and writeable by the www user, or the user that the web server runs as. In our example, we specified the directory webdav under the document root. We need to create this directory and set its ownership accordingly:

```
bash-2.05a$ sudo mkdir /Library/WebServer/Documents/webdav
bash-2.05a$ sudo chown www:www /Library/WebServer/Documents/webdav
```

Now deny other users access to this directory:

```
bash-2.05a$ sudo chmod o-rwx /Library/WebServer/Documents/webdav
```

All files created by the WebDAV module in this directory will now inherit these same permissions and ownership.

Setting Access Passwords

WebDAV-enabled locations should always require user authentication. With Mac OS X (client) using basic Apache HTTP authentication is the only option available for controlling access to Apache locations. The users and groups specified in the authorization file are separate from the system user accounts and groups. With Mac OS X Server, system accounts can be used. Mac OS X Server comes with an additional Apache module called mod_auth_apple. This module allows system accounts to be specified with the Apache "require user" or "require group" directives. Issues related to user and group authentication under Apache will be covered in Chapter 6. In our example, we have specified basic HTTP authentication, and the file /etc/httpd/.webdav.passwords to be used as the authentication file. To create the password file we use htpasswd and the -c option followed by the location where we want the password file created and the first user to be stored in the file.

```
bash-2.05a$ sudo htpasswd -c /etc/httpd/.webdav.passwords preston
New password:
Re-type new password:
Adding password for user preston
```

Additional users can be added to this file, but because the file now exists, it is no longer necessary to use the -c option. More information about basic and other forms of HTTP authentication is covered in the section on Apache in Chapter 6.

After all users have been added to the authentication file, we need to lock down the permissions on that file. The www user needs read access for verification purposes, the root user will need write access. Because we are storing password information, no other users should have access to this file:

```
bash-2.05a$ sudo chown root:www /etc/httpd/.webdav.passwords
bash-2.05a$ sudo chmod 640 /etc/httpd/.webdav.passwords
```

Setting up access control in this manner will work for both Mac OS X (client) and Mac OS X Server. Apache must be restarted for the configuration changes to take effect:

```
bash-2.05a$ sudo apachectl restart
/usr/sbin/apachectl restart: httpd restarted
```

Additional WebDAV Options

There are two more configuration options that are important to the security of WebDAV locations. The first one is an option for the WebDAV Apache module, the second is an Apache directive that can be used to limit the size of requests.

The DavDepthInfinity directive can be used to limit PROPFIND requests. WebDAV clients issue a PROPFIND request to retrieve information about a resource, or group of resources. A WebDAV client can specify a Depth value as an HTTP header to a PROPFIND request. If "Infinity" is specified in the depth header, the WebDAV module will build a response (in memory) for the resource, and all child resources, recursively. Under certain circumstances, this could present a problem. You can disallow recursive requests like this with the DavDepthInfinity directive. The syntax is

```
DavDepthInfinity On|Off
```

Place this directive under any WebDAV-enabled location, where you would place the WebDAV On directive. By default, infinite depth requests are not allowed.

LimitXMLRequestBody is a directive that can be used to limit the size of a request issued by a WebDAV client. This directive is actually a core Apache directive, but it applies because all WebDAV requests and responses are in

XML. The directive takes a single argument, the size in bytes for the maximum allowed request body size. To disable any size checking, specify zero as the argument. This directive only limits the size of a single request. Thus, it is still possible for a malicious user to fill up disk space with repeated requests.

Both of these directives can be useful in securing WebDAV locations, but realistically, they come with their share of usability problems. WebDAV security really boils down to whether or not you can trust your users. If you cannot, you might want to reconsider whether you should enable WebDAV on your web server.

Apple File Services

The remaining file-sharing services, AFS, NFS, and SMB, are generally more straightforward to configure. They are based on standard protocols and have a GUI configuration tool provided by Apple via the OS X Server Administration Tools. However, the fact that these services are easier to configure does not mean they are any less important to secure.

Apple File Service (AFS) provides file sharing for Mac OS Clients. AFS uses the Apple Filing Protocol (AFP) to control access and transport data. AFP is based largely on AppleShare IP, an older Apple file-sharing protocol used by AppleTalk. AFP has expanded AppleShare IP to handle Unicode file names and 64-bit file sizes.

AFS Security Model

AFS provides a robust user and group level authentication model. Objects within a share can be controlled on an individual level giving administrators tight control over their resources. When attempting to access AFS shares, a user must authenticate to the AFS server. After the user has been authenticated, access to objects is granted on a case-by-case basis. AFS has matured over the years to support encrypted authentication requests to prevent clear text passwords from transiting the network.

AFS can integrate with many authentication mechanisms. By default, Mac OS X supports NetInfo authentication and Kerberos. AFS also provides secure data transport via SSH.

AFS does not have IP-based access control. If you need to lock down access to AFS services based on source IP address, you will need to use an external mechanism such as a firewall to accomplish this.

Configuring AFS Via Server Settings

In the General tab under the Apple File Service window of Server Settings, configure a logon greeting. Although this greeting does nothing to enhance the technical security of your host, it is a legal barrier. By placing a banner that states that only authorized parties are allowed to access this data, you create an electronic Do Not Disturb sign. In the event of an attacker using your AFS shares, the banner will be valuable if you seek legal recourse.

Figure 7.1 shows the Access tab. Disable guest access and enable secure connections. With secure connections enabled, clients can tunnel AFS connections to the server via SSH. See "Making Secure AFS Connections" later in this chapter. Set the maximum number of connections to a reasonable amount based on your user base. Finally, set your authentication mechanism to whatever method your host is utilizing.

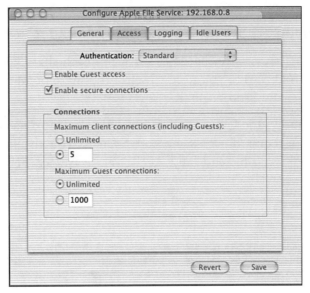

FIGURE 7.1   Access control for AFS in Server Settings.

Figure 7.2 shows the Logging tab. Enable the access log and select all events. This provides as complete an audit trail as possible. Finally, set an archival period that rotates logs in a timely manner based on your usage level.

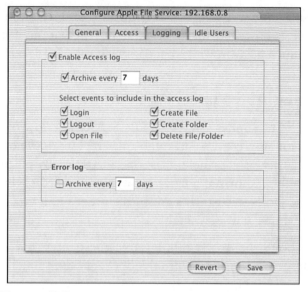

Figure 7.2   Logging control for AFS in Server Settings.

Be sure to turn on AFS in the main Server Settings window.

Configuring AFS Via Workgroup Manager

By default, all shares are shared by AFS. For each share you do not want provided through AFS, you need to select the share point and disable AFS sharing under the Protocols tab.

Figure 7.3 shows the General tab for a share. Least privilege dictates that only the minimum required access is granted. Unless you absolutely require write access, set all levels to read-only. At the very least, set the Everyone value to read-only.

Write Only

One of the potential values for any of the classes of access is Write Only. This allows you to turn a share into a drop box. Users can place files into the share, but they cannot read any files already there. This has novel application, but be aware that a malicious user could fill up a filesystem by repeatedly dropping files in the drop box.

Note

Under the Protocols tab, be sure to disallow guest access.

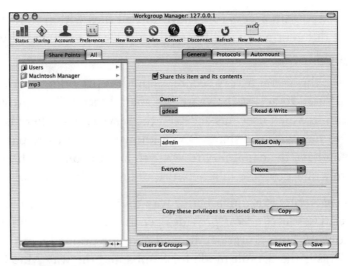

FIGURE 7.3   General settings for AFS in Workgroup Manager.

SMB File Services

Server Message Block (SMB) file sharing is commonly associated with
Microsoft Windows file servers. SMB was originally designed by IBM, and
has become the de facto standard for all Windows operating systems. Samba
provides services for NetBIOS-based applications. NetBIOS is an API that
provides local network browsing, addressing, and transport for network
aware applications.

Mac OS X provides SMB file services via the Samba package. Samba is an open
source SMB server that has been ported to many UNIX variants, including
Linux, FreeBSD, and Solaris. Samba is made up of many programs and a
few servers. smbd is the primary server daemon that actually controls the file
service of the host. nmbd is a daemon that provides NetBIOS name service and
browsing capabilities to the host.

SMB Security Models

SMB specifies two different security models. *Share Level Access* provides access
control on a share by share basis. A *share* is the term used in the SMB world to
describe the root of a network accessible folder. Share level access requires only

a password to gain access to a share and all files within that share. There may be a different password for read-only access versus read-write access to the share.

Obviously, this is not a very secure method of providing access to files. The password used to access the share is a shared secret. This provides no real way to determine which user has accessed the service. Also there is no fine-grained control to files within a share. If you know the read-write password for a share, you have the capability to write to any file on that share. This is completely unacceptable in a network of any reasonable size.

User Level Access is a much better way to control access to SMB accessible resources. User level access provides per user control to any resource or share. This allows for an accurate audit trail and fine-grained control of files and shares. This is the default mode for Samba and the way Mac OS X is configured.

Configuration Through Server Settings

SMB file sharing is disabled in a default Mac OS X Server installation. You must turn it on via Server Settings to use it. There are two security specific tabs in the Windows Services section. On the Access tab, you should ensure guest access is disabled (see Figure 7.4). Also, you should set a maximum number of connections to prevent a malicious user from making an infinite number of requests and eating up all system resources.

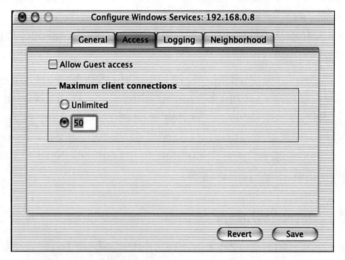

FIGURE 7.4   Access control for SMB in Server Settings.

The Logging tab allows you to control how much information is logged when SMB file sharing is enabled (see Figure 7.5). Unless your server will receive incredibly high amounts of traffic, you should set the logging level to Verbose in order to track everything users are doing.

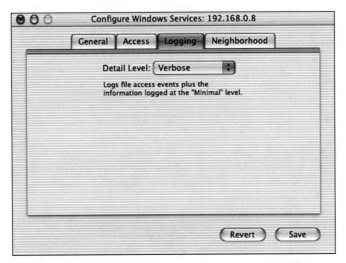

FIGURE 7.5 Logging control for SMB in Server Settings.

Configuration Through Workgroup Manager

By default, all shares are shared by SMB. For each share you do not want provided through SMB, you need to select the share point and disable SMB sharing under the Protocols tab.

Figure 7.6 shows the SMB configuration options in Workgroup Manager. Be sure guest access is not allowed. Also, unless necessary, set all access to read-only. If you do require read-write access, do not assign read-write access to everyone.

Each user that requires access to SMB shares will need to have their authentication mechanism changed. Mac OS X contains a general purpose password server which can be configured to talk to other authentication servers and applications requiring authentication. Figure 7.7 shows a user configured to use password server authentication via the Workgroup Manager.

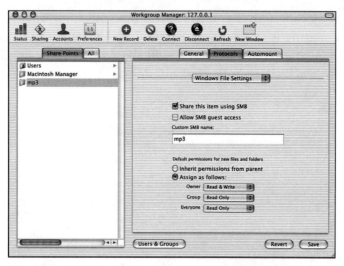

FIGURE 7.6   SMB options in Workgroup Manager.

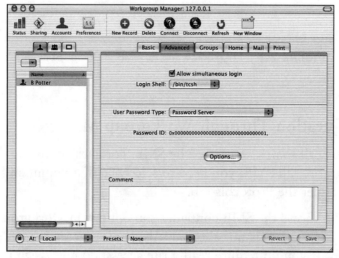

FIGURE 7.7   User configured to use password server.

WARNING

There are ramifications for configuring users to use password server. If a user requires SMB and AFP access from an Mac OS X client, the client must have an operating system revision at least Mac OS X 10.2; otherwise, AFP access will not work properly. Although this is an uncommon situation, it is something to be aware of.

Also, if the password service process dies, users configured to use password server authentication will not be able to log on. If users experience difficulty logging in, verify that `PasswordService` is running. If you find it is not running, launch it by typing `PasswordService -n`.

Configuration Through Terminal

Workgroup Manager creates a configuration file in /private/etc/smb.conf, which is seeded with the data you entered into the GUI. However, there are other security-specific Samba options that you cannot access via Workgroup Manager. To implement the following changes, you will need to edit smb.conf directly using your favorite text editor.

> **WARNING**
>
> Any change you make by hand to smb.conf will be overwritten the next time you modify your share settings via Workgroup Manager. If you plan to make manual edits to Samba, you should abandon the idea of using Workgroup Manager completely. It is best to delete Workgroup Manager from your system if you go this route (it can always be installed from the Admin Tools CD later).

smb.conf is structured in a hierarchical fashion. The following is an example of a smb.conf, which as been created by Workgroup Manager.

```
[global]
        client code page = 437
        coding system = utf8
        guest account = unknown
        encrypt passwords = YES
        local master = YES
        max smbd processes = 0
        server string = Mac OS X Server
        log file = /Library/Logs/WindowsServices/WindowsFileService.log
        log level = 2
        netbios name = mo
        workgroup = workgroup
[homes]
        comment = User Home Directories
        browseable = no
        read only = no
        create mode = 0750
[Users]
        path = /Users
        public = NO
        create mask = 0644
        directory mask = 0755
        read only = NO
        comment = macosx
```

The [global] section specifies directives that are common to the entire samba installation. The other sections are directives that apply to specific shares. The [homes] section is a special section for allowing users' home directories to be accessed via SMB. The other sections are standard Mac OS X shares and can be controlled at a high level via Workgroup Manager.

The directives in the default file are largely self-explanatory. The smb.conf man page contains a great deal of information for modifying your smb.conf.

IP Access Control

Samba allows you to control access to either the entire server or to specific shares via IP address. Hosts can either be explicitly allowed or denied depending on your requirements. The hosts allow directive allows access from the IP addresses specified. Conversely, the hosts deny directive restricts access. For example to restrict access to the entire smb server to only the 192.168.0.0/24 network, add hosts deny 192.168.0.0/255.255.255.0 to the [Globals] section.

These control statements can be added to the [Globals] section or any individual share. You should examine your security requirements for any SMB shares and limit control in as fine-grained manner as possible.

Veto Files

You may have files within a share you do not want to expose to users. Samba allows you to veto access to files and directories that match a certain pattern. These patterns must be delimited by /'s. Veto files can be specified at the [Globals] level or for any specific share. For instance, you may not want users to access their ssh keys via the network. You also may want to block any file that ends in .tmp. To accomplish this, add veto files = /.ssh/*.tmp/ to the [Globals] section.

Logging

By default, Mac OS X logs Samba activities to /Library/Logs/ WindowsServices/WindowsFileService.log. This location is configurable via smb.conf. There is generally no reason to change this.

Samba provides different logging levels depending on your need. Table 7.2 documents the different levels and what is logged.

TABLE 7.2 Samba Log Levels

LOG LEVEL	WHAT IS LOGGED
0	Errors only
1	Warnings and errors
2	Notices, warnings, and errors
3	Informational, notices, warnings, and errors
4	Debugging information

The default log level of Mac OS X is 2. This can be changed via the `log level` directive in your `smb.conf` file.

Network File System

Network File System (NFS) is a standard UNIX file service architecture. NFS is the final piece of Mac OS X's file-sharing system. NFS was designed by Sun Microsystems to provide transparent access to file systems across a network. UNIX clients can import NFS filesystems and the overlying operating system is basically unaware the filesystem is not local. This seamless integration is accomplished by using remote procedure calls (RPC). NFS originally ran only via UDP but has since been modified to use TCP.

The protocol was designed many years ago when network security was not as big a concern as it is now. NFS is inherently insecure due to its architecture. It is a difficult protocol to prop up with external security mechanisms and should never be deployed outside of a LAN environment.

When a host receives a request for a NFS share, the primary mechanism of security is the UID of the remote user. When a remote user attempts to access a file on an NFS server, the user is treated as the local user with the same UID. This was originally designed to work in a closed corporate environment with central user management. If a user had a UID of 1045 on their workstation, they would have a UID of 1045 on the NFS server.

This is a problem. With the advent of inexpensive PC's and free NFS clients, the level of authentication provided by the UID was lost. A remote workstation could spoof the UID of the client, including UID 0. Therefore, it is advisable to export filesystems read-only. Exports should be writeable only if you are sure you are in a closed environment and the security measures listed here are adhered to.

NFS also provides the capability to limit clients to select IP addresses. As with any service, you should limit access to only clients who require NFS filesystems.

NFS Structure

NFS is made up of three components on the server side: portmap, mountd, and nfsd. Portmap is effectively a phonebook that handles RPC requests from client machines. It tells the client which port the service it is requesting is listening on. Mountd examines which files systems should be exported, and verifies clients are allowed to connect. Once mountd has been satisfied, it forks a nfsd process and hands the client off to it.

Configuring NFS Through Server Settings

As Figure 7.8 shows, the configuration options in Server Settings for NFS are limited. Figure 7.8 shows that the configuration options allow you to control the number of servers spawned and the protocol to use. Unless you anticipate performance issues, select TCP as the protocol. This prevents potential spoofing in UDP packets in an effort to disrupt the NFS processes.

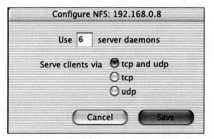

FIGURE 7.8   NFS options in Server Settings.

Configuring NFS Through Workgroup Manager

When a share is created, Mac OS X Server does not automatically export the filesystem via NFS. Figure 7.9 shows the Workgroup Manager configuration for a NFS exported filesystem. Add the IP addresses of the clients who need to connect to the server to limit access to NFS. Also, unless absolutely necessary, make the export read-only.

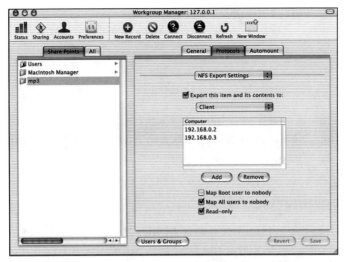

FIGURE 7.9 NFS options in Workgroup Manager.

Via this interface, you also have the capability to map users to the user nobody. At the very least you should map root to nobody to prevent clients from reading files they should not have access to by spoofing their UID. There is an option to perform this mapping in Workgroup Manager. Ideally, you should map all NFS users to a special NFS user with no privileges. This NFS user should not be trusted to perform any sensitive activities on a host, so this is the safest manner in which to export filesystems. Unfortunately, this is not possible within Workgroup Manager. You must configure NFS from the terminal to achieve this level of security.

Configuring NFS Through Terminal

Normally, NFS exports are controlled via `/etc/exports`. Under Mac OS X, the export information is controlled through netinfo. Use `nidump` to view the database.

```
bash-2.05a# nidump -r /exports .
{
  "name" = ( "exports" );
  CHILDREN = (
    {
      "name" = ( "/mp3" );
```

continues

```
      "opts" = ( "ro", "mapall=nobody" );
      "clients" = ( "192.168.0.2", "192.168.0.3" );
    }
  )
}
```

Exports can be saved to a file and then manipulated by hand to modify the user to your NFS user. The exports can then be fed back into netinfo via `niload -r /exports . < exportsfile`.

Re-Exporting Via AFS

NFS mounts are sometimes a fact of life. If your Mac OS X clients require data contained on a NFS share, the best way to secure the data is to re-export it via AFS. Mount the NFS share as a normal client on the Mac OS X server machine. Then, using the standard AFS sharing mechanisms, export the filesystems via AFS.

This setup allows for limited NFS exporting. The only NFS exposure is between the Mac OS X server and the host exporting the NFS file shares. Using AFS provides finer-grained control of data access and a more complete audit trail.

Personal File Sharing

Unlike Mac OS X Server, Apple File Sharing on Mac OS X does not have a graphical configuration tool. Enabling the AFS on Mac OS X is as simple as it gets. In the System Preferences, under the sharing pane, select the Personal File Sharing checkbox (see Figure 7.10).

If you must enable this service, there are a few additional steps that can be taken to reduce the risk it poses to your system.

First, remove the capability for others to log in as a guest. Although guest users do not have a great deal of power, they have the capability to write to certain folders (called drop-box folders) and there is no reasonable way to limit the amount of data that can be written. To completely disable guest logins, open `NetInfo Manager.app` and navigate to the config directory. There should be a subdirectory named AppleFileServer (see Figure 7.11).

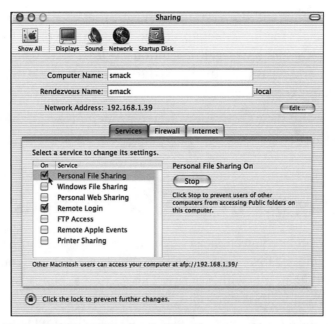

FIGURE 7.10   Enabling Personal File Sharing on Mac OS X.

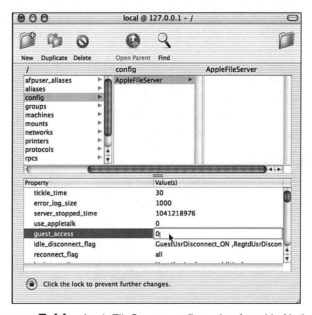

FIGURE 7.11   AppleFileServer configuration found in NetInfo.

Under this directory, there are many properties for the AppleFileServer. One of them is called `guest_access`. Set this value to 0 to disable users from logging in as guest.

While NetInfo is still open, you may want to set up a greeting to be displayed each time users log in. Although this does not do anything for the security of your system, it can be a legal precaution. At least state who is authorized to use the system and what they are allowed to do. To add a textual greeting, edit the `login_greeting` property.

Finally, be sure the `allow_root_login` property is set to 0, to disallow root logins through AFS.

Making Secure AFS Connections

Like many other connection services, AFS connections can be initiated right from the Finder. However, this built-in AFS client is more concerned with connectivity than it is with security. This section explores issues related to initiating secure AFS connections, from a client perspective.

Secure connections for AFS can be accomplished with SSH and port forwarding. All that is needed is a means of authenticating the remote host and a secure communications channel. SSH provides this, and does so quite well. Also, because AFS now works over TCP/IP, it is easy to use with the port-forwarding feature of SSH.

To initiate a connection, from the Go menu in the Finder, choose Connect to Server. This brings up the SLP dialog. Choose a remote host from the list, or enter the desired hostname or IP address in the address field, prefixed with the string, `afp://` (see Figure 7.12).

FIGURE 7.12   Initiating an AFS connection from the Finder.

The authentication dialog shown in Figure 7.13 contains an Options button.

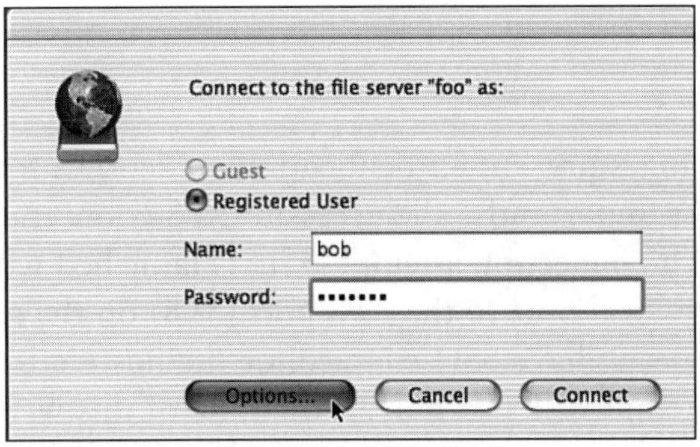

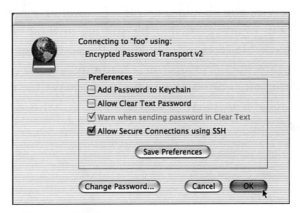

FIGURE 7.13   The AFS authentication dialog.

The options for AFS connections can be misleading. There is an option to allow secure connections using SSH (see Figure 7.14). However, checking this box does not necessarily mean your connection will use SSH.

FIGURE 7.14   AFS connection options dialog.

To ensure that every AFS connection attempt makes use of SSH, we need to modify a general preferences file. Each user has such a file located in `~/Library/Preferences/.GlobalPreferences.plist`. Edit this file and locate the `com.apple.AppleShareClientCore` key. This key has a dictionary object with various attributes related to AFS. In this dictionary, locate the key, `afp_cleartext_allow`, and make sure the value for this key is false.

```
<key>afp_cleartext_allow</key>
<false/>
```

Next, locate the key `afp_ssh_force` and be sure the value for this key is true.

```
<key>afp_ssh_force</key>
<true/>
```

These two changes prevent authentication credentials from being sent in the clear, and most importantly, all successful AFS connections are tunneled over SSH. With each connection attempt, SSH is launched with options to forward some arbitrary local port to the AFS port (548) on the remote server. If the remote host doesn't have SSH-enabled, or the host verification fails, the AFS connection attempt will also fail. At the time of this writing, it is not possible to adjust the arguments to SSH when used in this fashion.

Summary

OS X is an effective and robust platform for file services. However, file sharing is a service you should only offer if absolutely required. Understand the ramifications of any particular file-sharing method before deploying it. If you decide to use file services, only allow the access required, no more. Ideally, this means data is only provided on a read-only access. After you enable write access, proper configuration and auditing will make the difference between a secure and reliable installation and a resource that is a hazard to your entire organization.

## CHAPTER 8

NETWORK SERVICES

"They have an Internet for computers now?"
—*Homer Simpson*

Network security historically has been a topic reserved for devices at the edge of a network or for road warrior machines. Firewalls, Virtual Private Networks, and link-level encryption are generally difficult to configure and require third-party products. Mac OS X, however, brings simple and robust network security mechanisms to every server and workstation. Although the implementations are not without faults, they provide a mechanism every user can utilize to secure their host from network-based attacks.

Firewalling

Firewalls are typically network devices that control the flow of traffic. Companies will place firewalls in front of networks they want to protect in an effort to limit unwanted packets from entering or leaving that particular part of the network. This reflects the typical "security at the edge" idea employed in most enterprises.

However, this model is not bulletproof. A network attack that occurs within the border of your network firewalls can still pose a risk to your internal resources. In January 2003, a worm targeted at Microsoft's SQL implementation ravaged many corporate networks. After the worm propagated to one internal machine via some mechanism, it rapidly exploited the SQL vulnerability on every possible machine within each enterprise. The border firewall did nothing to stop the infection once it started.

Besides staying current with application and operating system patches, host-based firewalls can go a long way toward controlling threats from inside attacks. By running a firewall application directly on the host you are trying to protect, access can be controlled in a fine-grained manner.

Mac OS X has a built-in firewall called `ipfw` that operates at the kernel level. `ipfw` is a BSD-based firewall that has been used in FreeBSD for years. Apple has then leveraged this kernel-level firewall by implementing graphical tools to control it.

`ipfw` is capable of being a robust border firewall. However, that is not a typical deployment scenario for most Mac OS X machines. Apple's utilities are designed to protect the host itself, not an entire network. Regardless of your situation, you should use the firewall capabilities of Mac OS X. For a laptop using a public wireless network or a server providing QuickTime videos to an intranet, the host firewall allows you to enforce least privilege to each service running on a host.

This section examines the native firewall tools for Mac OS X Client and Server. Then we will dive under the hood and control `ipfw` from the terminal to handle nonstandard situations.

Using Built-in Tools

The tools provided in Mac OS X are designed to protect the core operating system and standard mail, web, and file-sharing applications that Mac OS X users usually deploy. They are effective at the services they know how to protect, but the tools are lacking in their capability to control the more advanced features of ipfw.

Mac OS X Client

In Mac OS X Client, the firewall is controlled through the Sharing System Preferences pane. By default, the firewall is turned off and allows all communication to and from the host. When you visit the firewall tab for the first time, any services you have running on the host will be checked to allow incoming connections. Even though the firewall is off, the configuration is tailored around your services. You cannot change this behavior. Any service that is enabled in the sharing tab is allowed through the firewall. Figure 8.1 shows the Firewall tab in the Sharing System Preferences pane.

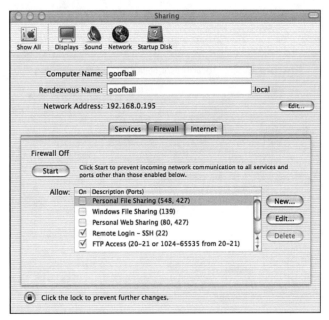

FIGURE 8.1   The Firewall tab in the Sharing System Preferences pane.

Also you may have services that are not listed in the default ruleset, such as AIM or Gnutella. These programs actually require some degree of inbound access. By clicking on the New button, you can add particular services by hand.

Figure 8.2 shows how to add support for Gnutella. If you have another service that is not in the standard list of services provided by Apple, you can add ports by hand by selecting Other from the pull-down menu (see Figure 8.3).

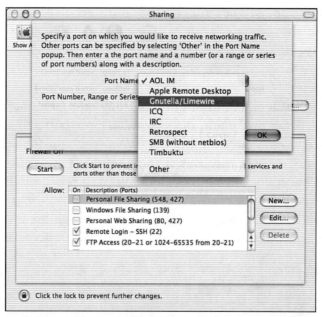

FIGURE 8.2   Adding Gnutella to the firewall rules.

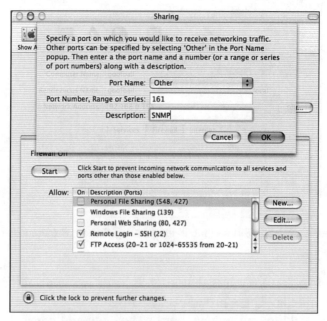

FIGURE 8.3   Adding other services.

If you are using FTP to transfer files, you will need to configure your host to use passive mode for the transfer itself. FTP is an old protocol that was designed before security was really a concern with network applications. An active mode FTP connection will result in the remote server making a connection to a random port on the client machine in an attempt to transfer the requested file. When the client machine is protected by a firewall, that inbound connection will fail. Passive mode FTP gets around this problem by forcing the client to initiate the connection for the file. Figure 8.4 shows how to configure passive mode FTP in the Proxies tab of the Network System Preferences pane.

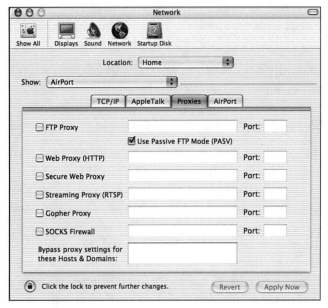

FIGURE 8.4   Forcing passive mode FTP.

After you have the correct services listed in your firewall rule, click on Start. The firewall is running and only allowing in the services you have specified in the ruleset.

WARNING

The firewall configuration GUI in OS X Client is very limited. It will only allow inbound TCP connections. All outbound TCP traffic is allowed, and all UDP traffic is dropped. Also, you do not have the capability to control *where* your connection is coming from. If you expect ssh traffic from just one host, the GUI does not allow that level of control. If your needs are not met by the basic firewall rules, see the section "Manually Configuring the Firewall" later in this chapter.

Mac OS X Server

The firewall configuration utility in Mac OS X Server has a completely different feel to it than the client utility. It allows for much more detailed firewall rules, including controls on IP addresses and logging information. It is still not a complete representation of everything `ipfw` can do, but it is much more appropriate for a firewall tool running on a server.

Due to the enhanced capabilities of Mac OS X Server's firewall utilities, you will have to do a bit more planning to create a functioning ruleset. Determine what services you want others to access and, if possible, what IP addresses those requests will be coming from. You also should determine what services the server needs to access as well. Using this list of services, source IP addresses, and destination addresses, you will create your firewall ruleset.

First, you should set up your overall firewall configuration options. On the Network tab in Server Settings there is an icon for a Firewall service. Click on that icon and select Configure Firewall to bring up the global firewall configuration options.

Under the General tab you can control how the firewall handles rejected packets. By selecting Send Rejection to Client If Connection Is Denied, the firewall service will send a TCP reset packet in response to queries to closed ports. This option speeds up client recognition that the port is closed and may avoid some client performance issues. However, it provides an attacker with detailed information on your firewall's configuration. It also may cause a denial of service (DoS) to the server in the event of large amounts of denied packets. Under extreme circumstances a server may become so preoccupied with sending reset packets that it is unable to service legitimate requests. However, in the event of a DoS attack, you may have many other problems as well that also are preventing service. Enable this option if you feel it is necessary.

In the same tab you can control logging. Logging traffic allowed or denied through your firewall can be useful for troubleshooting or tracking down an attacker. However, logging all denied packets can result in an attacker filling up your filesystem by sending large amounts of denied traffic. Similarly, if you decide to filter UDP traffic, then do not log all allowed packets. When a TCP session is allowed through the firewall, only the first packet is logged. The rest are allowed through transparently because the firewall understands that TCP is stateful. Because UDP is stateless, each packet that is allowed through the firewall is logged. This can result in huge amounts of data being logged, especially in the event of running streaming services over UDP. Only enable logging if you are troubleshooting or not concerned with running out of disk space. Figure 8.5 shows the General tab under the Configure Firewall pane.

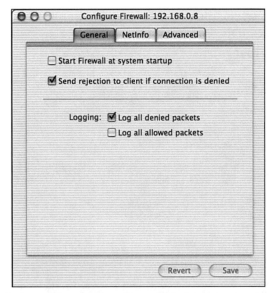

FIGURE 8.5 General configuration options for OS X Server firewall.

Under the NetInfo tab, the firewall service can be configured to allow only certain IP addresses to connect to the NetInfo process running on your server. By default all IP addresses are allowed access to NetInfo. Also by default, the NetInfo process listens on a random UDP port between 600 and 1023. This means the firewall must allow access to all ports between 600 and 1023 for the machines trusted to make NetInfo requests. By using NetInfo Manager, each domain can be bound to a specific UDP port. This allows the firewall to be much more restrictive in its access to NetInfo. If you must have network visible NetInfo domains, lock down the domains to specific ports and then filter on IP address for each domain. Figure 8.6 shows the NetInfo tab in the Configure Firewall pane.

Under the Advanced tab, the firewall can be configured to control UDP traffic. By default, all UDP traffic is allowed through the firewall. After filtering is turned on, the selected UDP ports are blocked. Unfortunately, UDP connections are stateless. This means the firewall cannot differentiate between a new inbound connection and a reply packet in an existing UDP stream. Blocking all UDP ports breaks any UDP traffic. By only blocking ports above 1024, you are effectively allowing inbound connections to UDP services. Ports that are open below port number 1024 must be controlled by a process running as a privileged user, for example a server. Conversely, by blocking access to the low numbered UDP ports, the firewall is attempting to control access to UDP server running locally while allowing outbound communication on UDP. If you choose to block UDP ports, you must configure specific allow rules for any services within that range.

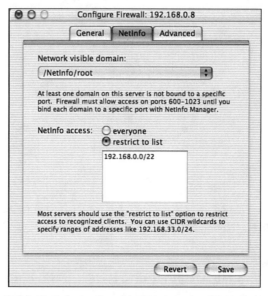

FIGURE 8.6   NetInfo configuration options for OS X Server firewall.

This tab also controls the configuration of ICMP reply messages. ICMP replies are commonly associated with the `ping` utility. When a client pings the server, an ICMP reply is issued by the server to inform the client the server is up. By blocking ICMP reply packets, clients cannot ping the server to determine reachability. Although this tactic may fool an unsophisticated attacker, it also makes troubleshooting difficult. Finally, this tab presents an option to control how the firewall handles IGMP messages. IGMP is used in environments where multicast applications are present. Generally you will know if you need to allow IGMP. Figure 8.7 shows the Advanced configuration tab in the Configure Firewall pane.

After the general properties of the firewall have been set up, the specific rules for your services need to be created. In the Server Settings Network tab, click Firewall Service, and select Show Firewall List.

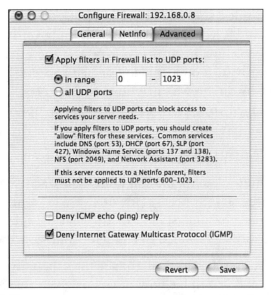

FIGURE 8.7   Advanced configuration options for OS X Server firewall.

By default the firewall denies all traffic. Any services that need to be accessed from the network need to have rules added to the firewall list. Clicking the New button creates a new rule and provides you with a window to configure it. For each service offered on the network, add a rule allowing access from required IP addresses. Figure 8.8 shows a rule that allows Apple File Sharing access from the 10.1.0.0/24 network.

FIGURE 8.8   Adding a rule to the firewall list.

After adding all rules, start the firewall by clicking the Firewall Service in Server Settings and select Start Firewall. Carefully verify that services on the server are accessible in a manner you expect. If there are problems, it is advisable to temporarily turn on logging of denied packets. Information about traffic that is dropped by the firewall is written to `/var/log/system.log`. After you have properly tuned your firewall, set the logging option to its original value.

Manually Configuring the Firewall

The graphical firewall configuration utility for Mac OS X Server and Client may be adequate for your needs. However, if you want more advanced capabilities or need to understand exactly what the firewall is doing, you can use the `ipfw` utility in Terminal to configure and view the firewall settings.

One of the most useful aspects of `ipfw` is the capability to show the current firewall ruleset and determine how often any given rule is being exercised. Here is example output from `ipfw show`:

```
bash-2.05a$ sudo ipfw show
00010     516     65224 allow ip from any to any via lo*
00030       0         0 deny log ip from 224.0.0.0/3 to any in
00040       0         0 deny log tcp from any to 224.0.0.0/3 in
00100       0         0 allow tcp from any to any 548 in
00100       0         0 allow udp from any to any 548 in
21433       3       196 allow tcp from any to any 22 in
21433       0         0 allow udp from any to any 22 in
65000       0         0 unreach net log tcp from any to any in setup
65000       1        77 unreach net log udp from any to any 0-1023 in
65535    2100    334718 allow ip from any to any
```

The first column is the rule number, the second is the number of packets that have matched the rule, and the third column is the number of bytes that have matched the rule. This ruleset was created by adding SSH and AFP to the Firewall List in the OS X GUI configuration. Note that the GUI configuration adds both TCP and UDP allow rules for services. This may or may not be acceptable to you.

NOTE

`ipfw` requires root level access for proper execution. Use `sudo` to execute these commands.

Rules can be dynamically added to the firewall ruleset by using `ipfw`. This manual mechanism for modifying the firewall ruleset provides for functionality above and beyond the GUI, including the capability to filter on source address and port, as well as destination address. For example, if you want to add a rule after the `ssh` rule to allow access to a local Internet Relay Chat server on port 6667 from any host on the 10/8 network, issue the following command:

```
bash-2.05a$ sudo ipfw add 21440 allow tcp from 10.0.0.0/8 to any 6667 in
```

This rule is active only until the firewall service is restarted. If this rule is to be made permanent, add it via the GUI. To delete the rule, use the following command:

```
bash-2.05a$ sudo ipfw delete 21440
```

The `ipfw` man page contains information on all the features in the firewall. If you need more features than the GUI offers, create a shell script with the required firewall rules in it. Then run the shell script at boot time to cause the firewall to load automatically. See "Static ARP," later in this chapter for an example of how to run a script automatically at boot time.

Kernel Configuration

There are firewall options in the kernel that can be controlled by the `sysctl` utility. Table 8.1 shows some of the more important options and what they control. All options are in the `net.inet.ip.fw branch`. Configure them as required for your server. Generally, these do not need to be changed from their default values.

TABLE 8.1 *sysctl* Values That Control the Firewall

OPTION	DESCRIPTION
Enable	Enables the firewall
One_pass	When set, packets are allowed to be processed by the firewall only once
Debug	Controls debugging output
Verbose	Turns on verbose logging
Verbose_limit	The maximum number of messages that will be logged when verbose logging is enabled

Alternatives to Apple

If you find the GUI supplied by Apple does not suit your needs and the command line interface to `ipfw` too clunky, there are other options. There are several shareware programs that provide alternative GUIs to that of Apple's. Brian Hill's BrickHouse utility is an excellent replacement for the stock Apple interface. BrickHouse is shareware and can be found at `http://personalpages.tds.net/~brian_hill/brickhouse.html`. Similarly, FirewalkX also presents an alternative method for configuring `ipfw`. FirewalkX is shareware and available from `http://www.pliris-soft.com/`.

Some companies, such as Network Associates, provide complete replacement firewalls for Mac OS X. `ipfw` does not yet make an effective stateful firewall. Commercial firewalls typically address weaknesses or missing features in `ipfw`. However, they may cost $50.00 (USD) or more per installation. For many, the built-in capability of `ipfw` is enough protection.

VPN

A Virtual Private Network (VPN) means different things to different people. There are also many reasons people will deploy VPNs. In general, a VPN is a mechanism for connecting a remote host or network to another in a secure and authenticated manner. Data within a VPN is generally encrypted (hence "private"). Also the connection between the two entities in a VPN connection is usually transparent, even if the networks are really on other sides of the planet (hence "virtual").

There are many different types of VPN technologies. Mac OS X has the capability to handle two of the major protocols used in VPNs: IPSec and PPTP. However, the graphical tools used to configure these protocols are limited (if they exist at all). To make full use of IPSec you will have to use command line utilities and a little elbow grease.

IPSec

IPSec is a powerful protocol. It has been through rigorous analysis and has proven itself through years of use. However, it is incredibly complicated and can frustrate even the most sophisticated security professional. Books have been written that discuss nothing but IPSec VPNs. This section is designed to get your feet wet with IPSec and show an example configuration. If you require information above and beyond what is presented here, see `http://vpn.shmoo.com/` for more IPSec resources.

Under the Hood

To properly set up even a simple IPSec connection you should understand what makes IPSec tick. IPSec is made up of two protocols: Encapsulated Security Payload (ESP) and Authenticated Header (AH). ESP provides confidentiality of data by encrypting it. AH, on the other hand, provides authentication and integrity of data on a per-packet basis. ESP and AH can be used independently or in combination, depending on your requirements.

IPSec can provide for tunneled or transparent connections between endpoints. Tunneled IPSec encapsulates an entire IP packet in another IP packet. This allows for a remote endpoint to act as a gateway to an entire protected network. For instance, tunneled connections are utilized when accessing an office network when you are traveling. A transparent connection merely protects the data in the packet and replaces the header information. Transparent mode connections cannot connect whole networks, only host to host communication.

When two IPSec hosts need to communicate, the first must form a *security association* (SA). An SA is a unidirectional relationship between IPSec hosts specifying various cryptographic information. Because an SA is unidirectional, at least two SAs must be present for a bidirectional conversation between hosts—one for outgoing communication and one for incoming.

A Security Policy Database (SPD) is a database of SAs and topology information. This effectively tells the host what traffic to encrypt, how to encrypt, and where to send it.

The Internet Key Exchange protocol (IKE) was created to facilitate the creation of SAs between hosts. Setting up SAs between hosts is time consuming. IKE allows for many hosts to be set up automatically. Under Mac OS X, the `racoon` utility handles IKE negotiations. After `racoon` has established SAs, the `setkey` utility is used to create SPD entries. `racoon` and `setkey` are terminal programs and have decent man pages.

racoon

`racoon` stores files in `/etc/racoon`. The following is an example racoon.conf used to talk to an IPSec gateway in tunneling mode. This example configuration is a minimum functional configuration for `racoon` to function. The file is broken into two parts. The first part, `remote`, specifies information about the IPSec gateway to which you connect. The second part, `sainfo`, controls how security associations are handled by racoon. Although this file looks complex, it is very effective for OS X to OS X IPSec connections. If you need to interoperate with other IPSec implementations, such as Checkpoint's VPN-1 or FreeS/WAN under Linux, consult the racoon man page and the documentation for the VPN endpoint for configuration options.

```
path include "/etc/racoon" ;
path pre_shared_key "/etc/racoon/psk.txt" ;
# "log" specifies logging level.  It is followed by either "notify", \
->"debug"
# or "debug2".
log debug;

# anonymous here means use these settings for all connections
# an IP address can be specified for specific gateways
remote anonymous
{
        exchange_mode aggressive,main;
        my_identifier user_fqdn "myemail@shmoo.com";
        nonce_size 16;
        lifetime time 1 hour;      # sec,min,hour
        initial_contact on;
        proposal_check obey;       # obey, strict or claim
        proposal {
                encryption_algorithm 3des;
                hash_algorithm sha1;
                authentication_method pre_shared_key ;
                dh_group 2 ;
        }
}
# again anonymous can be replaces with particular SA endpoint info
sainfo anonymous
{
        pfs_group 1;
        lifetime time 3600 sec;
        encryption_algorithm 3des ;
        authentication_algorithm hmac_sha1;
        compression_algorithm deflate ;
}
```

Run racoon at boot time. See "Static ARP," later in this chapter for an example on how to execute programs automatically when a machine boots.

The racoon.conf file references /etc/racoon/psk.txt. psk.txt should contain the shared secrets a user will use to make an IPSec connection. The file is simply a listing of email addresses and passwords. Because the passwords are not hashed, the file must be read-only by root to ensure passwords are not compromised. For example, the user in the preceding example may have the following entry in psk.txt:

```
myemail@shmoo.com          secret
```

racoon provides for mechanisms other than email address for identifying users in psk.txt. For example, rather than specifying an identifier of user_fqdn in racoon.conf, you can use the address identifier. By using address, the psk.txt file will contain IP address and password pairs. For example, a gateway at 10.0.2.3 may have the following entry in psk.txt:

```
10.0.2.3        secret
```

Launch racoon by executing the following:

```
racoon -f /etc/racoon/racoon.conf
```

Finally, security policies need to be added to the SPD. The easiest way to accomplish this is to create a file, /etc/racoon/ipsec.spd containing commands that will be fed to setkey. The example shown here is for a client IPSec machine. If you are running an IPSec gateway, your file will contain information for each client connecting. For this example, the client is at 192.168.0.100, the IPSec gateway is at 192.168.0.1, and all traffic is to be routed through the gateway. This is a typical setup for using IPSec on a wireless network:

```
spdadd 192.168.0.100/32 0.0.0.0/8 any --P out ipsec  esp/tunnel/ \
->192.168.0.100-192.168.0.1/require ;
spdadd 0.0.0.0/8 192.168.0.100/32 any --P in ipsec esp/tunnel/ \
->192.168.0.1-192.168.0.100/require ;
```

To load the security policy, use setkey in the following manner:

```
setkey -f /etc/racoon/ipsec.spd
```

At this point, you should be able to access the Internet through your IPSec gateway. If there are any problems, examine /var/log/system.log for errors.

PPTP

PPTP support under Mac OS X is more integrated into the GUI configuration utilities. Depending on your situation, it may be a more viable VPN option than IPSec. Microsoft operating systems historically have robust PPTP support, but little to no native IPSec support.

PPTP is an extension of PPP. It is a much simpler VPN protocol than IPSec. PPTP runs on top of a standard TCP connection on port 1723. The packet destined for the remote location is encapsulated in PPP. The PPP payload in turn is encapsulated in a Generic Router Encapsulation (GRE) tunnel and sent to the PPTP gateway. Unlike IPSec, there are not alternate ciphers to use or different encapsulation mechanisms. PPTP is a relatively inflexible protocol, but because of the ease of use on Windows platforms and the simple configuration, it is the VPN of choice for many.

PPTP Via Internet Connect

To configure a PPTP client in Mac OS X, use the Internet Connect utility. From the File menu, select New VPN Connection Window. Enter the name or IP address of the remote server, your username, and password for the PPTP connection. Figure 8.9 shows an example VPN Connection window. Click Connect, and all your traffic will now go through the PPTP connection. If the process fails, check the error logs on the PPTP server side.

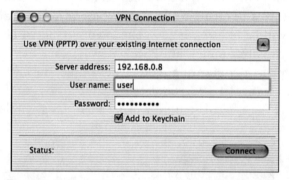

FIGURE 8.9   VPN connection via Internet Connect.

vpnd

Mac OS X server has a PPTP server, vpnd, built into the operating system. Apple has not advertised the existence of vpnd. There is a man page for the service, but there is no mention of it in the Mac OS X Server Admin Guide.

However, vpnd is a viable PPTP server. It can be set up quickly, and it easily integrates with Mac OS X Client machines. The man page is informative for setup, and it will likely be expanded in future releases of Mac OS X.

When clients connect to a vpnd server, the server assigns the clients IP addresses on the local subnet. This is basically a NAT for the tunneled client connections. These local IP addresses are where the rest of the network thinks the clients reside. In order to set up vpnd, you will need enough local IP addresses to handle your anticipated client base. Enter these IP addresses one at a time in /etc/ppp/pptp_addresses.

```
bash-2.05a$ sudo cat /etc/ppp/pptp_addresses
# Example pptp_addresses file
192.168.0.4
192.168.0.5
192.168.0.6
```

vpnd does not use NetInfo for authentication. A separate file, /etc/ppp/chap-secrets, must be created to store the authentication credentials for vpnd. Each entry in chap-secrets is made up of a username, the server name, the user's password, and the IP address associated with the user. If you do not wish to specify an IP address for each user, a * indicates that vpnd should use the first available IP address from those listed in pptp_addresses. Because the user's password is stored in the clear, this file should be readable only by root. Here is an example entry for a user, bob, in chap-secrets:

```
bob 192.168.0.1 secretpass *
```

Comment out the word nodetach from /etc/ppp/pptp_service. The entry of this word into the pptp_service file seems to be a bug that Apple will likely fix in a future release. Add the following lines to /etc/hostconfig to ensure the VPN service starts after rebooting:

```
VPNSERVER=-YES-
VPN_ARGS=""
```

Start vpnd manually with SystemStarter start VPNService. Test the service by connecting with a remote PPTP client. If there are any problems, vpnd logs to /var/log/system.log.

That is it. PPTP is much more straightforward to configure than IPSec, but the underlying architecture of PPTP is not as secure, scalable, or robust as IPSec. However, for a quick-and-dirty VPN solution, it works well.

AirPort Security

Easy, fast wireless networking is a major selling point with Apple's product line. Wireless networking capability is provided through Apple's AirPort product line, which has been designed from the ground up to fully integrate into the complete Apple image. This push for wireless networking has helped propel Apple users to the forefront of the wireless networking movement.

The original AirPort products were designed to conform to the IEEE 802.11b standard. AirPort cards and access points operate at speeds up to 11 megabits per second. The AirPort Extreme equipment uses the 802.11g standard, which is backward compatible with 802.11b. AirPort Extreme gear will work up to 54 megabits per second. Regardless of which version of AirPort equipment is used, the security mechanisms are the same.

Configuring WEP

Wired Equivalent Privacy (WEP) provides encryption and authentication for wireless connections. WEP uses a shared cryptographic key between a wireless access point and wireless station (such as a laptop with an AirPort card). The WEP key must be the same on the access point and stations for the station to properly associate to the access point.

WARNING

WEP is not exactly "Wired Equivalent Privacy." Several major flaws have been found in WEP that allow an attacker to use captured traffic to determine the cryptographic key. This has given many people the feeling that WEP is worthless.

Regardless of WEP's problems, you should always configure it. Cracking WEP is still a time-consuming task that takes a reasonable amount of expertise. A casual attacker who may be looking for targets of opportunity will bypass a WEP-protected network because it will take too long to break into it. Also, using WEP is a legal "Do Not Disturb" sign. Attackers who spend the time to crack your WEP key know they are breaking into your network—they have not stumbled accidentally onto your system.

WEP keys are either 64- or 128-bits long. Generally longer keys are much more secure than shorter ones. However, due to problems with the architecture of WEP, 128-bit keys are not as secure as they should be. Still, if your wireless equipment supports it, use 128-bit encryption.

NOTE

You may see references to 40-bit WEP. 40-bit WEP and 64-bit WEP are the same thing. Of the 64 bits used to encrypt the data, 24 bits are sent in the clear across the network. So only 40 bits are truly secret.

Your WEP key may be provided in ASCII characters or hexadecimal digits. ASCII keys are 5 characters long for 64-bit encryption or 13 characters for 128-bit encryption. If you are using hexadecimal, then a 64-bit key will be 10-digits long and a 128-bit key will be 26-digits long.

NOTE

Although ASCII and hex keys contain the same amount of key material, ASCII keys are generally less secure. Each ASCII character represents 8 bits of information for a total of 256 different characters. However, most people only use letters and numbers to form their keys. Assuming upper- and lowercase letters are utilized, that means only 62 characters are actually used to form ASCII keys. This is roughly 6 bits of data. So rather than supplying 40 bits of key material, ASCII keys really only make 30 bits of key material. The other 10 bits are already known. The moral of the story? Use hex keys where possible.

WEP is configured under the AirPort tab of the Network Preferences pane for your AirPort card. ASCII WEP keys should be entered in quotes (for example, "secrt"). Hexadecimal keys need to have a dollar sign prepended to the key (for example, $123456780a). Figure 8.10 shows a 64-bit hex key supplied for this network.

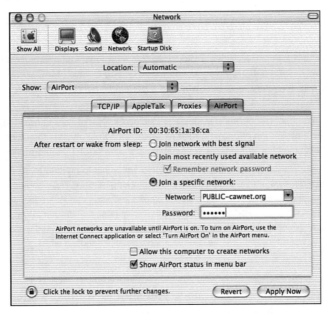

FIGURE 8.10   Configuring WEP in the Network Preferences pane.

Using LEAP

LEAP is a Cisco proprietary authentication protocol common on wireless networks. To use LEAP you need to use an access point that understands LEAP and provide a back-end authentication server. AirPort Access Point does not support LEAP natively and setting up a LEAP-enabled infrastructure is outside the scope of this book.

If your network uses LEAP, enter your LEAP username and password in the location where you would normally enter your WEP key. Your LEAP username and password should be separated by a slash and the entire string must be surrounded by angle brackets.

Static ARP

In any LAN situation, there is a danger of an attacker performing man-in-the-middle attacks against your traffic. In a wireless LAN, man-in-the-middle attacks are even more likely given the complete lack of control over physical access to the transmission medium. An attacker is likely to use an ARP spoofing attack to gain the ability to perform man-in-the-middle attacks.

NOTE

ARP stands for Address Resolution Protocol. ARP is a protocol that allows for a host to request information from local hosts regarding which IP addresses belong to which MAC address. A host broadcasts an ARP request asking every local host who has a certain IP address. The host with that IP address then sends an ARP reply with its MAC and IP address.

However, many modern operating systems, including OS X, are lazy in how they tie MAC addresses to IP addresses. Rather than performing ARP requests, they trust packets they receive. So if a host receives a packet, it assumes the IP/MAC address pair is valid and loads that information into its ARP table.

An attacker can use this to his advantage. If an attacker wants to pretend to be the gateway, he will send a packet to the victim host with a source MAC of the attacking machine but a source IP address of the gateway. The victim machine assumes that information is correct and adds that information to its ARP table. By sending false information to the gateway pretending to be the victim host, the attacker also can corrupt the ARP table on the gateway. At this point, all traffic between the gateway and victim is directed to the attacker. The attacker can then modify, view, or deny traffic as he sees fit. This is an ARP spoofing attack.

To combat ARP spoofing attacks, you should statically encode ARP entries for hosts you are likely to communicate with on your local network. The most important host you should statically encode is your local gateway. All traffic to the greater Internet goes through your gateway, so it is an ideal target for an attacker to perform a man-in-the-middle attack.

Using the `arp` utility in the BSD subsystem, ARP entries can be statically added to the ARP table to prevent ARP spoofing attacks. Assuming your gateway is 192.168.0.1 with a MAC address of 11:22:33:aa:bb:cc, add a static ARP entry by executing the following in a Terminal window. You can also use `arp` to verify the `arp` table.

```
bash-2.05a$ sudo arp -s 192.168.0.1 11:22:33:aa:bb:cc
bash-2.05a$ arp -an
? (192.168.0.1) at 11:22:33:aa:bb:cc permanent
```

The `arp` man page has a complete description of the functionality offered by the `arp` utility.

To avoid spoofing problems at boot time, the `arp` entries should be added at boot time. Create a StaticArp directory in `/Library/StartupItems` and add the following files:

StartupParamters.plist

```
{
   Description       = "Static ARP Entries";
   Provides          = ("Static ARP entries");
   OrderPreference = "First";
   Messages =
   {
     start = "Adding Static ARP Entries";
     stop = "Clearing Static ARP Entries";
   };
}
```

StaticArp

```
#!/bin/sh
# Script to add static ARP entries
StartService ()
{
    # add all static arp entries here
    /usr/sbin/arp -s 192.168.0.1 11:22:33:aa:bb:cc
}
StopService ()
{
    # delete static arp entries
    /usr/sbin/arp -d 192.168.0.1
}
```

continues

```
RestartService ()
{
    StopService
    StartService
}
RunService "$1"
```

StaticArp is a shell script that will be interpreted by the sh shell.
For more information on shell scripts, see the sh man page or
http://steve-parker.org/sh/sh.shtml.

Now, every time the host boots, the ARP entries for the gateway will be loaded
to the ARP table.

Software Base Station

Mac OS X 10.2 has the capability to act as a wireless base station. This enables
you to create a wireless network when you do not have a hardware access
point. This feature is referred to as a Software Base Station.

When creating a Software Base Station, you should enable WEP encryption.
The Software Base Station allows both 40-bit and 128-bit encryption. Again,
you can enter the key material in ASCII or in hexadecimal. Ideally, use a
128-bit hexadecimal key to make the best use of your key material. Figure 8.11
shows how to add WEP encryption to your Software Base Station. To bring
up this window, click on the AirPort icon in the menu bar and select
Create Network.

FIGURE 8.11   Adding WEP to Software Base Station.

Antivirus Protection

Defending against viruses is a fact of life on Windows machines. Virus writers have spent a great deal of time attacking the Intel/Microsoft platform. Viruses vary in type and effect on WinTel machines. Some viruses are destructive in nature and will destroy the operating system. Others are more benign and their effects go unnoticed. Regardless of their outcome, a huge antivirus industry has cropped up to defend WinTel hosts from infestation.

UNIX operating systems historically have not been susceptible to virus attacks. They have a much more rigid access control mechanism that prevents a user process from destroying the operating system in the same way Windows viruses can. Through the use of user accounts that operate with less privilege than the core operating system, malicious code running with user rights only affects data owned by the user. Further, virus writers have not devoted the amount of time to UNIX systems that they have to Windows hosts. UNIX hosts have been in the crosshairs of the hacker community for years. However, the hacker community has generally not employed viruses in its bag of tricks against UNIX systems because they are not likely to succeed.

Common Sense

These two factors make discussing antivirus on Mac OS X an odd situation. As security professionals, we would be remiss not to warn you of viruses and their potential for destruction. On the other hand, a little common sense and a few best practices will do more to prevent viruses on Mac OS X than an antivirus program will.

Viruses generally cannot infest a machine on their own. They need to be activated by performing some action or opening a document. By taking a few precautions with your daily computing, you can avoid the typical pitfalls that activate viruses.

Unknown Documents

Some document types, notably Microsoft Word, can have macros embedded directly into documents. When a document is opened, the macros run and add dynamic logic and activities to the document. However, the language that makes these macros possible also enables virus writers to access parts of your system, such as your address book, email client, and other documents you own.

Do not open any unknown document that may contain a macro. Regardless of how you received the document, if you do not recognize it, don't open it. Also, for programs that allow document types with embedded macros, turn on macro warning dialogs. Figure 8.12 shows Microsoft Word's Preference pane with Macro Virus Protection turned on. With this option enabled, a user will be prompted whenever a document with a macro is opened.

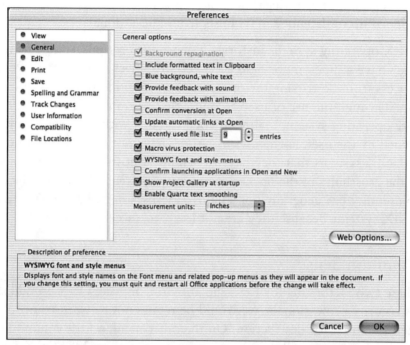

FIGURE 8.12   Enabling Word's macro virus protection.

Preview Panes and Embedded Objects

Many popular email clients have a preview pane that displays email in a frame in the mail client's window. Although this option is convenient for viewing mail quickly, it also executes any HTML that is present in the email and in some circumstances may actually automatically open attachments.

This execution is exactly what allows viruses to spread. To keep malicious code in email messages from automatically launching, you should disable the preview pane in your email client. This way you can delete emails with attachments without having to open them. As a rule of thumb, if you receive an email with an attachment from a person you do not know, your best bet is to simply delete it. Similarly, if you are contacting someone for the first time, do not include attachments. Mail.app allows you to disable its preview pane by double-clicking the bar that divides the index listing from the preview pane.

You also should prohibit the mail client from displaying images and embedded objects in emails after they are opened. This way even when you do open an email, malicious embedded objects will not execute. This is configured in the Viewing section of the Mail.app Preferences window (see Figure 8.13).

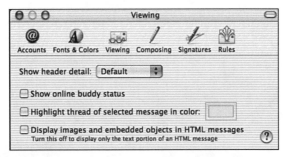

FIGURE 8.13   Disabling images and embedded objects.

Network Shares

Another way viruses end up on a host is via writeable network shares. Unless absolutely necessary, do not allow write access to shared data. This may seem like common sense, but far too often someone will "temporarily" create a share and never go back to shut it off. This share is then a vector for a network-based virus to attack your system.

Antivirus Software

Unfortunately, being diligent will not always protect you from virus infections. Either through a new propogation method or simply letting you guard down, it is likely a virus will eventually find a way to your system. By using antivirus software, you can protect yourself from the virii that make it past your primary defenses. Luckily, the Mac OS X antivirus space is competitive and the quality of the products that exist in the market are generally quite high. At the time of this writing, both Symantec (`http://www.symantec.com`) and Network Associates (`http://www.nai.com`) offer antivirus software compatible with Mac OS X 10.2. These companies are leaders in the antivirus field and their products will likely meet your expectations.

Summary

Securing your Mac OS X hosts from network attacks requires a broad approach. Firewalls, encryption, and antivirus software provide means for protecting your host and auditing the traffic hitting it. By being diligent and adhering to the principle of least privilege in your network communications, network-based attacks will be much less likely to succeed.

PART IV
ENTERPRISE SECURITY

## CHAPTER 9

ENTERPRISE HOST CONFIGURATION

Marge: "Well, Homer, I have to admit, you created something people really love.
You truly are an artist."
Homer: "No, I'm just a nut who couldn't build a barbecue."
—The Simpsons

Deploying Mac OS X in a small office setting is dramatically different from configuring tens or hundreds of workstations in a lab environment. In a small office, the threats are generally from the network, not from a malicious user sitting at the console. There are not issues regarding distributed authentication mechanisms, and there is usually not a need to create arbitrary connections between hosts; any relationships between machines are generally well-known and static.

However, in a lab or corporate environment, the situation is much less controlled. Central administrators want each user's experience to be the same. Users should authenticate against a common database of credentials. If the central authentication system is not NetInfo, Mac OS X must be configured to communicate properly in order to authenticate users. Finally, users should have the opportunity to discover local services in a secure and scalable fashion.

This chapter will cover some issues that may be encountered when deploying Mac OS X clients in an enterprise situation. First, customization of the login process will be discussed. Then we will dive into Rendezvous and its capability to find and use local services. Finally, Kerberos will be covered as a mechanism to implement secure enterprise authentication.

Login Window

When deploying managed client workstations, it is often desirable to customize the login screen. For some, this is only an aesthetic change to brand machines with an organization's logo. For others there are legal reasons for adding information to the login screen. When prosecuting an attacker who accessed a machine via the console and performed an illegal activity, defendants may claim they were unaware that the activity they were conducting was nefarious or off-limits. By displaying a banner at login time that documents what the host is to be used for, any confusion about what activities can and cannot be performed is removed.

The Login Window program controls the console login process. Even if a host is configured for automatic login, Login Window still runs and performs the automatic login. Login Window controls the graphics displayed, the test presented to the user, and any post-login activities that are common to all users.

Changing the Login Window Graphic

The loginwindow graphic is a simple 400×300-pixel TIFF file. Create the new graphic, containing whatever content you want. Then copy it to the location of the default loginwindow graphic by issuing the following command from a terminal window.

```
Bash-2.05a$ sudo cp mygraphic.tiff  \
/System/Library/CoreServices/SecurityAgentPlugins/loginwindow.bundle/ \
->Contents/Resources/MacOSXart.tif
```

Login Window will automatically use the graphic next time you attempt to log in. There is no need to restart Login Window. Note that there are other graphics in that directory that can be customized, based on your needs.

Adding a Login Banner

Adding a login banner using loginwindow is effectively a mechanism for hanging a "No Trespassing" sign on the host. This banner should provide an indication of who owns the host, what the host can be used for, and any contact information for the administrators of the host. This banner should be displayed prior to successfully logging in to ensure the user sees it.

NOTE

We are not lawyers. Because a login banner is largely a legal requirement, we recommend that you consult counsel prior to implementing a banner to ensure that you use the correct language.

To add a banner, you will need to edit `/Library/Preferences/com.apple.loginwindow.plist` with your favorite text editor as root or by using sudo. After the `<dict>` tag, add the following information:

```
<key>LoginwindowText</key>
<string>Your banner text goes here</string>
```

Again, you will not need to restart Login Window for this to take effect. Figure 9.1 shows an example login window with a banner at the top.

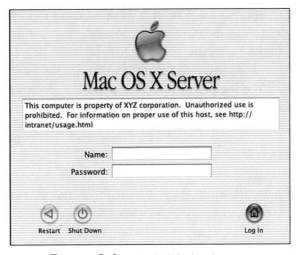

FIGURE 9.1   Login Window banner.

Using Kerberos Authentication

Rather than using NetInfo for authentication, loginwindow can be configured to require Kerberos authentication. (For more information on what Kerberos is, see the following section titled "Kerberos.")

For required Kerberos authentication, you will need to edit /etc/ authorization by using your favorite text editor with root privileges. In /etc/authorization, change this

```
<key>system.login.console</key>
<dict>
     <key>eval</key>                      \
-><string>loginwindow_builtin:login,authinternal,loginwindow_builtin: \
->success</string>
```

to this

```
<key>system.login.console</key>
<dict>
     <key>eval</key>                      \
-><string>loginwindow_builtin:login,krb5auth:authnoverify, \
->loginwindow_builtin:success</string>
```

There are other options for Kerberos authentication at login. For instance, you can force a user to log into a NetInfo domain and then into Kerberos. Further, you can even make Kerberos optional for the login process to give users control over their authentication mechanisms. (For more information on using Kerberos during the login process, see AppleCare document #107154.)

Kerberos

Kerberos is a network authentication protocol that allows clients and servers to authenticate each other with the use of a trusted third-party authentication server. Kerberos is commonly used in corporate and academic environments to provide authentication (and often encryption) for services such as telnet and email. It was designed to allow both the client to trust the server (and vice versa) without the client having to send a password (at least not an unencrypted password) across the network. Although it is not perfect, and certainly not simple, Kerberos does solve some basic security problems.

Kerberos is developed and freely distributed by MIT, and is installed with Mac OS X and Mac OS X Server. As a result, Mac OS X users can authenticate as Kerberos clients, whereas Mac OS X Server can make use of an existing Kerberos server as a means of authenticating users to certain services.

In this section, we will cover the configuration of Mac OS X as a Kerberos client and discuss some of the security issues surrounding the use of "kerberized" services on Mac OS X Server. Here, we do not provide an explanation of how the Kerberos protocol is designed to work. See Appendix C, "Further Reading," for a list of resources that provide such an explanation. Also the Mac OS X Server Administration Guide details the process of configuring certain services to authenticate clients using an existing Kerberos server.

Integrating Mac OS X Clients into a Kerberos Environment

First, as with any Kerberos setup, it is important to maintain accurate time. The Kerberos protocol makes use of time values as nonces in the authentication process. The key exchange process will fail if the client host is off by more than a few minutes. A good thing to do is use a time synchronization server, which can be configured in `System Preferences.app`. The process is explained in Chapter 11, "Auditing," in the section titled "The Importance of Time."

WHAT IS A NONCE?

In the world of cryptography, a *nonce* is a randomly generated piece of data. Nonces are often used in key exchange protocols as a means of preventing the replay or reproduction of an event or message.

When a Kerberos client authenticates with a service, part of the exchange includes a timestamp as a nonce encrypted with the session key. This process serves to prevent an attacker from replaying the issued Kerberos ticket at a later time.

Typically, Kerberos 5 clients on UNIX systems maintain an `/etc/krb5.conf` file that defines the realms and the locations of the Key Distribution Centers to use. On Mac OS X, this master Kerberos configuration file should be located in `/Library/Preferences/edu.mit.Kerberos`, and is not there by default. Usually, this file is supplied by an administrator and minimally contains a default realm definition; for example:

```
[libdefaults]
    default_realm = example.com
[realms]
    example.com =
    {
```

continues

```
    kdc = kdc1.example.com
    kdc = kdc2.example.com
    kdc = kdc3.example.com
    admin_server = kdc1.example.com
}
```

Additionally, each user can place a configuration file at the location `~/Library/Preferences/edu.mit.Kerberos`. This file is read first; if it does not exist, the system file is used.

Although command-line Kerberos applications (such as kinit and klist) are installed with Mac OS X, there is also an Aqua application for managing Kerberos tickets named `Kerberos.app`. This application is somewhat hidden in `/System/Library/CoreServices/Kerberos.app` (see Figure 9.2).

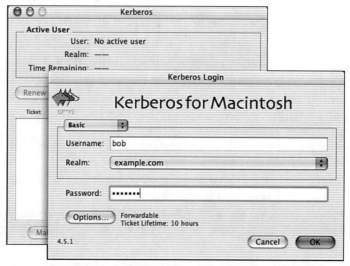

FIGURE 9.2   Kerberos for Macintosh ticket application.

This application is somewhat useless until you have created the Kerberos configuration file; however, after that is done, it can be much nicer to use in place of the various command line utilities.

Using Kerberized Services on Mac OS X Server

Mac OS X Server can make use of an existing Kerberos server for authentication to certain services. What it means for a service to be kerberized is that the application or server is modified to make use of the Kerberos libraries for authentication purposes; this is not always an easy process. Not all services on

Mac OS X Server are kerberized. At the time of this writing, the following services and applications can take advantage of Kerberos authentication:

- FTP
- AFP
- Mail, including IMAP, POP, and SMTP
- Mac OS X Login Window
- Telnet
- Macintosh Manager logins

> **NOTE**
>
> Although the man pages for rlogin and rsh mention that they support Kerberos, they do not. This is yet another case where man pages on Mac OS X are misleading.

The Mac OS X Administration Guide provides detailed instructions for setting up these services to make use of an existing Kerberos server.

Here, we will discuss what Kerberos does for these services as well as some of the security issues involved with using Kerberos that both users and administrators should be aware of.

Security Issues with Kerberos and Mac OS X Services

Kerberos essentially provides third-party authentication for TCP/IP network services. The main goal is to provide the capability for clients and services to authenticate each other using strong cryptography and to prevent clients from having to send out passwords onto the network. In this respect, Kerberos is successful; however, it is not perfect.

First, Kerberos is used primarily to provide authentication services. It does not provide confidentiality or integrity of data exchanged between the client and the service. Although Kerberos can be used to encrypt all network traffic, it usually is not used that way. On Mac OS X Server, configuring services such as Mail (including IMAP, POP, and SMTP), AFP, and FTP to use Kerberos secures only the authentication process, not all of the network traffic for that service. Keep this in mind: Kerberos is somewhat like a bulletproof vest; it provides protection for certain elements (such as passwords), but if an attacker is aiming for the head, it's all over. It is better than nothing, but not a perfect solution.

Second, Kerberos authentication is only as safe as the hosts involved; it assumes trusted hosts and an untrusted network. The Kerberos protocol is based upon previously established secrets. Both the client and the service have keys that are entrusted to a host that manages the Kerberos realm(s), known as the Key Distribution Center (KDC). If this host is compromised, so are all of the clients and accessible services. Likewise, if a client host is compromised, so is access to each service that has an outstanding ticket; in this case, the compromise is limited to the expiration date on the tickets. The main point here is that the use of Kerberos authentication adds another (possibly unnecessary) element of risk to a service. The security of the client host and the server are obvious elements to consider when evaluating the security of a service. By entrusting the responsibility of authorization for a service (such as AFP) to a remote Kerberos server, the security of the service now involves three hosts.

The security of most Kerberos deployments is dependant upon time. Thus, if an attacker can alter a host's concept of time, that system is then vulnerable to replay attacks.

Another seemingly silly, yet realistic, threat has to do with Kerberos client software. It is not uncommon for universities to run kerberized versions of telnet or ftp servers. If an attacker can get naive users to download malicious Kerberos client software, that user is doomed from the start. This scenario is not unrealistic; many users in this environment will consider the software a means to an end toward obtaining access to the service. Administrators truly concerned with the security of any services need to consider such things.

The Kerberos protocol is not completely immune to password-guessing attacks. Client keys are essentially protected by passwords. Although these passwords are not usually sent over the network, weak passwords are not immune to dictionary attacks. The attack works by an attacker requesting a ticket and performing an offline attack on the response. If compromised, the attacker can then impersonate the user, including access to any services. Attacks of this nature have been addressed with preauthentication mechanisms, but this depends upon the server's configuration. At least make sure that the Kerberos server software is up-to-date; many issues have been fixed with recent versions. Version 5 of the Kerberos protocol surfaced with MIT's 1.2 release of Kerberos. At the time of this writing, the MIT Kerberos distribution is 1.2.7. A popular document written by Steve Bellovin and Michael Merritt reveals some serious vulnerabilities with Kerberos versions 4 and 5 (http://www.research.att.com/~smb/papers/kerblimit.usenix.pdf). The Kerberos site hosted at MIT also contains a list of security advisories for recent releases of Kerberos (http://web.mit.edu/kerberos/www/advisories/index.html).

It may sound as if we are coming down hard on Kerberos. The main problem is that it is too complicated. There are alternatives, such as SSL and SSH, that are much easier to configure and set up than Kerberos. Securing AFP with SSH is discussed in Chapter 7, "File Sharing." Securing mail with SSH or SSL is discussed in Chapter 5, "User Applications."

Rendezvous

Apple was known for years for creating computers and an operating system that were easy to set up and use. At the network, much of this ease of use was due to AppleTalk, which allowed users to plug computers into a network and have them work without any configuration. AppleTalk transparently handled addressing responsibilities and service advertisement. No-brainer networking.

Fast-forward to Mac OS X and modern networking. Everything is now based on IP, and AppleTalk has been effectively shelved in favor of IP for availability and scalability reasons. However, there is still a desire to provide no-brainer networking in the modern age. Enter Rendezvous. Rendezvous allows the creation of "instant" networks of computers and smart devices simply by plugging them into the network. Rendezvous-aware devices automatically handle their networking needs without external services such as DHCP or DNS.

Rendezvous provides the following functionality:

- Automatic Addressing
- Naming and Name Service
- Service Discovery

Rendezvous provides addressing by utilizing the link-local netblock, 169.254.0.0/16, to randomly select an IP address. The host then ARP's to see whether another host on the network is using the same IP address. If a conflict is found, the host will choose another address until a free IP address is found. Historically, a DHCP or BootP server is required to handle addressing on a LAN. Rendezvous provides a mechanism to allow each host to allocate its own addresses.

The nameservice and service discovery go hand in hand with Rendezvous. Rendezvous uses multicast DNS with service discovery (mDNS-SD) to notify the network of hostnames and services available. By utilizing mDNS-SD, Rendezvous-enabled hosts do not require access to a central DNS server.

A host using mDNS-SD sends a multicast packet to the network with its host-name, IP address, and available services. The other hosts on the network cache this information for use later. A Rendezvous hostname is always in the .local domain so applications know the host is a local host. mDNS-SD uses multicast address 224.0.0.251 on port 5353.

Rendezvous Security

Using Rendezvous brings up some security concerns. First off, if a Mac OS X host fails to successfully contact its primary DNS servers, it will send a multi-cast DNS request for the address. In this situation, a local attacker could respond with a malicious DNS address in an attempt to dupe the client.

This attack can be remedied in two ways. First, the applications running on a host should make a distinction between hostnames acquired through normal DNS and those acquired through Rendezvous. Rendezvous hostnames for global names (such as www.cnn.com) should be considered highly suspect by the user and application. For example, Safari, Apple's web browser, shows web sites discovered through Rendezvous in their own pane so there is no confusion (see Figure 9.3). The other option is to use DNSSec for all nameservice lookups. DNSSec is a long way from being implemented on a global scale and is likely not a viable solution.

FIGURE 9.3   The Rendezvous pane in Safari.

Another potential vulnerability in Rendezvous is an attacker's capability to spoof traffic into a Rendezvous network from an outside network. Luckily, the creators of Rendezvous addressed this issue in the protocol specification. If an mDNS-SD packet does not have its TTL set to 255, it will be rejected by Rendezvous-aware devices. A TTL of 255 means that the packet has not been sent through a router. Remember, a router decrements the TTL of an IP packet when it passes the packet from one interface to another. A TTL of 255 is the highest possible TTL, and by definition it means that the packet has not been sent by an external party.

NOTE

Rendezvous-discovered services are no more or less secure than when they are discovered via normal routes. mDNS-SD is only a mechanism to find services, not use them. When a client attempts to access a service it found out about through mDNS-SD, such as a web site, all the security mechanisms are still in place for that service. If the web site requires a user/password combination to be accessed, it will still be required, regardless of whether the server was discovered through Rendezvous or whether the user entered the URL by hand into the address bar.

The same concept goes for other Rendezvous-aware applications such as iChat. iChat recognizes and presents users who are available via Rendezvous differently from other IM mechanisms. Still, iChat passes data in the clear and does not strongly authenticate users. iChat, or any standard IM client for that matter, is not a secure communication channel. Using Rendezvous does not make any program *more* secure.

Summary

Deploying Mac OS X in a large enterprise presents interesting challenges. Beyond file sharing and email service, issues such as service discovery, enterprise authentication, and banner presentation become more important as your network grows. Properly used, Rendezvous provides a secure mechanism for finding local services. Also, by using Kerberos and a customized loginwindow, users will authenticate in a common, controllable fashion. By understanding the tools at your disposal and understanding your needs, OS X can be made to scale reliably and securely.

## CHAPTER 10

DIRECTORY SERVICES

"If you don't find it in the index, look very carefully through the entire catalogue."
—Unknown, Sears, Roebuck, and Co. Consumer's Guide, 1897

As we have repeatedly stated throughout this book, Mac OS X has a great many features and capabilities that its predecessors only dreamed of. In the previous chapter, we spoke about several security configuration issues surrounding a Mac OS X host in a corporate or enterprise network. Most of these aspects have always existed in such networks, but were largely set aside or overlooked when dealing with Macintosh computers because the operating system (and its accompanying tools) were unable to provide an appropriate infrastructure. Mac OS X, of course, changed this. One of the places in which this is most evident in the enterprise is Mac OS X's support for various directory services. Not only can Mac OS X now host its own directory, it can participate in existing directories within the enterprise.

In this chapter, we will discuss some basics of directory services (including why they are used and general security issues) and then move on to much more specific discussions of Mac OS X's primary directory services: NetInfo and Open Directory. Finally, we will discuss some of the alternatives to the built-in directory services.

Yet Another "The Basics"

A *directory* in this context is a hierarchical data structure, which attempts to catalog all the available resources on a network, much like a phone book tries to catalog a city's phone numbers. Directories can store a variety of data: user credentials, supplementary user data, machine configurations, software configurations, and others.

There are several reasons why an organization might want to deploy an enterprise directory, most of which are related directly to the centralization of the data contained therein. First, with a properly deployed directory, users have access to all the resources their network has to offer and that they have permission to access. Just as it is easier to have everyone's phone numbers in a single book rather than in a million individual phone books (at one per person), it is easier to deal with an enterprise's resources when they can be found in one place. Second, administrators can often leverage the directory as a way to limit the number of management points required to control their networks, which can increase the stability of the network and decrease the stress of those same administrators. Another common use for directories is as a datastore for a single-sign-on (SSO) solution, often involving PKI (public key infrastructure).

As with most information systems, using a directory has security implications. Some aspects stem from the benefits of using a directory. This includes reduced human error from users and administrators because data is entered in fewer locations, reducing the chance that someone will fat-finger an important piece of data. Another benefit is that directories often make it much easier to deploy an organization's security policy; a single set of controls can rarely be deployed for an entire organization, but a directory's hierarchical nature makes it possible to get the most out of a single deployment.

The other aspects of directory services security pertain to the way in which the directory and its protocols are deployed. Among these are authentication, authorization, and data privacy. Authentication includes both the authentication of the user when reading or modifying objects in the directory and the client's ability to ensure that it is communicating with the proper server. Ensuring that users can modify only the things they are authorized to is also important. Finally, there should be concern for the privacy of the data that flows between the client and the directory server(s), especially sensitive information such as user credentials. As we shall see shortly, not all Directories are created equal in these respects.

NetInfo

Inherited from its NeXTStep roots, NetInfo is Mac OS X's default and primary directory service. A NetInfo directory (called a domain) is a hierarchical assemblage of individual databases. Each host (client or server) is a NetInfo domain unto itself and maintains at least one NetInfo database, called "local," which is the default NetInfo configuration for Mac OS X and Mac OS X Server.

Minimally, a NetInfo domain consists of a root domain (/) and any number of subdomains. In the default configuration, the root domain for each host is synonymous with its local domain. Other than the default configuration, there are two other common scenarios for NetInfo domains: a two-level hierarchy with a single root domain and multiple hosts beneath it, and a three-tier hierarchy with a single root domain with a number of "network" subdomains beneath it—each with a collection of hosts beneath it (see Figure 10.1).

Two-Tier NetInfo Hierarchy

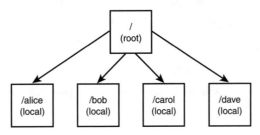

Three-Tier NetInfo Hierarchy

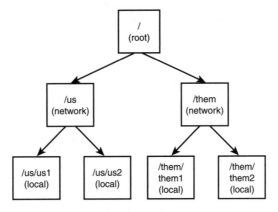

FIGURE 10.1 Common NetInfo hierarchies.

Each domain and subdomain in the hierarchy is given a "tag," or a name that can be used by clients to explicitly query a domain. There are three special tags: root, network, and local. As we have stated previously, on a single standalone host, the root and local domains are synonymous. In a two-tier hierarchy, both the root and network domains are synonymous. In addition, when a computer is configured to serve a domain via subnet broadcasts, it must use the "network" tag for the served domain. A host may bind to a parent domain (a domain that is one step higher in the hierarchy) by one of three methods: explicit IP address and tag, subnet broadcast, and DHCP assignment (see Figure 10.2). To configure a host to be a child of an existing domain is a relatively simple procedure:

1. Open Directory Access.app (`/Applications/Utilities/Directory Access.app`).

2. Authenticate the application by clicking the lock icon in the lower-left corner.

3. Select the Services tab.

4. Select the NetInfo line item and click the Configure button below.

5. Select the binding method required by the parent domain.

6. Click the OK button.

7. Check the check box next to the NetInfo line item.

8. Click the Apply button.

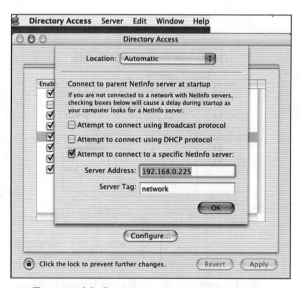

FIGURE 10.2   Binding to a parent domain.

For management of more complicated NetInfo domains, one must use
NetInfo Manager (`/Applications/Utilities/NetInfo Manager.app`).
By authenticating the application, an administrator has access to a number
of different NetInfo management options from the Management menu. To
modify the hierarchy itself, select the Manage NetInfo Hierarchy item from the
Management menu. A dialog box displays (see Figure 10.3) that allows an
administrator to create child and parent domains as well as clones of existing
domains (used for load balancing and fault tolerance).

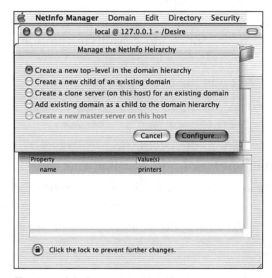

FIGURE 10.3   Modifying a NetInfo hierarchy.

NetInfo data is stored in the hierarchy as a series of attributes (or properties)
that are organized into directories (much like files are organized in a
filesystem). Table 10.1 describes the major NetInfo directories in a database
and their functions. These attributes can be viewed or modified via the GUI
(with NetInfo Manager) or through several command-line applications
(commonly known as the `ni*` applications). A number of other applications
and preference panes also indirectly modify the database. Administrators
should always beware when modifying any of the NetInfo attributes directly
because none of the applications that directly modify them perform any real
sanity-checking on the data entered. This makes it horribly easy to mess up the
database to the point the system no longer functions properly.

TABLE 10.1   Major NetInfo Directories and Their Functions

DIRECTORY NAME	DESCRIPTION
Aliases	Corollary to Sendmail's `/etc/aliases` file, contains directories specifying mail delivery aliases.
Config	Contains configuration data for a variety of Apple's services and daemons.
Groups	Corollary to the UNIX `/etc/groups` file, contains directories for each defined group.
Machines	Contains directories for each defined machine on the network; used for NetBoot and NetInfo integration.
Mounts	Similar to `/etc/fstab`, provides details of mountable resources (volumes) in the NetInfo domain.
Networks	Corollary to the UNIX `/etc/networks` file, contains a mapping of IP subnets to ascii names.
Printers	Corollary to the UNIX `/etc/printcap` file, contains information about lpr-based printer definitions.
Users	Loose corollary to the UNIX `/etc/passwd` and `/etc/master.passwd` files, contains directories for each of the users defined in the domain that contain a variety of user-specific properties.

When a machine looks up information in the NetInfo hierarchy, it first searches the local database for the data, then the parent domain, then the parent's parent domain, and so on. This feature can cause some interesting issues, particularly with regard to user accounts. User logins are queried from the hierarchy by usernames, which can cause unexpected issues when the hierarchy contains duplicate usernames or UIDs. In the former situation, the local user takes precedence, which can cause issues when users such as root attempt to log in to a workstation with the parent domain's root account password. The latter situation, with duplicated UIDs, is the most problematic situation because permissions to files are assigned by UID, not by name. This means that unless UIDs are carefully managed, two users with different names may end up with access to the same files with the same permissions, which is generally a bad thing.

This discussion is a basic overview of the way NetInfo works. Successfully deploying a functional NetInfo hierarchy demands attention and planning, as well as knowledge of a few topics we did not discuss here. Suggested readings for more in-depth knowledge can be found in Appendix C, "Further Reading."

Now that readers hopefully have a reasonable idea of what NetInfo is and does, we will dive into its security aspects. We will focus on the three major components discussed in the introduction to this chapter: authentication, authorization, and data privacy.

Authentication

Any discussion of NetInfo and authentication to its datastore is necessarily short. From any security standpoint it is lacking. The server performs no real authentication of a user prior to the user querying the hierarchy for any information, save for a sort of passive authentication using the _trusted_networks attributes at the root of each domain (we will discuss _trusted_networks in the next section, "Authorization"). No authentication of the server by the client is attempted either, except passively, by configuring the client to connect to a specific IP address and NetInfo tag.

This lack of authentication makes local network attacks against the NetInfo domain relatively easy. Besides clients being able to query for any data from the NetInfo without authenticating, it also means that it would be relatively trivial for malfeasants to set up a rogue NetInfo server for their devious purposes. Neither of these scenarios should make administrators very happy. It is for these reasons (and for general sanity) that access to NetInfo hierarchies should never be allowed from the Internet or any other untrusted network.

Authorization

As with authentication, the story of NetInfo and authorization is not very long or complicated. From previous discussions in Chapter 4, "What is this UNIX Thing?" we already know that localhost access to the NetInfo database allows any user to read any information, including password hashes. Other aspects of NetInfo's access control for a given domain or a directory therein are governed by two sets of attributes: the _writers* and _trusted_networks properties.

The _writers* Property

By default, only the root user can modify a NetInfo database. For various reasons, such as password management, it is necessary to allow non-root users to modify properties in the NetInfo hierarchy, which is accomplished with the _writers* property (see Figure 10.4).

The _writers* property comes in two varieties: _writers and
_writers_propertyname (for example, _writers_passwd). Both properties,
which can be found anywhere in a domain's directory structure, specify a list
of users allowed to write to a particular property or properties. Thus, setting
the value of _writers_passwd to bob in bob's NetInfo directory (/users/bob)
would let the user bob modify his password. If a directory contains the bare
_writers property, listed users can modify all properties in that particular
directory. Either form of the property can also accept an asterisk (*), which is
equivalent to specifying "all users."

FIGURE 10.4   The writers_passwd allows the user admin to modify its own password.

In general, administrators should not modify Mac OS X's defaults regarding
these properties. The operating system's defaults are very sane; tightening them
further will likely cause functionality issues, and relaxing them further will
likely only introduce additional unnecessary risks to the system. Also, if an
administrator finds herself seriously considering setting the _writers property
(indicating that all properties in the containing directory) with a value of '*'
(indicating all users), she should rethink things and possibly check herself into
the local loony bin.

The trusted_networks *Property*

The `trusted_networks` property, if it exists at all, is located at the root of a domain and sets the hosts that are allowed to query the domain database. If the property does not exist for a domain, then any host may query the domain's database. If the property exists but has no values set, only the localhost address may access the database. When set, the values can be specified as the network parts of classful addresses or individual host addresses (that is, 192, 192.168, 192.168.0, or 192.168.0.1).

Local domains in Mac OS X have their `trusted_networks` property blank, allowing only the local host to query the database (see Figure 10.5). If configured to provided configuration and authentication data for other systems on the network, Mac OS X Server does not include the `trusted_networks` attribute for its "network" domain.

To modify this default behavior, run the NetInfo Manager application; then select the root (/) of the domain to modify (parent domains can be selected by clicking the Open Parent globe icon in the toolbar). Next, authenticate the application and then select Add from the Edit menu; a new property will be added and highlighted in the lower pane. Change the new property's name to be `trusted_networks`; then set the value to the classful network address of the local network. Once done, save the changes, and then restart the NetInfo database using the Restart Local NetInfo Domains item from the Management menu.

FIGURE 10.5   Adding the `trusted_networks` attribute for Mac OS X Server.

The `trusted_networks` property provides only a small amount of additional security. Configuring the `trusted_networks` property should be of secondary concern to ensuring that no one can access anything on the local network from an untrusted network. But still, it does add some small bit of security with minimal pain and should be configured.

Data Privacy

Keeping data private as it bounces down the wire between the client and server is difficult with NetInfo. All traffic that transits the network is in the clear. Unfortunately, there is little one can do to secure this data; standard tunneling techniques with Stunnel or SSH do not function because of their reliance upon UDP and RPC in addition to TCP. Other than using IPSec to encrypt all traffic between the hosts (a jackhammer solution for a clawhammer problem), there is little an administrator can do to combat this.

Fortunately for us, Apple has transitioned (or is beginning a transition) away from NetInfo as a network directory service and protocol toward an implementation of OpenLDAP, which brings a myriad of potential improvements, not the least of which is security. This transition comes to us in the form of Apple's Open Directory.

Open Directory

One of the biggest things to understand about Apple's Open Directory is that it is not a directory service itself; in fact, there is, strictly speaking, no "it." Open Directory is instead an assembly of applications and daemons that together provide the features and functionality of a directory service. There is no single opendirectoryd (although in some respects lookupd comes near), or opendirectory.conf configuration file. Among the components of Open Directory are a framework (an API and libraries) for client access to data, a pluggable framework for discovering network resources (based on Apple's NSL API), a directory server (based on NetInfo and LDAP), and an authentication server. Another important thing to note is that some aspects of Open Directory (notably, the authentication server and the directory server) are only supported by Apple on Mac OS X Server, though intrepid users may enable the latter on the desktop version of the operating system as well.

Open Directory's provisions for client access to directory are embodied in DirectoryService.framework, and this framework's physical manifestation, Directory Access (`/Applications/Utilities/Directory Access.app`), an application we have already seen elsewhere in this chapter. The DirectoryService API allows developers to write clients that make use of the various datastores without needing to be cognizant of the underlying protocols. Datastores can be added to a system via an extensible pluggable architecture. DirectoryService.framework is open source and included with the Darwin project.

Network resource discovery is provided via Apple's Network Service Location (NSL) API. This API provides developers with a supple framework for accessing, cataloging, and displaying network resources, including both low-level raw data access and high-level GUI representation. Similar to the DirectoryService framework, NSL sports a pluggable architecture for locating resources in directories and on a network. The most accessible example of the use of the NSL API is the Connect to Server menu item in the Finder's Go menu.

Outwardly, Open Directory's directory server is an implementation of OpenLDAP (version 2.1.0). LDAP (Lightweight Directory Access Protocol) is perhaps the most common directory service in the industry, and OpenLDAP is an open-source implementation of this standard. Like NetInfo, LDAP is a hierarchical database that contains a variety of information, including user data and network resources. LDAP, however, far exceeds NetInfo's native capability to scale in breadth and depth of the hierarchy. It is also much more common on the non-NeXT, non-Apple networks of the world.

Despite its pretty LDAP exterior, the core of Open Directory's directory server is still NetInfo. A company named PADL Software (`http://www.padl.com`) created an LDAP wrapper for NetInfo (or a LDAP/NetInfo bridge), which supports LDAP-based (version 2 and 3) access to the NetInfo database. This wrapper permits a host of standard LDAP-based applications and tools to interact and utilize the underlying NetInfo database without having to port those same tools to a different protocol. This mapping of the LDAP protocol to the NetInfo architecture allows Mac OS X to integrate into enterprise networks in ways Mac OS never could, while leveraging the venerable NetInfo for support of legacy networks. By default, all (and only) non-"local" NetInfo domains are accessible via the LDAP protocol.

The remaining major component of Open Directory is its authentication server: Password Server. Password Server is a SASL-based (Simple Authentication and Security Layer) authentication server, which provides for encrypted network authentications (using several different protocols) as well as rudimentary password policies that include password expiration, forced password changes, minimum password lengths, and account disablement (see Figure 10.6).

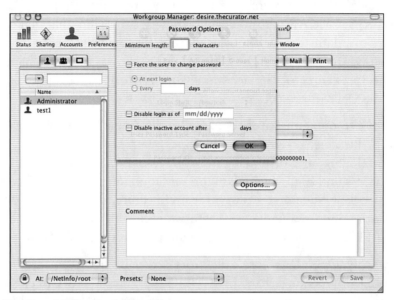

FIGURE 10.6   Password Server provides support for password policies.

In addition to these features, using Password Server also has the side effect of eliminating password hashes from NetInfo queries (the `nidump passwd . /` issue). One exception to this is the server's local root account, which is not stored in the Password Server. For this reason, no non-administrative shell or console access should be allowed to the server in a secure environment.

A full discussion of the theory and practice of LDAP is beyond the scope of this chapter and book, so we will assume that readers are familiar with its concepts and terminology. For those readers lacking this knowledge, we suggest checking Appendix C for additional material.

Connecting Mac OS X to an Open Directory Server

Like connecting Mac OS X to a NetInfo server, connecting to an Open Directory is relatively easy and done through the Directory Access application. To add Mac OS X to an existing Open Directory server, carry out the following steps:

1. Open the Directory Access application.
2. Select the Services tab.
3. Authenticate the application.
4. Select the LDAPv3 line item.
5. Ensure that LDAPv3 is enabled via the associated check box.
6. Click the Configure button.
7. If necessary, click the down arrow next to the Show Option label.
8. Click the New button.
9. Click the Edit button.
10. Fill in the Configuration Name text box appropriately.
11. Fill in the Server Name or IP Address text box appropriately.
12. If the server requires authentication (not the default) enable the Use Authentication When Connecting check box and enter the appropriate information.
13. If the server can use SSL encryption (not the default), enable the Encrypt Using SSL check box.
14. Select the Search & Mappings tab.
15. Select Open Directory Server from the pull-down menu labeled Access This LDAPv3 Server Using.
16. In the Search Base Suffix, enter the appropriate search suffix (for instance, `"cn=users,dc=example,dc=com"` for a server for the example.com domain).
17. Click the OK button.
18. Click the other OK button.
19. Click the Authentication tab.
20. Select Custom Path from the Search: drop-down menu.
21. Click the Add button.
22. Select the newly added LDAPv3 configuration (that is, `/LDAPv3/server.example.com`).
23. Click the Add button.
24. Click the Apply button.

Restart DirectoryServices (lookupd) by entering **sudo SystemStarter restart DirectoryServices** in a terminal window.

This process completes the configuration, and the host should be able to authenticate to the configured Open Directory server.

Authentication

Open Directory's LDAP/NetInfo bridge adds the capability to require users to be authenticated when querying the directory server, although not by default. Configuring slapd (Mac OS X's LDAP server, which carries the physical incarnation of the LDAP/NetInfo bridge) to require authentication, is a part of the access control mechanisms, so we will discuss this aspect more in the next section ("Authorization"). Users can authenticate against any one of three different services: simple, SASL (Password Server), or Kerberos. Simple authentication sends the user's distinguished name and clear-text password to the server. Apple's SASL-based server supports all the SASL standard authentication methods (CRAM-MD5, crypt, Digest-MD5, and so on), as well as a few additional methods added by Apple (such as NTLM, AFP, WebDAV digest, and others).

It should be noted that although the server's default configuration allows anonymous connections, password hashes are not available as they are with NetInfo access.

Authorization

Open Directory's LDAP implementation provides its access control through standard OpenLDAP ACLs, although in its default configuration, NetInfo authorization rules (via the _writers* and trusted_networks properties) take precedence.

To disable NetInfo authorization semantics, you can download an updated version of mkslapdconf (the tool that builds an appropriate slapd.conf file for the LDAP/NetInfo Bridge) from PADL Software (ftp://ftp.padl.com/private/mkslapdconf-PR-2984309.tar.gz). After the file has been downloaded, decompress the tarball, back up the existing files, and copy the files from the package in place, as follows (as the root user):

```
bash-2.05a# tar xzf mkslapdconf-PR-2984309.tar.gz
bash-2.05a# cp /usr/sbin/mkslapdconf /usr/sbin/mkslapdconf.orig
bash-2.05a# cp usr/sbin/mkslapdconf /usr/sbin/mkslapdconf
bash-2.05a# cp /usr/share/man/man8/mkslapdconf.8 \
->/usr/share/man/man8/mkslapdconf.8.orig
bash-2.05a# cp usr/share/man/man8/mkslapdconf.8 \
->/usr/share/man/man8/mkslapdconf.8
```

After the files are in place, back up the existing configuration file, create a new configuration file without the NetInfo semantics, and restart the LDAP server.

```
bash-2.05a# cp /etc/openldap/slapd.conf /etc/openldap/slapd.conf.orig
bash-2.05a# mkslapdconf -a -s -n > /etc/openldap/slapd.conf
bash-2.05a# SystemStarter stop LDAP
Welcome to Macintosh.
Stopping LDAP server
Startup complete.
Hangup
bash-2.05a# SystemStarter start LDAP
Welcome to Macintosh.
Configuring network
Initializing network
Setting host identifier
kern.hostid: 3232235745 -> 3232235745
Starting port mapper
Starting NetInfo
Starting LDAP server
Startup complete.
Hangup
bash-2.05a#
```

Further access control is managed via standard OpenLDAP semantics in the slapd.conf file. A simple general form of an ACL is

```
access to <something>
            by <who1> <access-level1>
            by <who2> <access-level2>
            ...
            by <whoN> <access-levelN>
```

Here, <something> is the Distinguished Name (DN) to which access is being controlled, <who> is the user(s) or group(s) that the rule applies to, and <access-level> is the permissions to grant to the indicated <who>.

> **NOTE**
>
> A Distinguished Name is a unique identifier used in LDAP directories to define the location of an object in the directory hierarchy, much like a file path defines the location of a file in a filesystem.

For example, to implement the OpenLDAP Project's recommended base ACLs, one would add the following to the end of slapd.conf after disabling the NetInfo authorization rules (as indicated previously):

```
access to attr=userPassword
     by self write
     by anonymous auth

access to *
     by self write
     by users read
```

The first ACL allows users to modify their own passwords and anonymous users to use the passwords for authentication. The second ACL allows users to write to their own user entry and authenticated users read-only access to anything. This also implicitly denies access by unauthenticated (anonymous) users.

This is just a simple example of OpenLDAP's ACLs. The access control syntax provides for much more complex and fine-grained control, but it is too complicated to adequately describe and demonstrate here. As usual, we suggest reviewing the additional documentation indicated in Appendix C.

Data Privacy

Like authentication and authorization, Open Directory's OpenLDAP front-end improves greatly upon the security of directory data as it transits the network. It begins with the SASL-based authentication mechanism, which can keep user credentials from being sent in the clear. The other major improvement is the capability to encrypt all traffic using SSL.

Enabling SSL encryption is an easy process for both a Mac OS X Client and a machine running Mac OS X Server. The client side of things, which we already discussed in the previous subsection, consists of checking a box in Directory Access, saving changes, and restarting DirectoryServices. Mac OS X Server is only a little more involved because it involves requesting and installing an SSL certificate. The process to create a certificate for the server follows the general process described in more detail in the section of Chapter 6, "Internet Services," named "Enabling SSL with Apache."

The first step is to create the certificate request:

```
bash-2.05a$ sudo mkdir /etc/openldap/cert.req
bash-2.05a$ sudo openssl req -new -nodes -keyout /etc/openldap/ \
->cert.req/ldapreq.pem -out /etc/openldap/cert.req/ldapreq.pem
```

Of note here is the -nodes flag, which indicates that private keys be stored in clear text, which is a requirement for OpenLDAP. After a certificate has been granted, the public and private keys, as well as a copy of the CA's signing key, should be placed in a securable location.

```
bash-2.05a$ sudo mkdir /etc/openldap/ca.key
bash-2.05a$ sudo cp ca.key /etc/openldap/ca.key
bash-2.05a$ sudo mkdir /etc/openldap/ldappub.key
bash-2.05a$ sudo cp ldappub.key /etc/openldap/ldappub.key
bash-2.05a$ sudo mkdir /etc/openldap/ldappriv.key
bash-2.05a$ sudo cp ldappriv.key /etc/openldap/ldappriv.key
bash-2.05a$ sudo chmod 0700 /etc/openldap/ldappriv.key
bash-2.05a$ sudo chmod 0600 /etc/openldap/ldappriv.key/ldappriv.key
```

Next, lines must be added to slapd.conf configuration file. Add the following lines to /etc/openldap/slapd.conf:

```
TLSCACertificateFile /etc/openldap/ca.key/ca.key
TLSCertificateFile /etc/openldap/ldappub.key/ldappub.key
TLSCertificateKeyFile /etc/openldap/ldappriv.key/ldappriv.key
```

After the additions are made, restarting the LDAP server enables SSL/TLS encryption.

```
bash-2.05a$ sudo SystemStarter stop LDAP
bash-2.05a$ sudo SystemStarter start LDAP
```

Some clients other than Mac OS X will additionally need a copy of the CA's signing certificate.

More Fun with Directory Access

Mac OS X's capabilities extend beyond just integrating with Apple's own directory services, though. With the DirectoryServices framework and the Directory Access application, Apple provides a way to integrate Mac OS X with a host of different service locators and directory services. This section will briefly describe each of these components and some of the benefits and drawbacks of each of the eight default protocols.

AppleTalk

This is a non-configurable component of Directory Access that provides access to the most common legacy protocol on Macintosh networks: AppleTalk. This support for a legacy protocol is its chief upside. This component includes support for locating network resources as well as authenticating (encrypted or not) to the hosts containing those resources. AppleTalk is not a directory service in the typical sense, but a network protocol that provides built-in subprotocols for resource location. AppleTalk's drawbacks, other than not being a real directory service, are that it is a non-IP protocol (in its pure mode, although the component also supports Apple File Protocol over IP) and that it does not scale in large or busy networks.

BSD Configuration Files

Another non-directory component, this selection allows Mac OS X to utilize the standard UNIX files (such as /etc/master.passwd, /etc/hosts, and so on) for user authentication and resource naming and location. The advantages of using BSD configuration files are mostly compatibility as well as a measure of increased security over NetInfo because user credentials cannot be enumerated if the files are adequately protected. The downside is that the files are useful only to the box on which they reside, and thus there is no real way to leverage them as a single point of configuration or management. Also, the built-in tools will not write information to any of the configuration files, so it must be done manually, an occasionally harrowing process.

LDAPv2

This is the first of the configurable components and is also the first that can integrate Mac OS X with a real directory service. LDAPv2 is a commonly deployed (though older and less capable than LDAPv3) directory service within the enterprise. True to its nature, LDAPv2 is a scaleable directory capable of handling a large number of objects in a deep hierarchy. It has a number of drawbacks, however, especially when compared to its descendant LDAPv3. One of the bigger drawbacks is only indirectly security-related: LDAPv2 implementations often vary considerably from the established standard, making it occasionally difficult to integrate directories from different vendors. More security-related is LDAPv2's lack of support for modern authentication methods or transport encryption. Mac OS X cannot write information to an LDAPv2 directory.

Like most directory services, proper deployment of an LDAPv2-based directory requires adequate education and planning prior to implementation; this learning curve is often steep enough to cause some administrators to flee in terror. Apple's current documentation for integration with Microsoft's Active Directory (one of the more common directory services in active deployment) is via this component (more information on this is in Appendix C). Novell also has information on integrating Mac OS X with its eDirectory (NDS writ large) product, which also utilizes the LDAPv2 plug-in (see Figure 10.7).

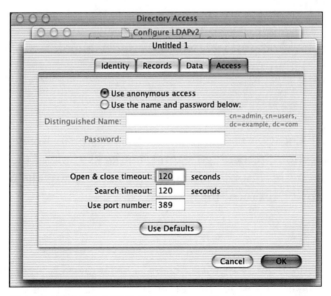

FIGURE 10.7   LDAPv2 has few configurable parameters.

LDAPv3

The LDAPv3 component is one of the great leaps forward for Mac OS X in business and enterprise networks. Like LDAPv2, it is a highly scalable directory service, but unlike LDAPv2, it supports both modern authentication mechanisms as well as transport encryption. Current LDAPv3 implementations also seem to be more reliant on the standards than are those of LDAPv2. LDAPv3 has few drawbacks, but it is currently less commonly used than LDAPv2. Beyond this, there also seem to be issues with different implementations of the transport layer security as well. Also, just like LDAPv2, there is a reasonably steep learning curve involved.

NetInfo

Yes, we have already talked about this beast, so a really brief overview is in order. The pluses: supported by a largish number of legacy NeXT and Mac OS X systems and is relatively easy to learn and deploy compared to other directory services. The minuses: no authentication mechanism for database queries, über simplistic access control, password hashes are available to any user unless an external authentication server is used, and no transport encryption.

Rendezvous

Like AppleTalk, Rendezvous is not really a directory service, but a resource and service location protocol, which we spoke about in much more detail in Chapter 9, "Enterprise Host Configuration".

SLP

SLP (Service Location Protocol) is like an ancestor to Rendezvous. It also is a service location protocol (go figure), but lacks some of the niftier features of its younger cousin. Prior to Mac OS X v10.2, SLP was the primary IP-based service discovery protocol for the Mac OS.

SMB

Our final entry from Directory Access is SMB (Server Message Block), probably one of the most ubiquitous protocols on business networks, due largely to the popularity of Microsoft's Windows operating system. Like AppleTalk, Rendezvous, and SLP, SMB is a resource discovery protocol (AppleTalk and

SMB are also network protocols). This component supports minimal configuration via the GUI (see Figure 10.8), allowing you to specify only the workgroup for the computer and the location of a WINS server (a type of name server). Additional parameters may be configured via configuration files. We spoke at more length about this protocol as Windows File Services (an open-source implementation of the protocol) in Chapter 7, "File Sharing."

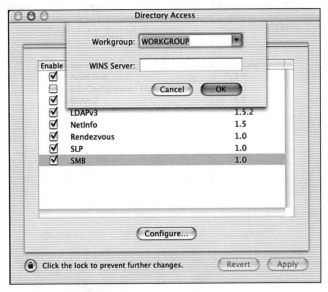

FIGURE 10.8   The SMB plug-in has limited configuration possibilities.

Summary

Not only does Mac OS X allow administrators to share information with other systems on their networks in unprecedented ways; now administrators can search for and access the data from those same systems as well. This chapter has described the security aspects of the core components of this new infrastructure, including NetInfo and Open Directory. Although NetInfo provides support for a protocol that has been with Mac OS X since it was still a strange port of the NeXT OS to the PowerPC platform, PADL Software's LDAP/NetInfo bridge extends this venerable directory to new heights and capabilities. Open Directory provides a wealth of authentication, authorization, and data privacy improvements that security-minded NetInfo administrators have long had on their wish lists.

This spirit of new horizons in capabilities, usability, and power are an ongoing theme in Apple's new operating system. We can only hope there is even more in store.

With the close of this chapter comes the close of our look at the security mechanisms in Mac OS X's core subsystems. The rest of the book focuses on auditing and forensics, which encompass day-to-day monitoring of logs, what to do when bad people happen to a system, and how to prepare for the eventuality before it happens.

PART V
AUDITING AND FORENSICS

## CHAPTER 11

AUDITING

"It depends on what the meaning of the word 'is' is."
—excerpts from Bill Clinton's Grand Jury testimony

No system or network service is 100% secure. Security is an ongoing process. All the precautions and steps taken during the installation and configuration of an operating system and its services are just the beginning. Routine audits of the system and services are critical. There are many ways to monitor the integrity of a system. An important part of auditing is the correct management and monitoring of log files. Sometimes, the default log settings for a system or service are not sufficient. Even then, log files are of no use unless they are routinely monitored.

The goal of this chapter is to point out the importance of logs, where Mac OS X stores log files, how to configure log settings for specific services, and how to set up automated monitoring of log files.

The Importance of Logging

The importance of logging and reading log files is often overlooked or ignored. Companies often invest a lot of time and money in intrusion detection systems and sometimes ignore log files. Permissions management, intrusion detection tools, and file integrity checkers are important aspects of managing host security. Although not as widely recognized, log files play just as much of a role in the management of host security. In fact, a lot of security tools rely on the analysis of generated log data.

Log files can be useful in tracking down break-ins, malicious activity, or abuse of the system. They also can be useful in bringing attention to critical circumstances that could lead to loss of data or services (such as a file system running out of disk space). Log files are sometimes the only way for applications or services to plead for help, so to speak. They can contain an audit trail of malicious activity. They can expose patterns of abuse or neglect. A professional can use log files to detect attack signatures and they allow an administrator to better combat intrusions or at least detect them.

Another thing to remember is that the configuration of logs is only the first step. All the logging in the world will not do any good if the log files are not monitored, or analyzed. It is not uncommon for logs to be cluttered with information that is not important. This is sometimes referred to as *noise*. There are tools that exist that can weed through this noise and highlight the areas of interest. One such tool is swatch, which we will discuss later in this chapter.

Logging is important, but it is not a complete way of detecting an attack. It is not uncommon for an attacker to alter the contents of log files in an attempt to cover up his or her tracks. In Chapter 12, "Forensics," we will discuss additional ways to audit the integrity of a Mac OS X host.

General Considerations

Before we address any logging configuration issues, there are some important concepts related to logging in general that we would like to highlight.

The Importance of Time

We recommend making use of a network time server for the consistency and accuracy of timestamps. Timestamps are an important element in log files.

From a security perspective, it can be critical to know the exact time an event occurred. Correlating a log entry to a real world event can be made easier with accurate timestamps. This becomes even more important in a networked environment. The correlation of log data across multiple computers that do not share a common concept of time can get very ugly. Using log data to support other log data on an unrelated network is more convincing with the use of a common time source. Log files also can be used in a legal setting where the importance of timestamp accuracy is obvious.

To enable NTP on Mac OS X, use System Preferences.app. Under the Date & Time pane, select the Network Time tab (see Figure 11.1). Be sure the network time server check box is selected and enter a hostname that provides the NTP time synchronization service.

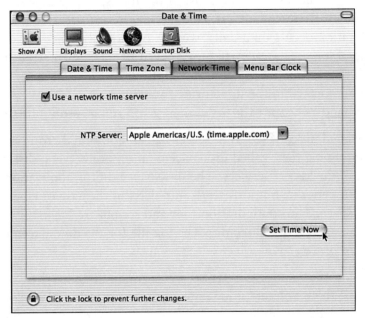

FIGURE 11.1 Enabling network time synchronization on Mac OS X.

> **NOTE**
>
> Besides using network time synchronization, we recommend using a common time zone for servers or machines that run critical services—for example, web, mail, and DNS servers. This is not necessarily as important for workstations. At a previous job, we all shared an office with the network engineer who decided to set all core servers to GMT (UTC) time. This made certain aspects of administration (including log management) easier. This engineer even set his wristwatch to GMT, which at times was the source of great confusion for him and entertainment for the rest of us.

Permissions and Access

Log files often contain information about a system (possibly multiple systems) that normal users have no business looking at. Some of the log files on Mac OS X are readable only by root or the admin group. However, many are readable by any user on the system. The Apache log files are world readable files. Most of the files under /Library/Logs/ are world readable. These log files should be readable only by root or admin users. Throughout this chapter, we will remind you of specific examples where log file permissions should be adjusted.

Log Rotation

Many of the system log files on Mac OS X are automatically rotated; this includes Apache log files and most of the files specified in syslog.conf. Rotating a log file involves renaming it, compressing it, and creating a new (empty) log file. Rotation occurs on a daily, weekly, or monthly schedule, depending on the volume of log data anticipated for a given file. These rotations are implemented as shell scripts, run by the periodic application /usr/sbin/periodic. The scripts are located in the directories /etc/periodic/daily, /etc/periodic/weekly, and /etc/periodic/monthly and run as cron jobs (see Table 11.1).

On a related note, Mac OS X Server has an additional cron-based facility for rotating log files, called diskspacemonitor. For servers, disk space issues can mean the loss of services. The diskspacemonitor application runs scripts similar to periodic, but also sends out alerts in the case of emergencies related to disk space. The configuration files and scripts are located in the /etc/diskspacemonitor/ directory. The log file for the diskspacemonitor application is /var/log/diskspacemonitor.log.

By default, the rotation scripts keep at most eight archives of any log file. Due to the high volume of log entries, the main syslog file is rotated daily. Thus, archived system.log files are stored for a week, and then deleted. For workstations, this is usually sufficient. However, for servers or systems running critical services, it is a good idea to set up a system for permanent storage of these archives.

TABLE 11.1 Mac OS X Default Log Rotation Schedule

FILE	SCHEDULE
/var/log/system.log	Daily
/var/log/httpd/access_log	Daily
/var/log/httpd/error_log	Daily

FILE	SCHEDULE
/var/log/ftp.log	Weekly
/var/log/lookupd.log	Weekly
/var/log/lpr.log	Weekly
/var/log/mail.log	Weekly
/var/log/netinfo.log	Weekly
/var/log/wtmp	Monthly

Log Archives and Secure Storage

Although many log files on Mac OS X are periodically rotated, the archives are eventually deleted after a certain amount of time has passed. How long you decide to maintain log data may depend on the sensitive nature of the services run, involved security policies, and administrative politics. Permanently storing log archives on optical read-only media allows for subsequent audits and freedom from tampering.

Log archives can contain sensitive information about systems, services, user activities, and networks. It is a good idea to encrypt any such files before storing them on read-only media. In the unfortunate event that this media is lost or stolen, there is little risk of unauthorized access to the contents of the log data.

With Mac OS X, it is easy to archive data to DVD or CD. Disk Copy.app can be used to create AES encrypted disk images (see Chapter 3, "Mac OS X Client General Security Practices"). Or, if your security policy has strict requirements, PGP or GnuPG also can be used for file encryption.

Logging Options and Configuration

There are many different applications and services that generate log files on Mac OS X. Most of these logs are configured in different ways, and reside in various places on the file system. This section discusses the most important of these logs, where they are located, and issues related to their configuration.

Syslog

Syslog is the main system message logger common on many UNIX platforms. Syslog is started automatically as part of the Mac OS X startup sequence through the startup item `/System/Library/StartupItems/SystemLog`. It runs as a daemon (a process that runs in the background) and manages a number of log files. The syslog daemon (syslogd) handles log messages from a variety of applications or services. When syslog receives a log message, it does one of the following with the message:

- Appends it to a specific file
- Forwards it to a syslog daemon on a different host
- Outputs it to `/dev/console`
- Outputs it to a set of users

Each syslog message has a level and a facility. The level denotes the importance, or severity, of the message. The facility is related to the message origin.

On startup, the syslog daemon reads its configuration from the file `/etc/syslog.conf`. This configuration states how the syslog daemon should handle any given message based on the message facility and level. The syntax for the syslog configuration file is relatively simple, and there is nothing peculiar about it from other UNIX syslog configurations. The man page for syslog.conf lists the levels and facilities supported on Mac OS X.

The default syslog configuration on Mac OS X places most of the received log messages in the file `/var/log/system.log`. This is the main syslog file. Messages related to ftp, mail, netinfo, lpr, and authorization are logged to separate files.

Changes to the syslog.conf file will not take effect until the syslog daemon is restarted. You can restart syslog by sending a hangup signal (`kill -HUP`) to the syslogd process id, or by using its startup item script:

```
sudo /System/Library/StartupItems/SystemLog/SystemLog restart
```

On Mac OS X, the system.log file is filled with messages of disparate origin. Important log entries, such as `sudo` commands, are mixed with messages that are not so important. It can be helpful to isolate some of the more critical events into separate files. When creating new syslog files, remember to adjust the rotation scripts accordingly. There are many adjustments that could be made to the default syslog configuration on Mac OS X. The following few suggestions are catered more toward security administration.

ACCURACY OF MAN PAGES

One thing Mac OS X is not known for is the accuracy of its man pages. At the time of this writing, the man pages for syslog, syslogd, and syslog.conf are not entirely accurate with respect to supported syslog facilities (some systems may not have man pages for syslogd or syslog.conf installed). Table 11.2 lists the facilities supported by the Mac OS X syslog daemon.

TABLE 11.2 Supported Syslog Facilities

Facility Name	Description
kern	Kernel messages
user	User-level messages
mail	Mail system
daemon	System daemons
auth	Security and authorization
authpriv	Private security and authorization
syslog	Messages generated by syslogd
lpr	Line printer
news	News system
uucp	uucp system
cron	cron daemon
ftp	ftp daemon
netinfo	NetInfo messages
remoteauth	Remote authentication/authorization
local0	Reserved for local use
local1	Reserved for local use
local2	Reserved for local use
local3	Reserved for local use
local4	Reserved for local use
local5	Reserved for local use
local6	Reserved for local use
local7	Reserved for local use

Isolating SSH Messages

To have syslog direct messages from the SSH server (sshd) into a separate file, modify (as root) the SSH server config file /etc/sshd_config so that the syslog settings are as follows:

```
SyslogFacility LOCAL0
LogLevel INFO
```

Next, edit /etc/syslog.conf (as root) and add a rule to direct messages from
local0.info into a new file:

```
local0.*                    /var/log/sshd.log
```

Finally, create the log file, set permissions, and restart the syslog daemon and
SSH server:

```
sudo touch /var/log/sshd.log
sudo chmod 600 /var/log/sshd.log
sudo /System/Library/StartupItems/SystemLog/SystemLog restart
sudo /System/Library/StartupItems/SSH/SSH restart
```

Isolating sudo Messages

By default, the sudo command on Mac OS X logs syslog messages to local2.
To have all such messages placed in a single file, adjust the syslog.conf file by
adding the line:

```
local2.*                    /var/log/sudo.log
```

Create the log file, set permissions, and restart the syslog daemon:

```
sudo touch /var/log/sudo.log
sudo chmod 600 /var/log/sudo.log
sudo /System/Library/StartupItems/SystemLog/SystemLog restart
```

Isolating xinetd Server Messages

The xinetd process is responsible for starting a number of Internet services,
such as ftp and telnet. To place xinetd server–related messages in a separate
file, adjust the xinetd configuration in /etc/xinetd.conf so that the
log_type parameter of the defaults section reads:

```
log_type                = SYSLOG local3
```

The default configuration files for all xinetd services use the default log_type
specified in this file. Next, adjust the syslog.conf file to have this facility
directed to a new file:

```
Local3.*                    /var/log/xinetd.log
```

Create the log file, set permissions, and restart the syslog daemon:

```
sudo touch /var/log/xinetd.log
sudo chmod 600 /var/log/xinetd.log
sudo /System/Library/StartupItems/SystemLog/SystemLog restart
```

Logging Network Services

With Mac OS X and Mac OS X Server it is relatively easy to deploy a variety of network services, many of which are for file sharing. This includes Apple File Services (AFP), Windows file sharing (SMB/CIFS), Network File System (NFS), and the Apache web server to name a few. Each of these services comes with its own degree of risk. However, the proper configuration and regular monitoring of log files goes a long way toward ensuring the integrity of these network services.

AFS

Logs related to the Apple File Service are located in the /Library/ Logs/AppleFileService/ directory. There is an access log (AppleFileServiceAccess.log) and an error log (AppleFileServiceError.log). The AppleFileService application handles the rotation of its own log files.

On Mac OS X Server, log settings for this service can be configured through the Server Settings.app, under File & Print, the Logging tab(see Figure 11.2).

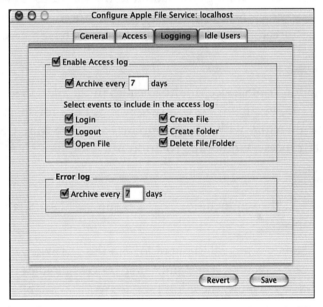

FIGURE 11.2 Mac OS X Server Log Configuration for Apple File service.

On Mac OS X, AFS access logging is disabled by default. Unlike Mac OS X Server, there is no graphical configuration tool for the logging configuration. However, log rotation and settings can all be configured through NetInfo

Manager.app. Log settings for AFS can be found under the local NetInfo domain, at `/config/AppleFileServer`. To enable the access log, set the `activity_log` key value to 1. The rotation schedule (in days) can be set with the keys `activity_log_time`, and `error_log_time`. By default, all events are logged. To change this, edit the value for the `logging_attributes` key.

By default, all these logs are world readable. It is recommended that their permissions be adjusted accordingly:

```
chmod o-r /Library/Logs/AppleFileService/*.log
```

FTP

Logs for the ftp service are handled by syslog and are rotated by periodic scripts. The ftp log file is `/var/log/ftp.log`. On Mac OS X Server, the ftp transfer log is located in the file `/Library/Logs/FTP.transfer.log`. By default, these files are readable only by root and the admin group.

Windows File Sharing (SMB/CIFS)

Mac OS X Server stores logs for samba in the file `/Library/Logs/WindowsServices/`. On Mac OS X, logs are stored in the directory `/var/log/samba/` directory. By default, both locations have world readable files.

Print Services

The log file for PrintServiceMonitor resides in the file `/Library/Logs/PrintService/PrintService.server.log`. Logs for shared printers appear in the same directory with an appropriate name. On Mac OS X Server, the print server process handles the rotation of its log files.

Mail Services

On Mac OS X, the sendmail log is `/var/log/mail.log`, and rotated by periodic scripts.

Mac OS X Server stores all the mail logs in the `/Library/Logs/MailService/` directory. The MailServer process handles the rotation of its own log files. By default, these log files are world readable.

Apache

Apache web server logs are located, by default configuration, in the `/var/log/httpd/` directory. There is an access log (`access_log`) and an error log (`error_log`). Logging is configured by editing the apache configuration files located in the `/etc/httpd/` directory. On Mac OS X Server, the directory

`/Library/Logs/WebServer/` contains hard links to the log files in
`/var/log/httpd/`. All these files are world readable.

DNS

The DNS server (bind) reads its configuration from the file `/etc/named.conf`.
Logging for this service is not configurable in the GUI. The Server Settings.app
only provides the capability to start and stop `named`. Administrators are
expected to understand how to configure the named.conf file directly. By
default, the named.conf file on Mac OS X Server contains no `logging{}`
section, which means `named` defaults to sending messages to syslog. These log
messages all begin with `named`. The named.conf file can be adjusted to send
messages to a specific syslog facility, or to a specific file. See the man page for
named.conf for details.

DHCP and SLP

DHCP and SLP services log all their messages to `/var/log/system.log`. Log
settings for the DHCP server can be configured through the Server Settings.app.
Log messages generated by the DHCP server begin with `bootpd`.

Log settings for the SLP Directory Agent also can be configured through the
Server Settings.app. All log messages from this service begin with `slpd`.

QuickTime Streaming Server

The QuickTime streaming server has an access log and an error log. The log
files, as well as the configuration information for this server, are all stored
under the directory `/Library/QuickTimeStreaming`. The log files are stored
in the Logs subdirectory. The application `/Applications/QuickTime
Streaming Server.app` can be used to adjust the log settings. By default,
all these files are world readable.

Software Update

Every update installed through the Software Update application is logged
to the file `/Library/Logs/Software Update.log`. The contents of this file
also can be viewed through the Software Update pane of the System Preferences
application. This log contains a timestamp, update or patch name, and any
version information.

DirectoryService

Logs related to the Open Directory server can be found in `/Library/Logs/
DirectoryService` on Mac OS X and Mac OS X Server. There is an access

log (`DirectoryService.server.log`) and an error log
(`DirectoryService.error.log`). In addition, the ServerStatus.app on Mac
OS X Server can be used to view the logs for various directory services such as
LDAP, NetInfo, and the Password Server. To view these logs, select the
Directory Servers option and choose the Logs tab (see Figure 11.3). The combo
box at the bottom of the dialog can be used to select which log file to view.

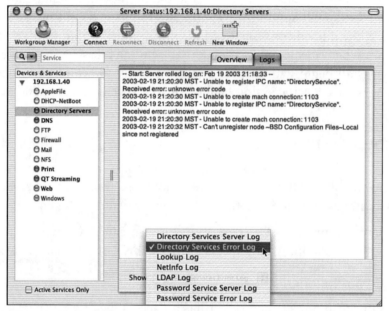

FIGURE 11.3   Viewing Directory Service logs from ServerStatus.app.

Watchdog

Watchdog is a process that serves to monitor critical services and relaunch
them if necessary on Mac OS X Server. The log file for the watchdog
process is found in the file `/Library/Logs/watchdog.event.log`. To
enable the Watchdog process, the following line should appear in the
`/etc/hostconfig` file:

```
WATCHDOGTIMER=-YES-
```

CrashReporter

CrashReporter logs detailed debugging information about applications when
they crash. Specifically, this log contains the date and time of the crash, the
name of the command, process ID of the application instance, error codes and

their meanings, backtrace information for each thread, and detailed register information. The following is an example of a crash log from Mail.app:

```
Date/Time:   2002-10-31 23:16:33 -0700
OS Version:  10.2.1 (Build 6D52)
Host:        trinity.local.

Command:     Mail
PID:         399

Exception:   EXC_BAD_ACCESS (0x0001)
Codes:       KERN_INVALID_ADDRESS (0x0001) at 0x74446972

Thread 0 Crashed:
 #0    0x9068ba74 in objc_msgSend
 #1    0x00027ba0 in 0x27ba0
 #2    0x907f3378 in -[NSConcreteNotification dealloc]
 #3    0x9080c0d8 in _delayedPerformCleanup
 #4    0x90162ac4 in CFRunLoopTimerInvalidate
 #5    0x901638dc in _CFRunLoopDoTimer
 #6    0x901493e0 in _CFRunLoopRun
 #7    0x9018157c in CFRunLoopRunSpecific
 #8    0x92ba34cc in RunCurrentEventLoopInMode
 #9    0x92bb326c in ReceiveNextEventCommon
 #10   0x92bda280 in BlockUntilNextEventMatchingListInMode
 #11   0x93082184 in _DPSNextEvent
 #13   0x930ca500 in -[NSApplication run]
 #14   0x930d2598 in NSApplicationMain
 #15   0x000045a4 in 0x45a4
 #16   0x00004424 in 0x4424

Thread 1:
 #0    0x9000600c in wait4
 #1    0x908317c8 in _waitForTermination
 #2    0x90021428 in _pthread_body

PPC Thread State:
  srr0: 0x9068ba74 srr1: 0x0000f030                  vrsave: 0x00000000
   xer: 0x00000000   lr: 0x00027ba0  ctr: 0x9068ba3c     mq: 0x00000000
    r0: 0x00027ba0   r1: 0xbfffedd0   r2: 0x44004280     r3: 0x018ad7b0
    r4: 0x906c6cdc   r5: 0x9069ce64   r6: 0x00000000     r7: 0x0166c720
    r8: 0x00000000   r9: 0x0001a608  r10: 0x74446972    r11: 0x201a91d4
   r12: 0x000800d8  r13: 0x00000000  r14: 0x00000000    r15: 0x00000001
   r16: 0x00000000  r17: 0x00000000  r18: 0x22004420    r19: 0x00000000
   r20: 0x00000000  r21: 0x00000000  r22: 0x001011a0    r23: 0x001012a8
   r24: 0x01665bf0  r25: 0xa0132894  r26: 0xa0132894    r27: 0x016a2678
```

CrashReporter logs appeal most to developers, but they can also be useful to administrators. Applications that are continually crashing can be an indication of something else that is wrong, misuse, abuse, or malicious intent. At the very least, knowing the timestamp, username, and the name of the application that crashed can be a good start to tracking down a problem.

To enable the system CrashReporter, the following line should appear in the /etc/hostconfig file:

```
CRASHREPORTER=-YES-
```

When a program (run as root) crashes, the log is stored in the directory /Library/Logs/CrashReporter. All crash logs for an application are stored in the same file. Crash logs, by default, are readable by any user on the system. This is true even of crash files generated by root. One way to prevent normal users from reading these files is to remove "others" permissions from the directory, as shown here:

```
sudo chmod o-rwx /Library/Logs/CrashReporter/
```

CrashReporter also can be enabled and disabled on a per-user basis. Normal users can enable CrashReporter through the Console.app. Under the main application menu choose Preferences, and select the Crashes tab as shown in Figure 11.4. When Automatically Display Crash Logs is enabled, the crash log is opened using Console.app. A user's crash logs are stored in the directory, ~/Library/Logs/CrashReporter.

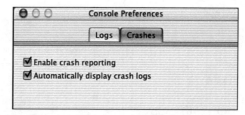

FIGURE 11.4   Enabling crash dumps with Console.app.

Monitoring Logs

Even the most verbose logging of an application or service is of no help if the logs are not eventually read and analyzed. Effective log analysis and monitoring can save you time, money, and reduce the chances of critical log messages being lost in the noise. The analysis of log data can be broken down into different stages, some of which may not apply in your situation. Logs can be monitored in real time for specific events or contexts. Specific log files can be reviewed by administrators for suspicious activities, or for the verification of expected events. Logs can be organized and archived for reference, correlation with other logs, or for future audits.

Mac OS X presents administrators with many different types of log messages and formats. Some are important, some not. The fundamental intent of the monitoring process can vary as well—for example, troubleshooting a hardware problem versus watching for denial-of-service attacks on your web server.

It is obvious from the first part of this chapter that Mac OS X does not offer any integrated log analysis facilities. Log files come in many different formats, are configured in disparate ways, and are scattered all over the file system. This is not uncommon, and it is not surprising that log analysis is often neglected under such circumstances.

Our goal in this section is to present a practical solution to log monitoring and notification on Mac OS X using swatch so that critical log events are less likely to be ignored. We will start by going over some basic tools that can be used to analyze log files. There are many tools designed to aid in the monitoring and analysis of log data. In addition, there are many books and online resources that address the subject in detail. A good online source for information and tools related to log analysis is www.loganalysis.org administered by Tina Bird and Marcus Ranum. See Appendix C, "Further Reading," for more suggestions related to log analysis.

The Basics

The intentions behind the analysis or monitoring of log data can vary significantly. However, there are some common applications and techniques that can be useful regardless.

Routine Audits

Log analysis and audits, however you define and structure them, should be performed on a regular basis. Eventually, the analysis of log data will expose something that requires immediate action or response. The configuration of scripts and monitoring tools should support the procedures for dealing with such events as defined in your security policy.

It can be useful to maintain a repository of tools, scripts, and reference material related to log analysis and known attack signatures.

Keep a reference of what log files are maintained and where they are located. Table 11.3 later in this chapter lists the locations of important log files on Mac OS X.

Command Line Tools

Some simple tools that can be used to dissect log files are the common UNIX `tail`, `cat`, and `grep` commands.

These programs can be used to quickly locate specific log messages, or to watch incoming log entries. For example, to see the last 10 lines in the main syslog file, use this line:

```
tail /var/log/system.log
```

To continually view new log events as they are appended to the file use the -f flag, use this:

```
tail -f /var/log/system.log
```

To see all the entries in the current system.log related to the lookupd daemon:

```
cat /var/log/system.log | grep lookupd
```

To count the raw number of requests in the current web server log from a specific host or IP address:

```
cat /var/log/httpd/access.log | grep -c <ip address>
```

Console messages can be very useful when troubleshooting, or for developers debugging applications. Mac OS X also comes with a graphical console application, `/Applications/Utilities/Console.app`. However, at the time of this writing it does not provide much in the way of monitoring. Console messages shown in this application reside in the file `/var/tmp/console.log`.

There also are some freeware tools available that display the `tail` output of any log file as part of the desktop background. One tool that works well is GeekTool (`http://sourceforge.net/projects/geektool/`) shown in Figure 11.5.

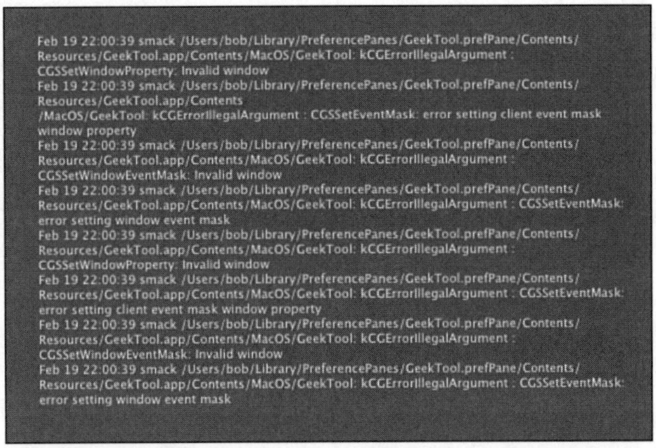

FIGURE 11.5   GeekTool provides quick reference to `/var/log/system.log`.

Automated Monitoring and Notification with swatch

Using `tail` to monitor log files for security related events is not only boring, it is not always practical. Automated monitoring and notification has obvious advantages.

First, it is automated. When known attack signatures are considered, computers can be quite effective in locating specific instances of them. Humans also are more prone to mistakes, and varied perceptions that computers are immune to.

The other major advantage is real time notification. There are some events that might warrant immediate attention. Although sometimes annoying, real time notification can save time, money, and possibly prevent intrusions.

swatch (Simple WATCHdog) is an effective tool for analyzing or monitoring all types of log files. It can be used to analyze an entire file, or to `tail` a file and filter the output. swatch uses a configuration file that consists of a list of patterns (triggers), and actions to perform when a pattern match occurs. An action can be echoing the log to the terminal, sending a bell to the terminal, executing a command, sending email to an administrator containing the log message, piping the log message to a command, or writing the log message to a local user. Actions can be throttled so that multiple occurrences of the same log message do not overload the action specified.

For our purposes here, we will cover installing swatch on Mac OS X and the configuration of some basic triggers for monitoring the system.log file. To build swatch as described in the next section, the Apple Developer Tools need to be installed.

Installing swatch

swatch requires four Perl modules that are not part of the default Perl installation on Mac OS X. Upgrading Perl with CPAN is relatively painless. Instructions for this can be found on Apple's developer site (`http://developer.apple.com/internet/macosx/perl.html`). The four additional Perl modules needed include:

```
Date::Calc
Date::Parse
File::Tail
Time::HiRes
```

First, download the latest swatch source. At the time of this writing the latest version of swatch is 3.0.4.

```
curl http://www.oit.ucsb.edu/~eta/swatch/swatch-3.0.4.tar.gz > \
->swatch-3.0.4.tar.gz
```

The MD5 checksum for the source is posted on the developer web site. Additional verification can be performed using knowngoods.org.

```
bash-2.05a$ openssl md5 swatch-3.0.4.tar.gz
MD5(swatch-3.0.4.tar.gz)= ce290dd2cae6ce834f59e24d97a30d3b
bash-2.05a$ curl https://www.knowngoods.org/search.php\?release= \
->swatch-3.0.4.tar.gz\&item=md5
ce290dd2cae6ce834f59e24d97a30d3b
```

Unpack the source with the following command:

```
tar xvfz swatch-3.0.4.tar.gz
```

To build and install swatch, do the following:

```
perl Makefile.pl
make
make test
sudo make install
```

Finally, change the permissions on the installed swatch scripts so that only root can execute them.

```
sudo chmod 500 /usr/bin/swatch
sudo chmod 500 /usr/bin/swatch_oldrc2newrc
```

swatch Configuration

There are many steps used to set up swatch to monitor a log file. We will go through the process of setting up a swatch configuration file for the main syslog file and look for a few specific events, as examples. Polishing the patterns and actions is something that takes a lot of time and testing.

First, it needs to be decided which events swatch needs to watch out for. This can be the hardest part of the configuration process. What is logged will vary widely with the nature of system, what users have access, what applications or services are deployed, and so on. It helps to generate an example of such events so that the pattern matching can be implemented correctly. Often this isn't possible on a production machine. In that case, it might be necessary to set up a test box that you can abuse and take note of the specific log messages you will be looking for.

Next, a configuration file needs to be created. With each trigger, an action must be specified. Some rules might warrant more intrusive types of notification. For example, email might not be sufficient if the DNS server crashes and fails to restart. You might have to have swatch execute a custom script that pages an administrator. You need to decide the target of an action. For example, if the action is email, it needs to be decided where that email will be sent.

Also, because swatch basically tails a file, it has to be restarted every time that log file is rotated. Fortunately, the command line argument `--restart-time` can be used to cause the swatch process to restart and `tail` the new file. Thus, for every configuration file created, you must take into consideration the rotation schedule of that log file.

For this example, we will produce a swatch configuration that will look for three types of events:

- System reboot
- `sudo` failures
- `ssh` login failures

When a system reboots, a message similar to the following is sent to syslog:

```
Jan 18 00:02:09 localhost reboot: rebooted by root
```

Thus, we could create the following trigger to send mail to an administrator each time log event is sent to syslog:

```
watchfor /reboot/
    echo=normal
    mail=admin@example.com,subject=----[ system reboot ]----
```

Following the same logic, we can create the following two triggers to detect sudo password failures and failed ssh login attempts.

```
watchfor /sudo*incorrect password/
    echo=normal
    mail=admin@example.com,subject=----[ sudo: denied access ]----

watchfor /sshd*Failed password/
    echo=normal
    mail=admin@example.com,subject=----[ ssh: login failure ]----
```

Because the default log rotation schedule for system.log on Mac OS X is 3:15 a.m., this instance of swatch should be started with a command line option such as `--restart-time=03:16`.

ENABLING SENDMAIL ON MAC OS X CLIENT

In this chapter (and others), we present some solutions that assume sendmail is running and can be used. By default, the sendmail process is not enabled on Mac OS X Client. However, enabling sendmail is relatively easy.

First, enable sendmail to start up automatically upon boot by editing (as root) the `/etc/hostconfig` file and changing the MAILSERVER line so that it reads:

```
MAILSERVER=-YES-
```

Next, edit the sendmail configuration file `/etc/mail/sendmail.cf` and add the following line:

```
DontBlameSendmail=GroupWritableDirPathSafe
```

This will inform sendmail to ignore certain constraints placed on the permissions of sendmail files. If you are not comfortable enabling this option, another solution is to change the permissions on the `/etc` and `/etc/mail` directory to deny group write privileges as follows:

```
bash-2.05a$ sudo chmod go-w /etc /etc/mail
```

Finally, to kick off the sendmail process, run the startup item script:

```
/System/Library/StartupItems/Sendmail/Sendmail start
```

To facilitate the management of swatch, we recommend creating a directory to store all these configuration files, for example, /etc/swatch/. It also makes sense to create a shell script that can be used to launch each instance of swatch with the correct arguments. This also makes it easy to launch swatch monitors during the boot process. Also, running swatch as root is not recommended. One solution is to create a swatch user and add that user to a group that has read access to each of the log files.

Creating triggers is a trial and error process. It is probably a good idea to dedicate a machine to be used to abuse and apply attacks to so that the effects can be recorded and used to create effective swatch triggers.

Log Location Reference

Table 11.3 shows log file locations for Mac OS X.

TABLE 11.3   Log File Locations for Mac OS X

APPLICATION OR SERVICE	LOCATION
AFS	/Library/Logs/AppleFileService/
Windows File Sharing (SMB/CIFS)	/var/log/samba/
NFS	/var/log/system.log
Apache	/var/log/httpd/
Firewall (ipfw)	/var/log/system.log
Directory Service	/Library/Logs/DirectoryService/
DHCP	/var/log/system.log
DNS	/var/log/system.log
SLP	/var/log/system.log
Software Update	/Library/Logs/Software Update.log
Kernel Panic	/Library/Logs/panic.log
Application Crash Logs	/Library/Logs/CrashReporter/
syslog	/var/log/system.log
ppp	/var/log/system.log
ftp	/var/log/ftp.log
lookupd	/var/log/lookupd.log

continues

TABLE 11.3 Continued

APPLICATION OR SERVICE	LOCATION
netinfo	/var/log/netinfo.log
lpr	/var/log/lpr.log
sendmail	/var/log/mail.log
cups	/var/log/cups/
lastlog	/var/log/lastlog
utmp	/var/log/utmp
wtmp	/var/log/wtmp

Table 11.4 shows log file locations for Mac OS X Server.

TABLE 11.4 Log File Locations for Mac OS X Server

APPLICATION OR SERVICE	LOCATION
AFS	/Library/Logs/AppleFileService/
Windows File Sharing (SMB/CIFS)	/Library/Logs/WindowsServices/
NFS	/var/log/system.log
Apache	/var/log/httpd/
Firewall (ipfw)	/var/log/system.log
Directory Service	/Library/Logs/DirectoryService/
Password Server	/Library/Logs/PasswordService/
LDAP Server (slapd)	/var/tmp/console.log
ServerSettings Daemon	/Library/Logs/serversettingsd.*.log
Print Services	/Library/Logs/PrintService/
Mail Services	/Library/Logs/MailService/
QuickTime Streaming Server	/Library/QuickTimeStreaming/Logs/
Watchdog Timer	/Library/Logs/watchdog.event.log
DHCP	/var/log/system.log
DNS	/var/log/system.log
SLP	/var/log/system.log
Software Update	/Library/Logs/Software Update.log
Kernel Panic	/Library/Logs/panic.log
Application Crash Logs	/Library/Logs/CrashReporter/
syslog	/var/log/system.log

APPLICATION OR SERVICE	LOCATION
ppp	`/var/log/system.log`
ftp	`/var/log/ftp.log`
lookupd	`/var/log/lookupd.log`
netinfo	`/var/log/netinfo.log`
lpr	`/var/log/lpr.log`
sendmail	`/var/log/mail.log`
cups	`/var/log/cups/`
lastlog	`/var/log/lastlog`
utmp	`/var/log/utmp`
wtmp	`/var/log/wtmp`

Summary

Logging is an important, and often overlooked, way to audit the integrity of a host. Log files are sometimes ignored altogether or critical entries missed because of a flawed auditing process. Log monitoring applications such as swatch can be used to improve the accuracy of audits and increase the response time needed for certain detected events. Mac OS X contains many services each with their own log files; Mac OS X Server contains even more. These log files are of little use if they are not regularly monitored. Administrators and users alike should know where critical log files are located, and actually monitor them. Tables 11.3 and 11.4 provide a good reference for the locations of log files on Mac OS X and Mac OS X Server.

CHAPTER 12

FORENSICS

"Only strong characters can resist the temptation of superficial analysis."
—Albert Einstein

Sometimes logging isn't enough; it can fail, or it can be incomplete, or it can be compromised. Sometimes it is simply too late by the time someone reads the log. And other times bad things just happen. That is where forensics comes in, giving users the capability to take snapshots of the forest before the tree falls, as well as allowing them to search the underbrush for fallen trees.

In this chapter we give you an overview of forensics and show how some open source tools can be used to monitor filesystem integrity and the options available for analyzing hard disk data in a postmortem situation.

An Overview of Computer Forensics

Computer forensics is a process that includes isolating, acquiring, preserving, documenting, and analyzing computer data for use as evidence. However, the analysis of a system can be conducted for various reasons with different goals in mind; the following are some examples:

- Investigation of a computer-related crime, often to collect needed legal evidence.
- Damage assessment after a break-in or exploit.
- Analysis of the specifics of system weakness to prevent future break-ins.
- Data recovery or evidence gathering from a corporate asset used by a naughty employee.

As computers continue to become more entangled in our daily activities, and more of our information is stored in bits than on paper, it should be no surprise that crimes involving computers will also increase over time. Computers are used as vehicles for crime and are often themselves the targets of crime.

Computer forensics encompasses more than just the actual process of analyzing any acquired data. There is a great deal of emphasis on, and concern over, the issues involved with each step of the process, from the initial acquisition to the final documentation and findings report. Although the circumstances surrounding an analysis will vary, with potentially different goals in mind, there are some core aspects common to any forensic analysis of computer data; digital evidence is first acquired, and then analyzed.

Acquisition

Computer forensics begins with discovery, realization, and a seizure of some kind. However, the initial set of actions taken in a forensic analysis case will vary depending on the persons involved, any defined incident response procedures, and usually on any learned facts leading up to the discovery. The decisions made at the onset of any incident can have a dramatic effect on the final results of a forensics examination.

First, prepare to document as much as possible. Maintain a log that includes details about where the data is stored, for what periods of time, and who has access to it. Such a log is known as part of the chain of custody. If the results of the analysis find their way into a legal setting, complete documentation in this manner will go a long way toward providing solid and convincing evidence for a case. Take note of *everything* about the environment, as trivial as it may seem. At the time, it may seem silly to document certain elements of the environment (such as the condition of the exterior case) but the goal is not to write flowing prose, it is to take multiple snapshots of the evidence or crime scene; part of those snapshots includes detailed descriptions of the environment. Who is to say that any one piece of information is more important than another before any real analysis is performed? Even the most experienced of examiners cannot possibly know what relevance the analysis may suggest concerning collected information. Keep an open mind at all times.

The main goal of the acquisition process is to capture and preserve the entire state of the system and to avoid any loss or tampering of data. This includes all contents of the hard disk(s) as well as the resident memory, state of the running kernel, network, application processes, and various aspects of the operating system. However, this is easier said than done if the system in question is up and running and providing a critical service.

Whether or not to shut down a system, and how, is often a topic of debate. Should the system be powered down? Should it be removed from the network? Obviously, if the system in question is a threat to other machines on the network, it should be isolated. However, sometimes the extent of any threat is not known. In the event that the system needs to be shut down, halt the operating system in the normal fashion but do not allow it to reboot; there may be self-destruct features in place designed to cover an intruder's tracks. The immediate loss of power stops the operating system in its tracks; however, it also can cause damage to the hardware, result in the loss of useful data, and possibly destroy any evidence residing in the running state of the system. Evidence exists in many forms and the wrong decision here can potentially lead to the loss of critical evidence. Essentially, there is no right answer to this problem; it boils down to one's best judgment based on the facts at hand, and the circumstances of the situation. In any case, document everything; you can always discard irrelevant information later.

The act of acquiring data usually involves a byte-by-byte duplication of any hard disks. There are commercial products today that provide write protection for the disk and allow an examiner to extract and archive the data to a more permanent storage medium. Subsequent copies should be made from the first copy so that the original data is handled as little as possible. The original drive as well as any archive(s) should be labeled and then placed in a secure location. The original data as well as the official extraction archive should never be given out for analysis. Analysis should only be done on copies of the data.

Analysis

In the world of computer forensics, the analysis and recovery is often the most exciting. There are various methods for analyzing a hard disk image, and any analyses conducted may differ depending on the goal. The goal may be to recover deleted files, to gather evidence against a person, or to find out how a compromised host was attacked and what can be done to prevent it in the future. In any case, there are some tools and procedures that are common to most kinds of forensic analysis.

Never perform analysis on the original data. As mentioned earlier, the original data should be copied once, and then stored in a secure location. All subsequent analysis of the data should then be performed on copies so that there is no risk of damage to the original disk. After the original data has been altered, it can be difficult, if not impossible, to establish any credibility in any of the findings.

Do not make assumptions, and keep an open mind. Until all the facts have been gathered, do not let assumptions affect your analysis procedure. For example, if a host is compromised, there may be evidence as to the nature of the attack or what was modified or attempted. Although log files can be tampered with to remove incriminating evidence, the intruder may not have been intelligent enough to do so. This isn't to say that a strict procedure should always be followed; that can also lead to an incomplete analysis. Keep an open mind and make decisions based on the facts.

Often an analysis will entail looking at the file structure. To be successful, an examiner should know the filesystem layout and be able to recognize something that looks out of place, or wrong. This includes file traits such as location, size, timestamps, and permissions. It may help to keep a complete filesystem listing for easier analysis and searching.

All aspects of a disk can be scrutinized, including any unallocated portions of the disk, unused data, and even swap space. Files that are deleted may still be recovered, and there are tools specifically designed to resurrect files that were deleted by the operating system.

When crimes involve computers, there is evidence left behind; sometimes this evidence is not so obvious. Computer forensics is all about finding that evidence. This entails acquiring seized data without modifying it, and then analyzing it by looking for specific files, revealing deleted files, analyzing logs, and basically performing a structured analysis of a system to determine the facts surrounding its involvement in a crime. The remainder of this chapter is devoted to practical information related to the forensic analysis of Mac OS X systems. This includes setting up Osiris to maintain periodic snapshots of the filesystem, using TASK to analyze a suspect host, and a list of important things to check for during any analysis of Mac OS X.

ARE FILES EVER COMPLETELY ERASED?

The best way to erase a disk is to format it, smash it with a sledgehammer, and send it on a course to the center of the sun. Assuming it is not intercepted, this should be effective. With the technology available today, electron microscopes can be used to recover the contents of a disk even after multiple low-level formats. However, keep in mind that this is not a common practice with most computer forensics professionals. There are ways to effectively delete files such that basic forensic software cannot resurrect them. See the sidebar "Using PGP to Effectively Delete Files" in Chapter 5, "User Applications," regarding the use of PGP utilities to effectively delete files.

Osiris

Osiris is a file-integrity management application that works quite well on Mac OS X. In a nutshell, Osiris can be used to periodically monitor the attributes of files so that an administrator can stay alert to changes that may indicate a break-in or an abuse of the system. Basically, the way it works is that Osiris is used to scan the filesystem on a regular basis. With each scan, the collected file attributes are stored in a database. With each new database, an application named `scale` is used to perform a comparison between the new database and the last trusted database. `scale` produces a flat-file report based on the differences between the two databases.

Osiris originally started out as a set of Perl scripts written by Preston Norvell. Eventually this project evolved into a more complete and configurable application (written in C) for monitoring the integrity of UNIX systems, including Mac OS X. However, the current release of Osiris is restricted in that it only supports a usage model to monitor a single host. Despite this limitation, Osiris can still be useful for monitoring changes to a system.

Although there are other solutions for checking file integrity, Osiris is the only open source solution that truly supports Mac OS X. Osiris includes sample configuration files for Mac OS X and Mac OS X Server and is HFS-aware with the capability to scan and compare file resource forks.

In this section, we will discuss some general security considerations concerning monitoring file integrity and go over how to set up and use Osiris on Mac OS X to monitor the integrity of a single host.

General Security Considerations

An Osiris database is just a collection of glorified file stat structures. With each scan, a new database is created that is a snapshot of the filesystem. Forensic examination can certainly benefit from having a collection of such snapshots. It is common for an examiner to look at the three timestamps associated with a file: the last modification time (mtime), the last access time (atime), and the last file status change (ctime). Analysis of these attributes can reveal a trail of activity. Having a collection of Osiris databases is kind of like having a hidden camera that periodically takes a snapshot of the environment. Having the last timestamp values for files is good, but having a timeline of these values is even better.

Another thing to consider is that because all the databases are stored on the monitored host, they run the risk of being tampered with, along with any generated comparison reports. Ideally, the data collected during a scan would never be written to disk, but securely transported somewhere else for analysis. Developing versions of Osiris support this concept of remote storage for databases; the current release does not. However, Osiris does have a MySQL module for storing scan data in a database, even a database on a remote host. Finally, an application such as Osiris does not possess any real-time monitoring capabilities. By real-time, we mean being able to respond to detected changes in less than a second. Because it usually takes more than a second to perform a scan and perform comparisons, any real-time monitoring is impossible and would require a more low-level integration with the operating system. Does this make applications such as Osiris useless? Not at all! Even scans as far apart as 24 hours can be valuable and may provide the first indication of an intrusion. Consider the following analogy: Suppose a bank installs perimeter security in the form of motion and heat-detection sensors. Additional precautions include locks on the doors, audible and silent alarms, video cameras strategically placed to capture every square inch of the interior, and multiple locked passageways leading to a vault protected by inches of steel and a sophisticated lock of some kind. No one element in this example serves to prevent every kind of penetration; they work to collectively provide a blanket of security for the valuables housed in the bank. Ideally, the installed perimeter security would thwart or detect any intrusion attempts but eventually a set of circumstances will exist in which it will fail. There are cases where firewalls and network intrusion systems can be compromised or ineffective. These systems are generally given more attention because the main goal is to keep the bad guys out altogether. When they do get in, we need to know about it and, if possible, what was compromised.

The bottom line is that every detection or prevention tool involved in maintaining the security of a host is important. The key to effectively managing host security starts with an understanding of how to apply the strengths of any used tools and how to fill in the gaps between their weaknesses. Each has its fair share of strengths and weaknesses; it is up to the administrator to recognize them and act accordingly.

Ideally, a host should be scanned and a database of the system created before it is ever placed on a network. This initial database should be burned onto read-only media and placed in secure storage. We realize that this is not always possible and often machines are already deployed. These machines can still benefit from the use of Osiris, but keep in mind that the reports only disclose information on the differences between previous scans, not any outside source; the key is to start with a trusted host.

VERIFYING THE INTEGRITY OF INSTALLED FILES

For already deployed systems, there are options for verifying the integrity of installed files before starting to use Osiris. First, you can verify them against the distribution CD. This is somewhat of an involved process that includes copying the files in question to a trusted machine, unpacking the archives that contain those files, and then comparing their checksums. Files are stored in package (.pkg) files that ultimately contain a compressed pax archive. The contents of a package can be extracted with the `gunzip` and `pax` commands. For example, to extract the BSD subsystem package off of the first Jaguar CD, first copy the `pax` file located at `/System/Installation/Packages/BSD.pkg/Contents/Archive.pax.gz` from the root of the CD volume to a temporary directory.

```
cd /tmp
cp /Volumes/Mac OS X Install Disc 1/System/Installation/Packages/BSD.pkg/
Contents/Archive.pax.gz .
```

Next, uncompress it and extract the `pax` archive.

```
gunzip Archive.pax.gz
pax -rf Archive.pax
```

This creates the directory structure that would have been installed from this package rooted in the `/tmp` directory. Comparisons can then be made against any installed files.

Another solution is to create a base database using Osiris (described in the next section), and compare it against a trusted database from another machine of the same installation. As long as none of the checksum values differ, it is known that the contents of the files are the same.

Finally, `http://knowngoods.org` maintains an exhaustive list of known good MD5 and SHA-1 values of executables for all released versions of Mac OS X and Mac OS X Server. The complete databases for each release also can be downloaded as text files and used to compare existing systems.

When talking about the verification of files (comparing checksums against known good values) on Mac OS X, one must consider the concept of pre-binding. Pre-binding is essentially a way to speed up the loading and execution of executables by resolving references to libraries. Because this information is stored as part of the executable, any updates to this pre-binding data will alter the value of a cryptographic checksum making it difficult to verify against known good values. Although this is somewhat of a problem, there are solutions for verifying executables on Mac OS X. See `http://www.knowngoods.org/macosx/prebinding.html` for more information on how to deal with checksums and pre-binding on Mac OS X.

Installing Osiris

This section discusses how to install and configure Osiris to monitor the integrity of a small set of system-critical files and applications on Mac OS X. This is a lightweight configuration that will require little maintenance and provide a reliable system for managing the security of any Mac OS X Client or Mac OS X Server installation.

The source for Osiris can be freely downloaded from http://osiris.shmoo.com. At the time of this writing, the current version is 1.5.2. Download and verify the distribution package with the following commands:

```
bash-2.05a$ curl -O osiris.shmoo.com/data/osiris-1.5.2.tar.gz

bash-2.05a$ openssl sha1 osiris-1.5.2.tar.gz
SHA1(osiris-1.5.2.tar.gz)= b9bd841934f23fc544fc8cbb745cb79fd07c89bb

bash-2.05a$ curl https://www.knowngoods.org/search.php\?release= \
->osiris-1.5.2.tar.gz\&item=sha1
b9bd841934f23fc544fc8cbb745cb79fd07c89bb
```

Now configure and build Osiris with the default settings. This installs the binaries in /usr/local/bin/ and configures Osiris to store scan information in local database files as opposed to a MySQL database.

```
bash-2.05a$./configure
bash-2.05a$ make
bash-2.05a$ make install
```

Next, we need to set up a repository where the configuration files, databases, and logs will be stored. A good place for this on Mac OS X is /var/db/ directory. Create an Osiris directory tree here and set some appropriate permissions with the following commands:

```
bash-2.05a$ sudo mkdir /var/db/osiris
bash-2.05a$ sudo mkdir /var/db/osiris/configs
bash-2.05a$ sudo mkdir /var/db/osiris/logs
bash-2.05a$ sudo chown -R root:admin /var/db/osiris
bash-2.05a$ sudo chmod -R 0750 /var/db/osiris
```

This ensures that only root has write access to the directory, while admin users can still read and compare the database files. If it bothers you to store the configuration or log files here, they can just as easily be placed somewhere else such as under the /etc directory.

Configuring and Automating Osiris

With Osiris installed, we can now configure and automate it to periodically perform a basic integrity scan. Osiris comes with a variety of built-in filters to allow only files matching specific attributes to be included in the database. However, for our purposes here, we are only going to scan the built-in system applications found in /bin, /sbin, /usr/bin, and /usr/sbin directories.

An Osiris configuration file consists of a sequence of directives and directory blocks. Each directive is either global or local to a specific block. If no directive is specified in a block, the global is used. Each directory block then consists of a list of rules that determine which files from that directory are logged to the database. If no rule matches, the file is ignored. When no rules are specified, the global rule is assumed. For a list of valid rules and syntax information, refer to the online documentation at http://osiris.shmoo.com/docs.

Under the configs directory, create a file named daily.conf with the following contents:

```
Database  /var/db/osiris/daily.osi
Verbose    no
ShowErrors no
Prompt     no
Recursive  yes
FollowLinks no

IncludeAll perm,mtime,ctime,inode,links,uid,gid,bytes,blocks,flags
Hash md5

<Directory /bin>
</Directory>

<Directory /sbin>
</Directory>

<Directory /usr/bin>
</Directory>

<Directory /usr/sbin>
</Directory>
```

The `database` directive specifies the path to store the scanned file data. The `verbose` and `showerrors` directives are turned off so that no output related to scanning progress or error messages are printed. The `recursive` directive sets the default scanning rule so that a recursive scan is conducted on each directory block, unless otherwise specified. Finally, the `followlinks` directive is turned off so that symbolic links are not traversed. The `IncludeAll` directive sets the default list of file attributes to monitor; in this example we monitor all except the last accessed attribute (`atime`). The `hash` directive specifies which checksum algorithm to use and must be one of `md5`, `sha`, `haval`, or `ripemd`.

This configuration will perform a scan of all system applications and should not take more than a couple of seconds to run. Each directory block is empty and thus will use the global `IncludeAll` rule specified at the top of the configuration.

Next, we need to add some lines to the periodic script so that `osiris` and `scale` are automatically run each day. Edit the file `/etc/periodic/daily/500.daily` and add the following lines to the bottom of the file:

```
# run osiris and compare against trusted database.

DATE='date +'%m-%d-%Y''

CONFIG=/var/db/osiris/configs/daily.conf
LOG=/var/db/osiris/logs/${DATE}.log

BASE_DB=/var/db/osiris/base.osi
DAILY_DB=/var/db/osiris/${DATE}.osi

/usr/local/bin/osiris -f ${CONFIG} -o ${DAILY_DB}
/usr/local/bin/scale -n -q -l ${BASE_DB} -r ${DAILY_DB} -o ${LOG}
```

The current release of Osiris does not have any built-in notification system. However, an application such as swatch can be run on the generated report file to look for specific files or attributes (see Chapter 11, "Auditing," for information about using swatch to monitor files). A more basic solution is to have email sent whenever the number of files that changed is greater than zero. This can be accomplished by appending the following additional lines to the daily periodic script:

```
DELTAS='grep "records that differ" ${LOG} | awk '{print $4}''

if test ${DELTAS} -ne 0; then
  mail bob@example.com -s "osiris report - ${LOG}" < ${LOG}
fi
```

With these additions to the periodic script, Osiris will run (as root) each day and will generate a new database, compare that database against the trusted database, and generate a report in /var/db/osiris/logs/ with the date as the filename. If any files have changed, the entire log will be mailed to the email address specified.

> **NOTE**
>
> If you are not comfortable running Osiris as root, feel free to create a special user and group specifically for handling the scans and comparisons. However, there are certain important files (such as /usr/sbin/init) that can only be read by the root user. Although we can understand any reservations, we feel it is more important to have a complete database. The files that would be missed are very important files to keep tabs on.

Finally, we need to prime this system by creating the initial database used for all the comparisons. This can be done with the following command:

```
bash-2.05a$ sudo osiris -f /var/db/osiris/configs/daily.conf -o /var/ \
->db/osiris/base.osi
```

The generated databases will be roughly 100K and will eventually take up disk space. One option is to not save the databases with unique names. The periodic script can be adjusted to write the daily scan to the same filename each day. Likewise, the log files will also build up and can be rotated in a similar fashion as the system logs.

All database files are created with permissions of 0600 and all scale report files are created with permissions of 0400.

When a legitimate change occurs, such as a software update, the scale report may contain many entries for changed file attributes. The reported entries can be reduced by changing the periodic script to use a more current database file as the trusted database; don't forget to review the changes before assuming a newer database is to be trusted.

Using Osiris to Monitor SUID Files

Along with sample configurations included with Osiris is a configuration file that can be used to monitor SUID applications. Maintaining a separate database specifically for SUID and SGID applications is probably not a bad idea. The file is named suid.conf and can be found in the `/configs/` directory of the Osiris source tree.

This sample configuration file can be used to determine any added, removed, or altered SUID or SGID files on the entire disk. However, such an intensive scan can take a few minutes and almost approaches the annoyance of a virus scanner.

Using *scale*

The `scale` application is used primarily to compare database files, but there are some features of `scale` that can make it a handy tool for forensic examiners.

As a simple example, to compare the two databases cain.osi and able.osi, do the following:

```
bash-2.05a$ scale -l cain.osi -r able.osi -o scale.log
```

The output file is optional; results will be printed to standard output if no output file is specified. Ideally, `scale` will produce a report file stating zero changes like the one shown here:

```
osiris database comparison
Sat Feb 8 19:12:45 2003


[ database: /var/db/osiris/base.osi ]

 records:     809
 source:     config file

created on:  Sat Feb 8 18:29:46 2003
created by:  root
created with: osiris 1.5.2

[ database: /var/db/osiris/02-08-2003.osi ]

 records:     809
 source:     config file
```

```
created on:  Sat Feb 8 19:12:45 2003
created by:  root
created with: osiris 1.5.2

[ file differences ]

[ new files (0) ]
[ missing files (0) ]

records compared:  809
records that differ: 0
new records:        0
missing records:    0
```

scale also can be used to print the entire contents of the database. To see an ls style listing, use the -p option. To see every attribute of every file in the database, use the -x option. The following example prints all attributes for the file /bin/ls found in the database named base.osi:

```
bash-2.05a$ scale -x base.osi | grep "(/bin/ls)" -A 16
path: (/bin/ls)
checksum: md5(2f6c62439d1a56b27a52a2478c4ecbf6)
user: root
group: wheel
device: 234881033
inode: 123111
permissions: -r-xr-xr-x
links: 1
uid: 0
gid: 0
mtime: Jan 30, 2003 10:18
atime: Jan 30, 2003 10:18
ctime: Jan 30, 2003 10:18
device_type: 0
bytes: 27668
blocks: 56
block_size: 4096
```

Specific attributes can be isolated with further grep statements. For example, to see the last modification time for that same file:

```
bash-2.05a$ scale -x scan.osi | grep "(/bin/ls)" -A 16 | grep mtime
mtime: Jan 30, 2003 10:18
```

Forensic Analysis with TASK

Often a forensic examination of a system is contracted out to specialists who charge thousands of dollars; and some situations may warrant such an expense. Likewise, you can collect an arsenal of expensive hardware and software to put in your forensic toolkit, but this is not always necessary. There are open source forensic tools that can be considered quite effective. The most common of these open source tools is TASK, developed by @stake (http://www.atstake.com). However, TASK does not have support for HFS+, the default filesystem on Mac OS X. Thus, the reality is that any hard-core analysis of a Mac OS X system demands the use of commercial software or services; something we will not cover in this book. However, we will not leave you empty handed.

In this section, we will provide information about what elements of TASK can be used on Mac OS X, and other issues involved in a postmortem situation on Mac OS X.

Overview of TASK

TASK (The @stake Sleuth Kit) is basically a filesystem analysis toolkit that contains applications that allow for the analysis of many different types of filesystems for both UNIX and Windows. In the event that a live analysis is necessary, TASK can also be used to conduct certain types of analysis on a running system.

Collectively, the TASK command line tools work off hard disk data collected with the common UNIX dd command. Some of the most prominent features include:

- View deleted files.
- Reveal detailed information about files and the structure of the filesystem.
- File checksum verification tools.
- File sorting based on type and extension.
- Timeline creation based on file activity of modified, access, and change timestamps that are associated with every file.

One of the more useful TASK applications that can be used on Mac OS X is mactime, used to construct a timeline of file activity. mactime is discussed later in this chapter.

Getting the Data

Before we start, it is recommended that a machine be used solely for the purpose of creating the disk image, or copy of the target filesystem. We will refer to such a machine as the "imaging" system. Obviously, this system needs to be trusted and should not be connected to a network. The imaging system will be used to create a checksum of the original filesystem, do a byte-for-byte copy of the disk, and then verify the copy with another checksum. The original disk should then be locked away and any further copies should be made from this master copy.

Another thing to consider is how to write-protect any disks before they are ever connected to the imaging system. There are commercial products available that provide write protection for disks. Sometimes the drives themselves have the capability to disable write operations.

The copied image may be quite large. There are many hard disk vendors that now make external FireWire drives with capacities greater than 120GB, which should be sufficient for storing a disk image. Before copying data, the disk that will be used to store the copy should be cleared. This can easily be accomplished with the dd command. For example, assuming the disk used to store the copied disk is located at /dev/disk0s10, use the following command to wipe any pre-existing data:

```
dd if=/dev/zero of=/dev/disk0s10
```

Finally, we would like to boot the imaging system such that the target drive is not mounted, only discovered. An easy way to do this is to boot into single user mode. This also ensures that the system doesn't find its way onto a network.

To boot into single user mode, boot while holding down the Command-s keyboard sequence. Once in single user mode, check and mount the root filesystem with the following commands:

```
/sbin/fsck -y
/sbin/mount -uw /
```

Next, start the automounter with this command:

```
/sbin/autodiskmount -v
```

> **NOTE**
>
> We would like to remind the reader that the system used for analysis should not only be trusted, it should also only contain disks necessary for the analysis process. The use of the automounter command in the preceding code line discovers and attempts to mount any found disks.

If not already known, locate the discovered target disk from the output of the automount daemon. The `diskutil` application also can be helpful in locating this. The following is an example of using `diskutil` to look at the main disk:

```
bash-2.05a$ diskutil list disk0
/dev/disk0
   #:              type name          size     identifier
   0: Apple_partition_scheme          *14.1 GB disk0
   1:   Apple_partition_map           31.5 KB  disk0s1
   2:        Apple_Driver43           27.0 KB  disk0s2
   3:        Apple_Driver43           37.0 KB  disk0s3
   4:      Apple_Driver_ATA           27.0 KB  disk0s4
   5:      Apple_Driver_ATA           37.0 KB  disk0s5
   6:       Apple_FWDriver           100.0 KB  disk0s6
   7:   Apple_Driver_IOKit           256.0 KB  disk0s7
   8:        Apple_Patches          256.0 KB  disk0s8
   9:       Apple_HFS OS X (10.2)     14.1 GB   disk0s9
```

Assuming the disk is disk2, first compute a MD5 checksum of the target disk and save it to a file so it is not easily lost.

```
openssl md5 /dev/disk2 > original.md5
cat original.md5
MD5(/dev/disk2)= 81ff7a34cbecb764a211582608073172
```

Next, copy everything from the target disk onto the repository using the `dd` command. For example, if your repository was /Volumes/extfw, you would use the following command:

```
dd if=/dev/disk2 of=/Volumes/extfw/seizure-master.img
```

Go and get a cup of coffee, this will probably take a long time to copy depending on the size of the disk.

Finally, compute the MD5 of the copy and verify that it is the same as the original determined earlier:

```
openssl md5 /Volumes/extfw/seizure-master.img
MD5(/Volumes/extfw/seizure-master.img)= 81ff7a34cbecb764a211582608073172
```

Now we are ready to analyze the copied data. Do not forget to immediately shut down the imaging system, label the target drive, and lock it up somewhere safe. All copies for analysis should now be made from the image that was just created.

Analysis with TASK

First, acquire a copy of the target image to be analyzed. Do not forget to verify the MD5 sum against the original that was initially taken from the actual disk. To prevent the image file from being modified, change the permissions to read-only. This can be done through the GUI with GetInfo, or on the command line as follows:

```
bash-2.05a$ chmod 0440 seizure-copy1.img
bash-2.05a$ chflags uchg seizure-copy1.img
```

Next, mount the image with Disk Copy.app by clicking the image, or using the following on the command line:

```
bash-2.05a$ hdiutil mount seizure-copy1.img
```

> **NOTE**
>
> Some UNIX systems allow a "noatime" option to mount so that access timestamps are read-only. This can be useful for optimization purposes, but it is also convenient for forensic analysis. The `mount` command on Mac OS X does not have such a feature so keep this in mind when performing analysis of file timestamps. Specifically, any symbolic links will be dated according to the mount time.

Before we begin any analysis, we need to first download and install TASK. TASK can be downloaded from the @stake web site `http://www.atstake.com/research/tools/task/`. At the time of this writing, the current version of TASK is 1.60. The included Makefile works just fine on Mac OS X.

```
bash-2.05a$ tar xvfz task-1.60.tar.gz
bash-2.05a$ cd task-1.60
bash-2.05a$ make
```

This places all the applications in the `bin/` directory. However, most of the TASK applications operate directly on the disk image and thus require foreknowledge of the filesystem. As mentioned earlier, HFS is not on the list of currently supported filesystem types but there are some tools that can still be used.

> **NOTE**
>
> Although HFS and HFS+ are not supported by TASK, TASK applications have been known to work on Mac OS X UFS partitions. However, we recommend that any efforts to analyze UFS filesystems be treated as disparate attempts and not to rely on the ability for that information to be trusted or used in a legal setting.

Analyzing the Filesystem

A lot can be learned about a system by just browsing the filesystem. Because there are not a lot of nifty open source tools available for examining Mac OS X systems, we will try to provide more than a few valuable tips about what to look for in a potentially compromised host.

First, and foremost, look at log files. It may not be necessary to put on your detective hat when you have a blatantly obvious sequence of events revealed by entries in a log file. Chapter 11 contains a listing of log files and their locations for Mac OS X and Mac OS X Server. Log files can be tampered with though, so do not be quick to jump to conclusions.

NetInfo is the default store for users and groups on Mac OS X. If a host has been compromised, an attacker will sometimes create new accounts, possibly a duplicate root account. The NetInfo database file is located in the `/var/db/netinfo/` directory. The default database is local.nidb. The command line tool `nicl` can be useful in examining the contents of this database. For example, to print the users and their UID values from a NetInfo database on `/Volumes/seizure-copy1/`, use the following command:

```
nicl -raw /Volumes/seizure-copy1/var/db/netinfo/local.nidb -list /users
```

To see the list of groups and the GID values, use a similar command:

```
nicl -raw /Volumes/seizure-copy1/var/db/netinfo/local.nidb -list /groups
```

Things to look for include unrecognized groups or users, duplicate UID or GID values, and non-root users with UID of zero. Here is a useful way to search specifically for users with a UID of zero:

```
nicl -raw /var/db/netinfo/local.nidb -search / 0 -1 uid 0
```

Other things that can easily be extracted from the NetInfo database file include the `trusted_networks` setting at the root of the domain. By default, this is an empty list. To view the value of this field, use the following command:

```
nicl -raw /var/db/netinfo/local.nidb -read / trusted_networks
```

Likewise, the list of machines entries in the database can be viewed with the following command:

```
nicl -raw /var/db/netinfo/local.nidb -list /machines
```

Although the `nicl` command line application is quite clunky, it can be useful as demonstrated here. For more information about `nicl`, reference the man page.

Like most UNIX systems, there are typical configuration files under the `/etc/` directory. The `/etc/hostconfig` file contains system configuration settings. The `/etc/hosts.allow` and `/etc/hosts.deny` files contain settings for TCP wrappers. The `/etc/xinetd/` files should be audited as well. Another prime target are crontab files, and the periodic scripts that get run daily. The root crontab file is located in `/etc/crontab`. On Mac OS X, this file starts out with only three entries to run the daily, weekly, and monthly periodic scripts.

Logs for crashed applications are stored in `/Library/Logs/CrashReporter/` directory. Unless crash dumps are turned off in `/etc/hostconfig`, every time an application crashes a detailed log is created.

The version of the operating system, including the build version, is located in the file, `/System/Library/CoreServices/SystemVersion.plist` (keep in mind that this information can easily be modified).

Startup items are located in `/System/Library/StartupItems` and are started by the SystemStarter process on boot. It is a good idea to check these and make sure that there is nothing out of the ordinary here. Specifically, audit each script file to be sure nothing sneaky is going on. Each startup item has a directory and a shell script of the same name as that directory.

The time zone setting is designated by the symbolic link `/etc/localtime`, which points to a time zone file in `/usr/share/zoneinfo/`.

Another useful thing to do is to perform a SUID and SGID audit of the system to look for any such applications that are out of the ordinary. This can be done easily enough with the `find` command, as follows:

```
find /Volumes/seizure-copy1 -type f \( -perm -02000 -or -perm -04000 \)
```

Appendix A, "SUID and SGID Files," lists the installed SUID and SGID files on Mac OS X and Mac OS X Server.

Although the filesystem does not show everything about the state of the system when it was operational, an examiner can piece together a lot of what was going on. This could include the nature of an attack, what was exploited, and maybe any backdoors that were put in place. An understanding of the organization of the filesystem, and what would be considered out of the ordinary, is invaluable.

Looking at Timestamps

The `mactime` application that is part of TASK can organize the files in the image according to their modification time. Because `mactime` relies on TASK applications that do not understand HFS, we need to use an additional timeline application based off of an application from The Coroners Toolkit (which TASK is an extension of). This application is mac-robber and can be downloaded from the @stake site `http://www.atstake.com/research/tools/mac-robber-1.00.tar.gz`.

Unpack mac-robber and build it as follows:

```
bash-2.05a$ tar xvfz mac-robber-1.00.tar.gz
bash-2.05a$ cd mac-robber-1.00
bash-2.05a$ make GCC_OPT="-O2 -Wall"
```

Next, run the mac-robber tool on the target image to collect the timestamps:

```
bash-2.05a$./mac-robber /Volumes/seizure-copy1/ > seizure-copy1.mac
```

This produces a text file that the TASK application, `mactime`, can understand and use to print a chronological file listing. Next, provide this file as an input to `mactime`. By default, the timeline is printed to standard output so it is a good idea to redirect it to a file. It is recommended that the appropriate time zone be specified with the `-z` option. This can make understanding the analysis and correlation with other data less painful.

```
bash-2.05a$ mactime -z MST7MDT -b seizure-copy1.mac > \
->seizure-copy1.timeline
```

If the UID and GID values are bothersome, there are options to specify the group and password files to be used so it can recognize UID and GID values. These must be extracted from the NetInfo domain.

The output of the `mactime` application is a listing of files organized by their timestamps. That is, the first entry is the oldest timestamp; the last entry is the most recent timestamp. The timestamps include the last modification time (mtime), last access time (atime), and the last change time (ctime). Thus, it is possible for a file to appear three times in this list if all three of its timestamps are different. Seeing the files organized in this fashion can sometimes reveal what operations were performed on the system. It also can be used and correlated with known events. For example, if you know the web server stopped working at a specific time, the timeline in this file will reveal what parts of the filesystem were being operated on.

Here is a snippet of a sample timeline generated with mactime. At the top is the timestamp value. Each of the five files in this example share the same access timestamp (atime). Each entry consists of seven columns of information about the file. The first column is the size (in bytes) of the file. The second column denotes the timestamp; in this case all are last-access time values as a result of the daily periodic scripts being run. The third column is the file permissions. The fourth and fifth columns are the UID and GID values, respectively. The sixth column is the inode number for the file and the last column is the file path.

```
Sun Feb 09 2003 03:15:08

3094 .a. -r—r—r— 0   0   28137   /etc/defaults/periodic.conf
724 .a. -rw-r—r— 0   0   7878    /etc/syslog.conf
1389 .a. -r-xr-xr-x 0  0   28138   /etc/periodic/daily/100.clean-logs
0    .a. -rw-r—r— 0   0  155923   /etc/dumpdates
337 .a. -rw-r—r— 0   0   27062   /etc/networks
```

Summary

One good way to prevent a host from being compromised is to completely disassemble it and bury the parts in your backyard. In most cases this is not an option and it is better to be prepared for the worst, just in case. In this chapter we saw some less-than-glamorous ways to examine a host for intrusions or abuse. Applications like Osiris can be used to monitor the integrity of files. Beyond that, there are more intrusive methods to examining a system for evidence that may indicate what was compromised and how. Although the forensic toolkit TASK does not fully support Mac OS X, portions of it can still be used to examine a Mac OS X disk image.

This chapter discussed practical ways to detect a potentially compromised host, as well as methods and tools that can be used to look for damage. In the next chapter we will discuss more general issues related to incident response.

CHAPTER 13

INCIDENT RESPONSE

"I am pleased to dedicate this emergency warning system.
In the, uh, off chance of a nuclear disaster, this sign will tell you,
the good citizens of Springfield, what to do."
—Mayor Diamond Joe Quimby

After you have identified anomalous behavior on a host, you still have
to deal with it. It is tempting to spend the majority of your time configuring
your monitoring and auditing tools. However, if you do not respond quickly
and accurately you may do more harm than the incident that sparked your
response. Too often a company is able to detect an intrusion within minutes
only to follow up with a multi-day response that flails around and
accomplishes little.

This chapter provides some groundwork to help you tune your incident
response activities. Incident response is a complicated topic. Your incident
response needs will vary wildly based on your technical resources and your
business needs. This chapter touches on the high points of incident response,
including the incident response lifecycle and resources for further research
and learning.

What Does Incident Response Mean to You?

Like any other part of computer security, you must respond to incidents in a manner proportionate to your risk. If you maintain a handful of desktop computers and control data of minimal relative value, you will not need a complex incident response team and thick documents full of formal procedures. Conversely, if you maintain a nationwide IT enterprise, you will need to have a solid incident response plan and a coordinated team of individuals ready to act on a moment's notice.

Incident response is not strictly an internal event. There are external incident response teams who help coordinate activities during large scale attacks and correlate previous trends with existing activities. Possibly the most famous of these external teams is the Computer Emergency Response Team Coordination Center (CERT/CC) at Carnegie Mellon University. CERT/CC was formed in the aftermath of the Morris Worm, a rapidly propagating worm which infected the Internet in 1988. CERT/CC is a federally funded program with a mission to assist the community as a whole in dealing with computer incidents. Most notably, CERT/CC releases advisories whenever an especially critical vulnerability or worm is discovered. In general, the information coming out of CERT/CC is high quality and useful to any security professional, even if he or she is not directly involved in incident response procedures. More information about CERT, its mission, and its advisories can be found at `http://www.cert.org/`.

The Forum of Incident Response and Security Teams (FIRST) is a coalition of Incident Response Teams (IRTs) from around the world. It is a forum where many IRTs, both internal and external, come together and share information. Founded in 1995, FIRST has grown to over 100 members. For more information on FIRST and how to join, visit `http://www.first.org/`.

Finally, many vendors have their own incident response teams to assist their customers. Large software and hardware vendors provide this incident response service not only to provide expert technical assistance but also to limit public relations problems due to security vulnerabilities in their systems. If you experience an incident due to a flaw in a product, you are much less likely to be angry with the vendor if the vendor is responsive to your problem and assists in your response. Apple has a security team that is trained to provide technical help during a security incident. This support may or may not come at a price. Apple's policy has changed from time to time to either providing free support during an incident or charging a fee. See `http://www.info.apple.com/usen/security/index.html` for information about contacting Apple and any possible fees.

Most people reading this book will not require a formal, dedicated incident response team. There are several books on the subject of incident response, including *Incident Response* by Kenneth R. van Wyk and Richard Forno (O'Reilly & Associates, July 2001) and *Incident Response: A Strategic Guide to Handling System and Network Security Breaches* by E. Eugene Schultz and Russell Shumway (New Riders Publishing, 2002). This chapter focuses on the incident response needs of small to mid-sized IT installations. If you have a large organization with high security requirements, I encourage you to find a more complete discussion of incident response.

Incident Response Life Cycle

Incident response is not an acute event. It should be a lifecycle so that your incident response capability is constantly improving. You should always learn something from an incident and feed that information back into your process. This idea of a lifecycle is a critical component in all aspects of security, and incident response is no different.

There are many different incident response lifecycle models. Depending on what book you read or what presentation you attend, there will be any number of steps (usually between four and seven) and the steps will involve various classifications of activities. The steps provided here are simply one way to view incident response. What exact lifecycle you choose to follow is not important, because they are all basically the same. What is important is that you customize the lifecycle to your environment and continue to make improvements as you learn more about the process.

Incident response can be broken down into the following phases:

- **Preparation.** This phase involves the creation of policies and procedures, training users, and practice incidents.
- **Detection and Assessment.** This is where the incident is first detected and reported to the incident response team. During this phase the scope of the incident is determined.

- **Response.** Here the incident response team (and other players if necessary) works to minimize the effects of the incident and to return the system to normal operations.

- **Postmortem.** Finally, the team must learn from what has happened and feed that information back into the incident response process.

The incident response lifecycle is shown in Figure 13.1.

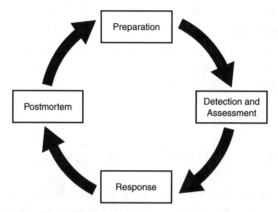

FIGURE 13.1   The incident response lifecycle.

Let's look at each of these phases in more detail.

Preparation

Being properly prepared for an incident is incredibly important. Dealing with a security breach can be an extremely stressful experience. It can be difficult to think straight and communicate effectively. The more preparation you do up front, the quicker you will be able to recover after an incident has started.

When preparing for an incident, remember that the continuity of your business operations is your primary responsibility. Although it may be fun to play a game of cat and mouse with an attacker, it likely will not further your business's goals. Unless otherwise stated, resuming secure, reliable service should be your number one goal throughout the response process. Under certain circumstances, however, you may need to reprioritize the importance of business continuity. For instance, if an attack has been particularly financially damaging, it may be in the company's best interest to allow the attack to continue in order to gain enough forensic data to be able to track down and document the attackers. Regardless, you must do what is best for the business during the incident, not what is best for the security of the system.

Asset Identification

The first thing you should do is make a list of all your assets and what services they provide. Although this sounds simple, it can be a surprisingly difficult task even in a small organization. Assets to be identified include

- Servers
- Routers and switches
- Telecommunication circuits
- Modems
- Firewalls

On all servers, document what services are running. Then tie those services to technical and business owners. Be sure to notify the owners of their respective services so they are aware they are becoming part of the incident response process. The technical owner of the service is the one who provides practical assistance as you assess and respond to the incident. This person should be the domain expert for the given service. Be aware that there may be several technical service owners for any given host. For example, if a host has a mail and web server running, there may be one person responsible for the mail service and one responsible for the web server.

The business owner is an individual who understands the business impact of the service. This person can assist you during the assessment and response phase to help actively determine the state of the business while the incident progresses. Again, there may be multiple business service owners for a given host.

Finally, identify an owner for the system as a whole. This person is typically the one responsible for the hardware and the operating system of the machine. In a small organization the technical service owner and the system owner may very well be the same person. But as an organization grows, you will find that these roles may diverge to multiple people.

For your telecommunication circuits, document the purpose of the circuit and any identifying information regarding the circuit, such as IP address and circuit ID. It is common for network engineers to store this information directly in the router configuration so it can be found easily. This is great as long as the router is functional. If an attack renders the router useless, or you are unable to log in, the data is unreachable. Store the information in a different location to make sure it is reachable.

> **NOTE**
>
> Be prepared for the worst. Too often, organizations store critical documents, such as contact information, on a central server. If you are unable to get to the server because of the incident, your preparation suddenly became useless. Print a hard copy of your incident response documents in case the network or central server becomes unusable.

Be sure to have contact information for the circuit itself and whoever is on the other side of the connection. This means you should have contact information for the telecommunication provider who is supplying the circuit itself (for example, Verizon, who provides your T1). You should also have contact info for the entity that is attached to the other side of the circuit. If the circuit is providing Internet access, this would be your ISP. If the circuit connects your office to another office, this would be a technical contact at the remote site.

Escalation Procedures

After you have documented your assets, there are still other individuals who you need to account for. During an incident, communication is key. Not only do the technical players need to communicate, but upper management needs to be appraised of what is happening. An incident will likely interrupt some part of your business operations for a period of time. Upper management will be sensitive to these issues and should be updated on a regular basis. Without proper communication, you may find yourself suddenly under pressure by a member of senior management who feels there is no progress being made.

First, identify the managers of the service and business owners from the inventory phase. These individuals will need to be contacted if the service or business owners cannot be contacted. They should also be notified in the event of an incident that their employees are tasked with assisting in resolving the problem. Then, identify management within the company who will need to know about incidents as they happen. This list will likely include a member of your legal department and a member of your public relations department.

After you have identified the required members of management who will be notified at some point during an incident, be sure to discuss with them their role in the response process. They need to be made aware they are part of the incident escalation process so they are not completely surprised when they get a phone call during a response.

Finally, be sure to have valid contact information for appropriate law enforcement agencies. It is unlikely that you will have to call law enforcement during an incident. However, if a situation reaches the point where you need help, you should have contact information on hand. Depending on the type of data your company deals with, you will want to list different agencies. Local police will generally not be useful except in the event of a physical intrusion. Various FBI field offices participate in the National Infrastructure Protection Center and can offer assistance during and after an incident. See http://www.nipc.gov/ for a complete listing of NIPC's mission and office locations. If your organization handles financial data such as credit card numbers, the Secret Service may be an agency you can work with. The Secret Service has a web site at http://www.secretservice.gov/, which lists its contact information and provides insight into threats to the financial sector.

Chain of Custody

When dealing with an incident, there is always the possibility your company may take legal action against the attackers. Whether the action is criminal or civil, having valid and trusted evidence will be a key factor in successful prosecution of the case. If the case actually goes to trial (few do, but better safe than sorry) the defense will likely attempt to refute the integrity of the evidence. With electronic evidence, this is even more of a possibility than it is with physical evidence as data can be changed without difficulty.

Any physical evidence that is collected during the course of an incident should have a documented chain of custody document. A chain of custody document specifies who had control of the evidence when, how the evidence was stored, and how it was transferred between individuals. Unless the evidence is in secured storage, there should always be two people present with the evidence. It is easy for one person to lie about changing data. It is much less likely for two people to act in coordination to subvert evidence. Having two people present with the evidence will help judges and juries believe the chain of custody document.

The chain of custody document should accompany the evidence at all times. The document should allow line item entries for each transition in the evidences state or location. Each line should have a place for time, date, location, description of the activity, who was present, and signatures. Create blank forms for chain of custody documents and keep them handy for when there is an incident. If you do not have access to forms, grab any piece of paper and start documenting the chain of custody. When describing the activity, be as explicit as possible to avoid confusion later. Figure 13.2 shows an example blank entry from a chain of custody document.

```
Time:                        Date:
Location:
Activity:


Notes:


Witnessed: _____    Witnessed: _____
```

FIGURE 13.2   An entry from an example chain of custody document.

Technical Procedure

Having a detailed technical procedure can make the difference between a
chaotic incident and a smooth and short event. Based on your company's
assets, the importance of your IT infrastructure, the technical knowledge of
your employees, and the architecture of your network, your response procedure
will differ from that of other companies. Regardless of your precise situation,
the procedure should address the following issues.

DETECTION

The procedure should indicate where you expect to detect an intrusion. It
should provide details of how that infrastructure is maintained, who controls
it, and what their escalation procedure is. The procedure should instruct the
members not to modify any system during the detection phase.

After an incident is detected, the procedure should provide clear instructions on
how to assemble the incident response team to proceed to the assessment phase.

ACCURATE ASSESSMENT

The procedures in the assessment phase should concentrate on a quick and
accurate determination of exactly what is going on. These directions will be
free-form to allow the team to act as necessary; however, there should be a time
limit the team has before the situation escalates to management. If the assessment phase continues for too long without moving to the response phase, the
damage from the incident may become more severe. Also, this is the phase
where a chain of custody document should be started in case the situation
turns into an incident.

QUICK AND FULLY CONTAINED RESPONSE

In the response phase, the procedures need to provide a roadmap to a quick and complete response. Time is of the essence in order to maintain business continuity. If a machine has been compromised, provide directions for unplugging the host from the network and notifying the system and business owners. The procedures should also state that the machine should be backed up completely by an out of band mechanism before a complete examination is done. This will likely involve powering down the compromised host, removing the hard drive, mounting it read-only on another host, and making a copy of the data.

NOTE

For information on copying a disk to another host for forensics purposes, see Chapter 12, "Forensics."

Also the procedure should describe the steps necessary to restore service. Restoring from a known good backup is a good way to get a spare machine in a usable state to resume service. It is recommended that you determine how the attacker entered the system and patch the hole before bringing the new host online.

In the event the attack is a network-based denial of service (DoS) attack, the procedure needs to define where to add access control mechanisms to limit the scope of the attack. It should also instruct the team to contact your Internet providers to assist you in stopping the DoS.

Instruct the team members to be as discrete as possible when responding to the incident. It may take days to determine what happened during the course of an incident, and limiting knowledge of the events to a need-to-know basis helps keep insiders from interfering with the investigation. Keeping information private also limits any public relations problems you may have as a result of the incident.

Finally, ensure that proper communication with appropriate players is occurring throughout the process. Upper management will be easier to deal with if they are kept in the loop about the events as they transpire.

FEEDBACK

After the response is complete, the procedure needs to specify a timeframe in which a postmortem must be completed. It is important to use the incident to improve your infrastructure and incident response process. This feedback stage is required to complete the incident response lifecycle.

Detection and Assessment

Detecting an incident can be tough. The first problem is having a mechanism in place that can detect strange and malicious activity. The second problem is verifying that activity is actually an attack and not an overreaction to a mundane problem.

There are many ways to identify strange activity. Hopefully you have implemented an integrity verification program such as osiris, which can alert you when a critical system file has changed. (See Chapter 12 for more information on integrity verification programs.) At the very least, an integrity verification program will alert you that something is wrong. Another useful metric for finding an attack is the amount of bandwidth used on your telecommunications circuits. If there is an abnormal change in traffic, either too much or too little, something may be amiss and should be investigated. Also, you should be monitoring the availability of all your services. If a service goes away, or new services are discovered, an investigation should be performed.

Even if all your monitoring tools indicate that nothing is wrong, do not discount the value of intuition. Many incidents were caught because things "didn't feel right." Users and administrators get a feel for a system over time and develop an uncanny ability to determine that the system has changed. If you hear discussions from users of sudden system instability or strange activity, you should raise your level of awareness and investigate.

As a security professional, we frame everything in terms of security. When analyzing an incident, many security professionals begin the process assuming the incident is a security breach and will examine the incident as if it were a breach. As the saying goes, if you look hard enough, you will always find what you are looking for. If you think an incident is a security breach, you will likely focus on the data points that indicate security problems and may miss the data points that indicate the problem is really a harmless software bug. Approach each and every incident with an open mind.

During your preparation process, you identified the technical owners of various systems and services. Feel free to call them in during the detection process to help assess the situation. They can put the problem in a different context that will help you determine the true nature of the incident.

Minimizing Change

Valuable data is often destroyed during the incident response process because the individuals involved at the early stages of the incident do not understand how easy it is to delete or alter useful data. Sometimes administrators will delete files they feel are unimportant to try and restore the system to a workable state before they understand the scope of the incident. Or if trojaned binaries have been installed on a host, executing a subverted command may trigger events designed to cover the tracks of the attacker. Simply logging in to a machine or rebooting it may make tracking the attacker almost impossible.

Incident responders at every step need to be instructed to be as hands-off as possible to preserve data. Activities committed with the best of intentions can hinder the investigation. Let the security experts do the forensic analysis. Instruct administrators and engineers that when in doubt, do nothing until the incident response team can examine the situation. For a complete discussion of forensics on Mac OS X, see Chapter 12.

Point Person

Another pitfall many encounter during an incident relates to a lack of clear leadership. When a decision needs to be made quickly, it is difficult if several people are arguing over who has authority to make the decision and what the merits of the decision are. After an incident has been declared and the response team has been convened, a leader for the incident should be appointed. This person has complete authority over the activities of all team members during the incident. Obviously, this coordinator must be someone who is trustworthy and handles stress well. By having a point person handling the events, precious seconds can be saved and team members' activities will be more focused.

Response

Depending on the nature of the incident, your actions in the response stage will range from straightforward to highly complex. Remember that your primary goal in the response phase is to resume normal business operations as effectively as possible. Tracking the attacker is secondary. There are several common activities that most response processes go through. By properly executing these activities, both responsibilities will be addressed.

Isolating the System

A compromised host is a liability to your entire network. Until you can prove otherwise, you should assume that the host has been completely compromised and attackers are actively using the machine. By unplugging the host from the network, you remove the capability of the attackers to access the host. You also limit the capability for the host to be used as a jumping point to other hosts inside or outside the network.

Disconnecting a host from the network will obviously result in a service interruption. Be sure any business owners are notified of the outage caused by the incident.

WARNING

Unplugging the host from the network may trigger a logic bomb on the compromised system. Because the common practice when a machine is compromised is to unplug the network cable, some attackers may launch a program that watches for loss of ethernet connectivity. After connectivity is lost, the program will trigger a series of events designed to cover the tracks of the attacker or to simply destroy the box. If you are not overly concerned about destroying evidence, then this is not something to worry about. If you are, you may consider isolating the machine on a nonroutable VLAN if it is attached to the switch. This keeps the ethernet network up but isolates the machine.

Also, if you have several hosts serving the same purpose, such as in a cluster or web farm, be aware that the other hosts may have fallen victim to the same attack. Examine them for signs of intrusion and disconnect them if necessary. Redundant hosts may provide no redundancy in the case of security breaches.

NOTE

Load balancing devices are common in web farms and other similar connection-based transactions. These load balancers may cause strange effects during an attack. If an automated tool was used to compromise a host, the request was handled by the load balancer before it was passed to a particular server. This would cause only one machine in the farm to actually be compromised even though all the hosts may be vulnerable to the attack.

Backing Up the System

Preserving the precise system state before examining the compromised host is an important step in determining what happened during a break-in. Not only does it provide evidence, which can be used if the attacker is prosecuted, it provides a copy of the system in a "known-bad" state for aggressive examination. If, during the course of investigating the incident, you trigger a Trojan horse or other mechanism that deletes the attackers tracks, you can restore the host from the known bad copy and begin your examination again. Never use the original compromised media to perform your forensic analysis, always work from a copy.

See Chapter 12 for a complete discussion on backing up disks for use in forensic examination.

Vulnerability Assessment and Mitigation

By examining the host and the audit trail generated throughout the incident, you hopefully will be able to determine how the attacker entered the system.

Once you have identified the manner of compromise, determine how you are going to address the vulnerability. This may be as complicated as a custom code fix or as simple as simply disabling a service. Be sure to look at other machines similar to the compromised one and fix them if applicable.

You must address the vulnerable service before a new host is put on the network. By not fixing the vulnerability, you are inviting another incident.

System and Service Restoration

After you know how the machine was compromised and have identified a mitigation technique, the focus now moves to restoring service. Using a known good backup of the host, rebuild a host to replace the compromised machine. Build the machine offline and remove the vulnerabilities before deploying the host. If you have enough people on your incident response team, you can work on restoring the host from a backup in parallel to previous steps. Restoring from backup can take a long time depending on your backup media and how organized your tapes are. Starting the restoration before the vulnerability assessment is done will shorten your time to recovery.

If you cannot determine how the attacker entered the system, continue to the service restoration portion of the response phase. After you restore from a known good copy of the host, examine the system and look for any security vulnerabilities that may have existed prior to the attack. Attackers will sometimes patch vulnerable services on a host to keep other attackers off the machine. If you find a vulnerability on the known good system, then patch the service before making the system live.

If the assessment of the compromised machine indicates that the attacker had access to authentication credentials, such as passwords or cryptographic keys, you should change these credentials on any other host that contains them or relies on them for authentication. Even an encrypted password database can be examined offline by an attacker and used in later attacks.

Postmortem

After the incident response team has verified that the incident has been contained properly and service has been restored, use the incident to refine your infrastructure and processes. First and foremost, try and take a break after the incident. Responding to a security event is a stressful and tiring experience. It is best if your entire team can rest for some period of time to recharge their batteries and have some time to think about the prior events on their own.

Usually a good night's sleep is all that is needed to return everyone to a normal stress level and allow for a successful post mortem.

Gather up all the team members who were involved in the incident and have a frank debriefing about what happened. There are really two discrete aspects of the postmortem process: analysis of the event itself and analysis of the incident response process.

Analysis of the event should concentrate on why the event happened and how to prevent similar events in the future. The "why" may be more difficult to find than you would think. If an attacker entered through a host which was missing a security patch, it is easy to point at the lack of the patch as the reason for the break-in. However, the missing patch may be indicative of a larger problem such as improper patch management or a gap in auditing capability. After the causes are identified, use whatever project management technique your company employs to create and track the projects designed to address them.

Analysis of the incident response process should focus on friction points that occurred during the incident. Typically there will be problems with an out-of-date escalation procedure, confusion of roles, and technical failings in the response phase. List all the problems the team finds, and then find a solution for each of these problems. Feed these solutions back into your incident response lifecycle to improve and streamline it.

NOTE

Postmortems should concentrate on facts, not faults. They can be difficult because there may be hurt feelings, feelings of guilt, or even anger among some of the team members. Enforce a positive attitude at the meeting and keep discussions focused on the job at hand, not at the people involved. Everyone makes mistakes. It is important to learn from those mistakes. Incident response is a lifecycle designed to turn mistakes into a learning tool for later incidents.

Summary

No matter how secure your installation is, you still need to be prepared for security incidents. At some point your infrastructure will be attacked and you will have to deal with the results. Being prepared and keeping a level head throughout the incident will go a long way toward quickly resuming normal business operations. Incident response is a lifecycle. By using each incident to improve your infrastructure and your process, incidents can at least be productive even if not enjoyable.

PART VI
APPENDIXES

SUID AND SGID FILES

The Set-User ID (SUID) and Set-Group ID (SGID) bits allow an application to be run as the user or group that owns the application. In most cases, the owner is root. The main reason for this is to give users the capability to modify files or have access to resources that require special privileges. The unfortunate aspect of this is that such applications can often be exploited to perform malicious operations or used to access private information. SUID and SGID files should not be treated lightly. Administrators should know which files on their system are SUID or SGID, especially those owned by root. The security implications of SUID and SGID files are covered in more detail in Chapter 4, "What Is This UNIX Thing?"

Like many operating systems, Mac OS X has a number of installed SUID and SGID files. Many of these programs do not necessarily require such permissions; some are not even useful. This appendix provides a listing of all the installed SUID and SGID files. In addition, it provides suggestions for dealing with some of these files to improve the security of your system(s).

Table A.1 lists all the SUID and SGID files installed with Mac OS X and Mac OS X Server, and their ownership information. All listings in this appendix are based on Mac OS X and Mac OS X Server version 10.2.3, build 6G30.

TABLE A.1 Installed SUID and SGID Applications

FILE	OWNER	GROUP	SUID	SGID
/bin/df	root	operator		X
/bin/ps	root	wheel	X	
/bin/rcp	root	wheel	X	
/sbin/dmesg	root	kmem		X
/sbin/dump	root	tty	X	X
/sbin/mount_nfs	root	wheel	X	
/sbin/mount_smbfs	root	wheel	X	
/sbin/ping	root	wheel	X	
/sbin/ping6	root	wheel	X	
/sbin/rdump	root	tty	X	X
/sbin/restore	root	tty	X	X
/sbin/route	root	wheel	X	
/sbin/rrestore	root	tty	X	X
/sbin/shutdown	root	operator	X	
/sbin/umount	root	wheel	X	
/usr/bin/at	root	wheel	X	
/usr/bin/atq	root	wheel	X	
/usr/bin/atrm	root	wheel	X	
/usr/bin/batch	root	wheel	X	
/usr/bin/chfn	root	wheel	X	
/usr/bin/chpass	root	wheel	X	
/usr/bin/chsh	root	wheel	X	
/usr/bin/crontab	root	wheel	X	
/usr/bin/fstat	root	kmem		X
/usr/bin/login	root	wheel	X	
/usr/bin/lppasswd	daemon	admin	X	
/usr/bin/nfsstat	root	kmem		X
/usr/bin/passwd	root	wheel	X	
/usr/bin/quota	root	wheel	X	

FILE	OWNER	GROUP	SUID	SGID
/usr/bin/rlogin	root	wheel	X	
/usr/bin/rsh	root	wheel	X	
/usr/bin/setregion	root	wheel	X	
/usr/bin/smbutil	root	wheel	X	
/usr/bin/su	root	wheel	X	
/usr/bin/sudo	root	wheel	X	
/usr/bin/top	root	wheel	X	
/usr/bin/uptime	root	kmem		X
/usr/bin/w	root	kmem		X
/usr/bin/wall	root	tty		X
/usr/bin/write	root	tty		X
/usr/libexec/authopen	root	wheel	X	
/usr/libexec/chkpasswd	root	wheel	X	
/usr/libexec/load_hdi	root	wheel	X	
/usr/libexec/load_webdav	root	wheel	X	
/usr/libexec/ssh-keysign	root	wheel	X	
/usr/sbin/DirectoryService	root	wheel	X	
/usr/sbin/lsof	root	kmem		X
/usr/sbin/netstat	root	wheel	X	
/usr/sbin/pppd	root	wheel	X	
/usr/sbin/pstat	root	kmem		X
/usr/sbin/scselect	root	wheel	X	
/usr/sbin/sendmail	root	smmsp	X	
/usr/sbin/traceroute	root	wheel	X	
/usr/sbin/traceroute6	root	wheel	X	
/usr/sbin/trpt	root	kmem		X
/Applications/Utilities/ Disk Utility.appContents/MacOS/ Disk Utility	root	admin	X	

continues

TABLE A.1 Continued

FILE	OWNER	GROUP	SUID	SGID
/Applications/Utilities/NetInfo Manager.app/Contents/MacOS/ NetInfo Manager	root	admin	X	
/Applications/Utilities/ODBC Administrator.app/Contents/ Resources/iodbcadmintool	root	admin	X	
/System/Library/CoreServices/ AuthorizationTrampoline	root	wheel	X	
/System/Library/CoreServices/ Classic Startup.app/Contents/ Resources/TruBlueEnvironment	root	wheel	X	
/System/Library/CoreServices/ Finder.app/Contents/Resources/ OwnerGroupTool	root	wheel	X	
/System/Library/Filesystems/ AppleShare/afpLoad	root	wheel	X	
/System/Library/Filesystems/ AppleShare/check_afp.app/ Contents/MacOS/check_afp	root	daemon	X	
/System/Library/Filesystems/ cd9660.fs/cd9660.util	root	wheel	X	
/System/Library/Frameworks/ ApplicationServices.framework/ Versions/A/Frameworks/ PrintCore.framework/Versions/A/ Resources/PrinterSharingTool	root	wheel	X	
/System/Library/Printers/ Libraries/aehelper	root	wheel	X	
/System/Library/Printers/ IOMs/LPRIOM.plugin/Contents/ MacOS/LPRIOMHelper	root	wheel	X	

FILE	OWNER	GROUP	SUID	SGID
/System/Library/Printers/ Libraries/csregprinter	root	wheel	X	
/System/Library/PrivateFrameworks/ Admin.framework/Versions/A/ Resources/readconfig	root	wheel	X	
/System/Library/PrivateFrameworks/ Admin.framework/Versions/A/ Resources/writeconfig	root	wheel	X	
/System/Library/PrivateFrameworks/ DesktopServicesPriv.framework/ Versions/A/Resources/Locum	root	wheel	X	
/System/Library/PrivateFrameworks/ NetworkConfig.framework/Versions/ A/Resources/NetCfgTool	root	wheel	X	

In addition to the applications in Table A.1, Mac OS X Server has the following SUID and SGID applications shown in Table A.2.

TABLE A.2 Installed SUID and SGID Applications with Mac OS X Server

FILE	OWNER	GROUP	SUID	SGID
/usr/sbin/NeST	root	wheel	X	
/usr/sbin/networksetup	root	wheel	X	
/usr/sbin/ PrintServiceAccess	root	wheel	X	
/usr/sbin/systemsetup	root	wheel	X	
/Applications/Utilities/AppleShare IP Migration.app/Contents/MacOS/ AppleShare IP Migration	root	admin	X	X

The information in the Tables A.1 and A.2 will probably change with future releases or updates to Mac OS X. The following command can be used to locate all SUID and SGID files on a system. This command also can be useful to locate any such files that may have been added since the initial installation.

```
sudo find / -xdev \( -perm -02000 -or -perm -04000 \) -ls -type f
```

SUID Files

The applications shown in the list that follows are all SUID apps that we
suggest be removed. The remote applications (rcp, rdump, rrestore, rlogin,
rsh) are of no real use on modern UNIX systems. The "ch*" applications
(chfn, chpass, chsh) allow users to change their shell, finger information, and
other credentials. Some administrators may not want their users to have such
capabilities. Also, these applications are useless in most cases because Mac OS
X defaults to storing this information in NetInfo, not the /etc/passwd file on
which these applications operate. The sliplogin application has a dirty past
that has lead to unauthorized access exploits. Previous versions of Mac OS X
shipped a sliplogin program that contained a buffer overflow.

If you do not feel comfortable removing these programs, at least change them
so that they are not SUID.

- /bin/rcp
- /sbin/rdump
- /sbin/rrestore
- /usr/bin/rlogin
- /usr/bin/rsh
- /usr/bin/chfn
- /usr/bin/chpass
- /usr/bin/chsh
- /usr/sbin/sliplogin

The applications in this next list should probably have their SUID bits
removed. All these are applications that should really only be used
by administrators.

- /usr/bin/at
- /usr/bin/atq
- /usr/bin/atrm
- /usr/bin/batch
- /usr/bin/crontab
- /usr/sbin/netstat

- /usr/sbin/traceroute
- /usr/sbin/scselect
- /sbin/dump
- /sbin/restore
- /sbin/route

SGID Files

The applications in the list that follows should probably have their SGID bits removed. It was suggested previously that the remote applications (rdump, rrestore) be removed, or at least their SGID bits removed. The wall and write applications have a history of being exploited and are not necessary.

- /usr/bin/wall
- /usr/bin/write
- /sbin/dump
- /sbin/rdump
- /sbin/restore
- /sbin/rrestore

COMMON DATA SECURITY ARCHITECTURE

The Common Data Security Architecture (CDSA) is an architecture-independent cryptographic framework and a set of layered security services for use on desktops, servers, and even PDAs. Originally designed by Intel Architecture Labs, the CDSA is now managed by the OpenGroup (www.opengroup.org) and is being refined with the help of many companies (including Apple). Apple has an implementation of the CDSA as part of the Darwin project.

This appendix provides an overview of the structure of the CDSA. It takes a peek into its design, function, and how users benefit from its integration into the operating system. The CDSA is quite complex. As such, a detailed dissection of it requires a book all to itself. Our goal here is to provide the reader with a brief overview of the CDSA. It is our belief that the CDSA will become more significant, from a security perspective, as Mac OS X continues to be developed.

Benefits of the CDSA

The CDSA exposes a complete set of cryptographic modules (and managing modules) for the management of keys, certificates, data stores, and the enforcement of trust policies. The intent is for these elements to be tightly coupled with the user environment of the operating system. Furthermore, the CDSA allows for applications to get as serious about security as they want. That is, applications can involve themselves with the nitty-gritty of the security related implementation, and to the degree desired. However, it is important to note that the CDSA is not a panacea of security tools. For example, an exploit against the TCP stack is the responsibility of a different element or access control mechanism. The CDSA does not attempt to address such issues.

Some practical benefits of the CDSA include

- **Extensibility.** The architecture is not rigid or constrictive. One of the main objectives of the CDSA is to offer a security solution that is interoperable. This is demonstrated by Apple who has adopted the use of the CDSA and extended it for their purposes on Mac OS X.

- **Open architecture.** The source code for the CDSA is made available under an Intel license, which is basically another BSD-style license with export extensions. This license is considered open-source by the Open Source Initiative (OSI) and can be downloaded from SourceForge (www.sourceforge.net). The primary benefit is the typical open-source theory that the code is not only easily accessible for review, but can quickly be patched in response to exposed vulnerabilities.

- **Modularity.** Modularity ties into extensibility. That is, the architecture is layered and made up of cooperative modules in a way that facilitates adding and incorporating new modules.

CDSA Structural Overview

The CDSA is made up of three layers, the top-most layer is the most abstract. The bottom layer provides the basic building blocks of the architecture. This includes implementations for ciphers or encryption algorithms, hashing algorithms, storage management, and code to manage the details of digital certificates. The top-most layers provide high-level system security services for managing certificates, disk encryption, secure transmission of data, and tunneling protocols. The three layers of the CDSA, starting with the bottom-most layer, are

- Add-in Modules
- Common Security Services Manager (CSSM)
- Security Services

Add-in Modules consist of the most low-level routines and implementations. Custom modules can be added, registered, and integrated for use by the top-level API.

The Common Security Services Manager is the core of the CDSA and exposes an API for accessing the features of the Add-in Modules.

The Security Services layer is a high-level abstraction of the functionality made available by the CSSM. Applications can make direct use of the CSSM, but are not required to.

Figure B.1 shows the CDSA architecture.

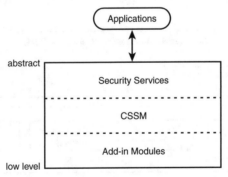

FIGURE B.1 Major layers of the CDSA architecture.

Add-in Modules

Add-in Modules consist of an organized collection of cryptographic algorithms, low-level certificate routines, and data storage implementations. This section of the CDSA can be extended to support new algorithms, as well as the integration of custom service modules.

Here is a generic real-world example. Suppose Company X has a security policy that necessitates the use of some particular hardware token product. This product can be integrated into the security framework by addition, registration, and use of a storage module.

Common Security Services Manager (CSSM)

The Common Security Services Manager is the core of the CDSA. The CSSM provides a gateway to the primitive implementations below it through a complex API. When applications that make use of the API issue requests, the CSSM routes those requests to the correct Add-in Module. You can think of the CSSM as a black box that bridges the gap between an application's requests and a complicated set of implementations capable of satisfying those requests.

In addition, the CSSM provides an extensible Service Provider Interface (SPI) that allows for the integration of custom Add-in Modules.

The CSSM bridges this gap with a set of exposed services. These services are functionally partitioned into categories (see Figure B.2).

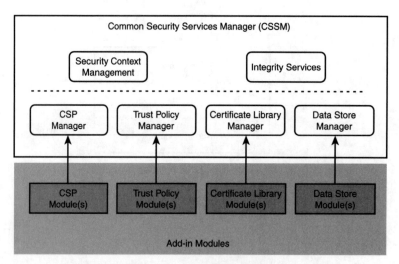

FIGURE B.2   Service categories of the CSSM.

The types of modules managed by the CSSM are as follows:

- Cryptographic Service Provider (CSP)

  Cryptographic service modules provide encryption, digests or check-sums, and digital signatures—as well as the management of private keys.

- Trust Policy (TP)

  Trust policy modules define policy. They define the clearance level required to perform certain operations, or gain access to certain pieces of information. This is where the security needs of the using authority can be implemented.

- Certificate Services (CL)

  The cert modules provide for operations common to digital certificates, including cert manipulation, revocation lists, signing, and verification of memory resident certificates.

- Data Storage (DL)

  Data storage modules provide secure storage for various types of security-related data, including certificates and keys. The storage medium can also vary from memory to a specific hardware device.

There are actually more elements central to the function of the CSSM. Two of the more important ones include

- Security Context Services
- Integrity Services

Security Context Services manage input data from the requesting application. From a user perspective, this component is what enables an application to make use of more than one Add-in Module at the same time.

The integrity services component is responsible for defining a security perimeter for the CDSA. This service is used by the CSSM, Add-in Module managers, Add-in Modules, and CDSA-aware applications for the verification of themselves, and other components of the CSSM. Add-in Modules must go through a bilateral authentication process involving a certificate signed by the manufacturer of the module. This must be done before making the module available to the system.

This is a very rough breakdown of the CSSM, but is sufficient for our purposes. The CSSM is further divided into additional functional sections, including module managers. For more information about the CSSM, consult the actual CDSA specification made available by the OpenGroup (www.opengroup.org).

Security Services

These are services that sit on top of the CSSM and expose yet a higher-level API that might appeal more to application space. Applications can interface directly with the CSSM, or they can take a step back and interface with the security services. This is how the CDSA allows for applications to get as involved with the details of the security architecture as they want to.

This layer of the CDSA also allows for custom implementations that can cater more to the needs of the applications making use of CDSA services. This is also where the services of the CDSA can be made available to programming environments other than C, for example, a Java interface.

Figure B.3 presents a generic diagram of the CDSA with all the layers discussed here.

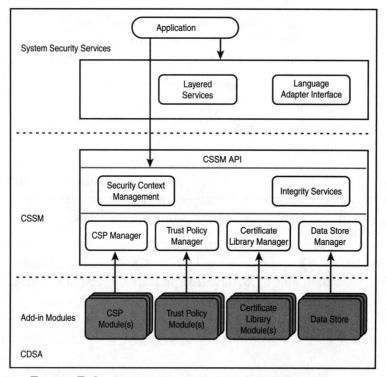

FIGURE B.3   Simplistic breakdown of the CDSA architecture.

Apple's CDSA Security Services

Now that you have a basic understanding of what the CDSA is and how it is organized, let's use that understanding to see how the CDSA implementation on Mac OS X demonstrates the power of this framework and in turn supports some fairly attractive built-in security features.

More than likely you have discovered the keychain application
(/Applications/Utilities/Keychain Access.app). This nifty little
program can save your passwords, lock them away, and then produce them just
when you need to use them. In addition, many applications present the option
to store a password on your keychain. For many users, this is the only aspect of
the keychain application they see. How do those applications know you have a
keychain, how do they know how to interact with it, and how does it actually
protect your passwords? The details of the keychain application are discussed
in Chapter 5, "User Applications," but the relevant discussion begins here with
the Security Services layer of the CDSA implementation on Mac OS X.

Apple's implementation of the CDSA includes additional Security Services
and default Add-in Modules (see Figure B.4). The Security Services provide a
high-level API and serve to abstract commonly used CDSA functionality. The
Add-in Modules provide implementations for the lower-level operations used
by those security services. Some of the Security Services that are currently
implemented by Apple include

- Keychain
- Authorization
- Secure Transport
- Certificate, Key, and Trust

The Add-in Modules implemented by Apple include

- Apple CSP
- Apple DL
- Apple File CSP/DL
- Apple X509 CL
- Apple X509 TP

The keychain API supports applications such as KeychainAccess.app, but
more importantly, makes keychain access available to all the CDSA-aware
applications. For example, Mail.app has the option to put the password you
use to authenticate to a mail server into your keychain. This service not only
stores passwords, but also allows for the storage of public and private keys.
The Apple File CSP/DL Add-in Module is what is actually responsible for the
secure storage of keychain data.

The Authorization service is used to restrict access to various critical elements
of the system. For example, when a user launches the SoftwareUpdate application, he is prompted for an administrative username and password before being

allowed to install software. This is done through an Authorization service. Likewise, there are applications that can allow or deny access to certain operations through the use of this API. The System Preferences application is a good example.

Secure Transport services include a full implementation of the Secure Sockets Layer (SSL) version 3, and Transport Layer Security (TLS) version 1. SSL is a popular secure transport protocol used to secure the transmission of data in applications such as mail and web browsers.

The Certificate, Key, and Trust services provide the capability to operate on and verify certificates, create public and private keys, and to implement trust policies.

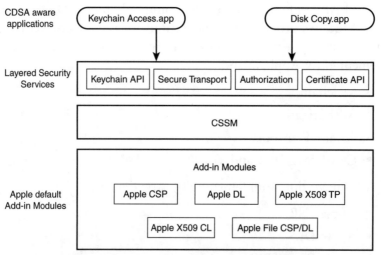

FIGURE B.4 Apple's CDSA Security Services.

Having an integrated security framework will continue to put more applications, such as the keychain and file encryption, into the hands of the common user. Taking complex functionality, such as SSL, out of applications and placing them into libraries and toolkits is a good thing. Taking that functionality and implementing an architecture that unifies those services across applications and system utilities is even better. The extensibility of the CDSA will continue to be more and more useful as security becomes more of a core element of application use rather than just an afterthought.

A Note to Developers

Most software developers will find interest in the top portion of the CDSA as opposed to the actual implementation of the CSSM, or the Add-in Modules. Although developers can interface directly with the CSSM API, the layered services, including Apple's APIs should be sufficient for most applications.

Another aspect of the layered services is the concept of a language adapter. The APIs exported by the CSSM are written in C, but a language adapter can wrap the API such that it is made available to other programming environments.

For those familiar with NeXT development, you will not be surprised to find out that Apple has implemented such a framework. The Security.framework is located in `/System/Library/Frameworks/` along with the other frameworks that are installed with the operating system. The source for this framework is available from the open-source corner of Apple's developer site. If the Mac OS X development tools package is installed, you will have some interesting header files under this system directory in addition to the framework itself.

The security framework is actually packaged as a multipart project named "Security." Not surprisingly, this project contains multiple targets. This code also is part of Darwin and is available via CVS under the module name `/Security`.

The following are available under this module:

- Complete source for the CDSA
- The Security Server (includes Authorization)
- Keychain API
- Secure Transport API
- All of Apple's Add-in Modules

Information about how to obtain the source code for Apple's CDSA implementation can be found at Apple's developer site:

`http://developer.apple.com/darwin/projects/cdsa/`

FURTHER READING

In this book we have covered many topics related to Mac OS X security. However, an exhaustive analysis of each of those topics would require entire books to themselves, not chapters.

This appendix is a collection of additional resources applicable to Mac OS X security. In addition, we have set up a web site (`http://www.macsecurity.org/thebook`) for updated information and example configurations found throughout this book.

Chapter 1—Security Foundations

- Mel, H. X and Doris M. Baker. *Cryptography Decrypted.* Addison-Wesley, 2000.

  A good introduction to cryptography. This book explains concepts and algorithms fundamental to many of the applications and protocols used by Mac OS X.

- Schneier, Bruce. *Secrets and Lies: Digital Security in a Networked World.* John Wiley & Sons, 2000.

  This is a good book that serves as a guide for the wide range of risk and threats related to computer security.

- Viega, John and Gary McGraw. *Building Secure Software: How to Avoid Security Problems the Right Way.* Addison-Wesley Professional, 2001.

  Poorly written software continues to be a threat to the security of any system. Despite this, and the growing popularity of computer security, there are actually few books on the subject. This is by far the most complete and useful book available.

Chapter 2—Installation

- http://www.macosxhints.com/

  Some of the best reading on installations can be found on the Mac OS X Hints web site's Install section.

- http://www.apple.com/server/

  For Mac OS X Server installation and general knowledge, Apple has some very useful PDFs on its web site.

Chapter 3—Mac OS X Client General Security Practices

- http://www.macsecurity.org

  With the rise in popularity of Mac OS X, many web sites related to general usability of the OS have surfaced—a couple are devoted specifically to security issues. MacSecurity.org has been around since before Mac OS X was released and contains documents, tools, and news related to Mac OS X security. Interested administrators and users should also note the MacSec mailing list hosted on this site, which is a moderated mailing list for discussing Mac OS security issues.

- http://www.securemac.com

  This is another very good resource for Mac OS X security-related information. Like MacSecurity.org, this site contains news, tools, hints, and links to other security related information about Mac OS X.

- http://www.apple.com/support/security
  http://www.info.apple.com/usen/security/
  security_updates.html

  Apple, of course maintains its own pages for security information and these are two of the most useful. The first URL is Apple's general security information and suggestion page, and the second is a page listing all the security updates Apple has released since Mac OS X v10.0.

- http://www.sans.org/rr/mac/
  SANS has an entire section of its "Reading Room" devoted to Mac-specific papers.

Chapter 4—What Is This UNIX Thing?

- Garfinkel, Simson, Alan Schwartz and Gene Spafford. *Practical Unix & Internet Security*, 3rd Edition. O'Reilly & Associates, 2003.

  This book is an excellent reference for general UNIX security. Although Mac OS X has its own peculiarities, it shares many common elements with other versions of UNIX.

- Potter, Bruce. *Practical Security in a Networked UNIX Environment*. `http://www.shmoo.com/wp/pract/`.

  The Shmoo Group (`http://www.shmoo.com`) has a collection of whitepapers, one of which deals with UNIX security, including this one by founder, Bruce Potter.

- Jepson, Brian and Ernest E. Rothman. *Mac OS X for Unix Geeks*. O'Reilly & Associates, 2002.

  This is a good reference, specifically for Mac OS X UNIX issues.

Chapter 5—User Applications

- `http://www.shmoo.com/~tbird/metaweather.html`

  Tina Bird maintains this listing of security resources for Vendor and Open Source Projects. It contains a great deal of information about patches and alerts for some software that is installed with Mac OS X.

- `http://www.freebsd.org/security/index.html`

  Mac OS X shares a lot of code with FreeBSD and in the past some FreeBSD security advisories have also been a concern for Mac OS X. See this page for the latest FreeBSD security advisories. This site also contains the mailing list instructions specifically for announcing security advisories with FreeBSD.

- `http://www.gnupg.org`

  This is the official site for GnuPG, which contains complete information related to GnuPG and GnuPG development.

- `http://macgpg.sourceforge.net`

  This SourceForge project site is devoted to GnuPG applications and bundles for Mac OS X.

- `http://www.pgp.com`

  PGP Freeware products and information for Mac OS X can be found at this, the PGP Corporation site. It includes technical specifications, whitepapers, and source code.

- `http://developer.apple.com/macos/security.html`

  For developers, Apple has a section of its developer web site devoted specifically to security. This includes information about APIs and other frameworks that help support the strong security found in many of the built-in applications.

Chapter 6—Internet Services

- Laurie, Ben and Peter Laurie. *Apache: The Definitive Guide*, 3rd Edition. O'Reilly & Associates, 2002.

  We said there are entire books written about Apache, and there are; FatBrain lists some 40+ books available. Of these, this is the one we most recommend, which certainly lives up to its name.

- `http://www.macdevcenter.com/pub/a/mac/collections/webserving.html`

  Another good source of information specifically geared toward Apache on Mac OS X is this nugget from O'Reilly & Associates' *MacDevCenter*.

- Viega, John, Matt Messier and Pravir Chandra. *Network Security with OpenSSL*. O'Reilly & Associates, 2002.

  For those interested in a lot more information on OpenSSL this is a bible.

- Costales, Bryan and Eric Allman (Contributor). *sendmail*, 3rd Edition. O'Reilly & Associates, 2002.

  Because no books are currently available for Apple's MailService, we can only recommend this book for those wishing to use sendmail. It is the bible of sendmail and the only book many administrators ever use. For those less masochistic, there are other MTAs available with their own books to help administrators along.

- Barrett, Daniel J. and Richard Silverman. *SSH, The Secure Shell: The Definitive Guide.* O'Reilly & Associates, 2001.

  For anyone interested in the SSH protocol, this is the only book to buy.

- http://www.xinetd.org

  This is the official xinetd web site and a bountiful source of information.

Chapter 7—File Sharing

- Eckstein, Robert, David Collier-Brown and Peter Kelly. *Using Samba.* O'Reilly & Associates, 1999.

  This is the best Samba source we have found in a single book.

- http://www.webdav.org

  This is the official web site for WebDAV, and should be the first stop for anyone wanting to learn about it.

- Stern, Hal, Mike Eisler and Ricardo Labiaga. *Managing NFS and NIS*, 2nd Edition. O'Reilly & Associates, 2001.

  This is a good book with lots and lots of information for users of NFS shares.

Chapter 8—Network Services

- http://www3.sympatico.ca/dccote/firewall.html

  This is a good resource for configuring various aspects of Mac OS X built-in firewall (ipfw).

- Zwicky, Elizabeth D., Simon Cooper, D. Brent Chapman, and Deborah Russel. *Building Internet Firewalls*, 2nd Edition. O'Reilly & Associates, 2000.

  This is one of the best books available on general firewall theory.

- Potter, Bruce and Bob Fleck. *802.11 Security.* O'Reilly & Associates, 2002.

  This book has some good Mac OS X-specific configuration help in it as well as a wealth of other practical information.

Chapter 9—Enterprise Host Configuration

- `http://www.zeroconf.org`

  This is official site for the Zeroconf working group.

- `http://developer.apple.com/macosx/rendezvous`

  This is Apple's site for its implementation of the Zeroconf standard.

- `http://web.mit.edu/macdev/www/kerberos.html`

  Because Apple provides nearly none, perhaps the best source for information on Kerberos is that provided by MIT itself.

- `http://docs.info.apple.com/article.html?artnum=107154`

  The Apple Knowledge Base Document that explains how to set up the Login Window to do Kerberos authentication.

- `http://docs.info.apple.com/article.html?artnum=107155`

  The Apple Knowledge Base Document that explains how to configure common services (such as mail) to use Kerberos authentication.

Chapter 10—Directory Services

- `http://www.apple.com/server/resources.html`

  Among the several documents available, Apple has some decent documentation on NetInfo, Open Directory, and Active Directory integration.

- `http://homepage.mac.com/ackman/wwdc/`

  This is a fun and educational QuickTime movie on Directory Services by the University of Colorado that was presented at WWDC last year. It is not on any specific topic, but is good for an entertaining introduction to the possibilities.

- `http://www.mines.edu/students/m/mheck/`
  `netinfo_user_guide.pdf`

  This is a relatively old document on NetInfo from the NeXT days, but its one of the most thorough documents we've ever found.

- `http://developer.apple.com/techpubs/macosx/Networking/Open_Directory/`

  This is Apple's developer documentation for Open Directory.

- `http://conferences.oreillynet.com/cs/macosx2002/view/e_sess/3298`

  This is a presentation on Open Directory and NetInfo from O'Reilly's Mac OS X Conference by a couple of Apple chums.

- `http://www.novell.hu/faq/macosx-edir_1.pdf`

  This is Novell's official guide for integrating Mac OS X into its enterprise directory.

Chapter 11—Auditing

- `http://www.loganalysis.org`

  The log analysis site, maintained by Tina Bird and Marcus Ranum, provides access to great deal of information and software related to log analysis. The hosted mailing list can be very helpful, and has a low signal to noise ratio.

- `http://docs.info.apple.com/article.html?artnum=122015`

  The Mac OS X Server Admin Guide is an acceptable reference for up-to-date information regarding logging configuration issues and locations of log files.

Chapter 12—Forensics

- `http://osiris.shmoo.com/docs/`

  Complete documentation and the latest source for Osiris can be found online at this site. This includes the configuration file specification, sample configurations, and filter definitions. There is also an osiris-users mailing list.

- `http://www.atstake.com/research/tools/task/`

  @stake maintains complete documentation and reference material for TASK online.

- Kruse, Warren G. and Jay G. Heiser. *Computer Forensics: Incident Response Essentials.* Addison-Wesley 2001.

  This is a good source of information about computer forensics in general, including Windows and UNIX.

Chapter 13—Incident Response

- `http://www.sans.org/rr/incident`

  SANS has some good articles on incident handling from its membership.

INDEX

G

H

I

www.informit.com

YOUR GUIDE TO IT REFERENCE

New Riders has partnered with **InformIT.com** to bring technical information to your desktop. Drawing from New Riders authors and reviewers to provide additional information on topics of interest to you, **InformIT.com** provides free, in-depth information you won't find anywhere else.

Articles

Keep your edge with thousands of free articles, in-depth features, interviews, and IT reference recommendations— all written by experts you know and trust.

Online Books

Answers in an instant from **InformIT Online Books'** 600+ fully searchable online books.

POWERED BY

Catalog

Review online sample chapters, author biographies, and customer rankings and choose exactly the right book from a selection of over 5,000 titles.

www.newriders.com

Publishing
the Voices
that Matter

OUR AUTHORS

PRESS ROOM

| web development | design | photoshop | new media | 3-D | server technologies |

EDUCATORS

ABOUT US

CONTACT US

You already know that New Riders brings you the **Voices That Matter**.

But what does that mean? It means that New Riders brings you the

Voices that challenge your assumptions, take your talents to the next

level, or simply help you better understand the complex technical world

we're all navigating.

Visit **www.newriders.com** to find:

▶ **10% discount** and **free shipping** on all book purchases

▶ Never-before-published chapters

▶ Sample chapters and excerpts

▶ Author bios and interviews

▶ Contests and enter-to-wins

▶ Up-to-date industry event information

▶ Book reviews

▶ Special offers from our friends and partners

▶ Info on how to join our User Group program

▶ Ways to have your Voice heard

New
Riders

WWW.NEWRIDERS.COM

VOICES THAT MATTER

HOW TO CONTACT US

VISIT OUR WEB SITE

WWW.NEWRIDERS.COM

On our web site you'll find information about our other books, authors, tables of contents, indexes, and book errata. You will also find information about book registration and how to purchase our books.

EMAIL US

Contact us at this address: **nrfeedback@newriders.com**

- If you have comments or questions about this book
- To report errors that you have found in this book
- If you have a book proposal to submit or are interested in writing for New Riders
- If you would like to have an author kit sent to you
- If you are an expert in a computer topic or technology and are interested in being a technical editor who reviews manuscripts for technical accuracy
- To find a distributor in your area, please contact our international department at this address: **nrmedia@newriders.com**

- For instructors from educational institutions who want to preview New Riders books for classroom use: Email should include your name, title, school, department, address, phone number, office days/hours, text in use, and enrollment, along with your request for desk/examination copies and/or additional information.
- For members of the media who are interested in reviewing copies of New Riders books: Send your name, mailing address, and email address, along with the name of the publication or web site you work for.

BULK PURCHASES/CORPORATE SALES

The publisher offers discounts on this book when ordered in quantity for bulk purchases and special sales. For sales within the U.S., please contact: Corporate and Government Sales (800) 382-3419 or **corpsales@pearsontechgroup.com**. Outside of the U.S., please contact: International Sales (317) 581-3793 or **international@pearsontechgroup.com**.

WRITE TO US

New Riders Publishing
201 W. 103rd St.
Indianapolis, IN 46290-1097

CALL US

Toll-free (800) 571-5840 + 9 + 7477
If outside U.S. (317) 581-3500. Ask for New Riders.

FAX US

(317) 581-4663